Teaching Economics As If People Mattered

A Curriculum Guide to the New Economy

Tamara Sober Giecek
with United for a Fair Economy

United for a Fair Economy
29 Winter Street
Boston, MA 02108
Phone 617-423-2148 • Fax 617-423-0191
Email: info@faireconomy.org • Web: www.faireconomy.org

Acknowledgments

Special thanks to Laura Delmore, Renee Sarrao, and all of the field-testers for their hours of hard work reviewing the original materials and test-piloting them in the classroom.

Grateful acknowledgment is also made to Bill Bigelow for his contribution of Lesson 15, "Globalization: The Race to the Bottom."

Thanks to Edith Bross for timely and accurate research assistance and Martha Maitlaw for expert proofreading, with the 2007 edition.

Teaching Economics As If People Mattered

By Tamara Sober Giecek with United for a Fair Economy
2007 edition edited by Steve Schnapp

Research, Design and Layout: Chris Hartman
Cover photo by Ellen Shub

Printed in the United States

ISBN 0-9659249-4-7

Published by United for a Fair Economy
29 Winter Street, 2nd Floor
Boston, MA 02108
www.faireconomy.org
617-423-2148

United for a Fair Economy is a national, independent, nonpartisan, non-profit organization. UFE raises awareness that concentrated wealth and power undermine the economy, corrupt democracy, deepen the racial divide, and tear communities apart. We support and help build social movements for greater economic equality.

Contents

Foreword: "Why?" The Art of Asking Questions iv

Introduction v

Tips for Using These Lesson Plans vi

Lesson 1: Defining Economics 1

Lesson 2: What is Income and Why Do Some People Earn So Much More of It Than Others? 5

Lesson 3: Signs of the Economic Times 10

Lesson 4: Distributing Income: You Be the Judge 24

Lesson 5: Income Levels and How They've Changed Over the Past 25 Years 27

Lesson 6: Viewing Income Through Gender and Race Lenses 38

Lesson 7: How Much More Do CEOs Make Than the Average Worker? 43

Lesson 8: The Widening Pay Gap, What the Experts Say, What Government Can Do About It, and How It Affects the Business Cycle 52

Lesson 9: Monetary Policy and the Role of the Federal Reserve Board 60

Lesson 10: What is Wealth and Who Owns How Much of It 66

Lesson 11: How Savings Accounts and Stocks Function 75

Lesson 12: Born on Third Base 79

Lesson 13: Economic Boom for Whom? 87

Lesson 14: Power Shift Led to Rule Changes 97

Lesson 15: Globalization: The Race to the Bottom 108

Lesson 16: America: Who Really Pays the Taxes? 120

Lesson 17: Closing America's Racial Wealth Gap 135

Lesson 18: Democracy, A Game for the Elite? 153

Lesson 19: The Consequences of Economic Inequality and What's Been Done about Them in the Past 157

Lesson 20: Economic Inequality, Why Should We Care? Because Knowledge Without Action Leads to Despair 168

Lesson 21: What Can You Do: Real Policies that Lift the Floor, Level the Playing Field, and Address the Concentration of Wealth and Power 174

Resources for Teachers 178

Foreword

"Why?" The Art of Asking Questions

Meizhu Lui

When children are still small, they love to pester their parents with the question, "Why?" They are thrilled with their discovery that they have the capacity to question, and that they can get explanations from big people who have more experience and information than they do.

As they grow older, it is our responsibility as teachers in both classrooms and informal settings to encourage them to continue to ask questions, and to see that an answer leads to more questions: like an onion, understanding comes as we keep peeling away the layers.

Every one of our student interacts with the economy every day. "I'm going to buy that ipod on credit — got to have it now!" "The price of gas keeps going up." "My friend is at his summer home in the Hampshires." "My dad says he can't afford the tuition at the college I want to go to." But are they asking why these things are happening, why our economy works this way?

One hears that this is the most prosperous nation in the world, and it is. And yet, in the last few decades, our economic system has produced a few hundred billionaires, at the same time that more and more families — 37 million in 2006 — live in poverty. This has been accomplished not because it is a law of nature that "the rich get richer and the poor poorer," but because laws made by people disproportionately benefit the already wealthy, and do not lift those at the bottom or strengthen the middle class. Teachers and students who use this curriculum will identify the mechanisms by which we choose to distribute the vast resources of this country.

But why has our country created these rules? Are they fair? Should just a few have their wealth shoot through the roof? Or should prosperity be widely shared? These are the values questions that you as teachers know best how to pose. And the dialogue that will follow will be essential to our future as a self-governing, democratic society. Through their own answers, students will decide what rules they want to live by, and whether they will participate in the processes of rules change.

Since it's founding more than a decade ago, United for a Fair Economy has been leading workshops for adults that draw on people's own experiences and add information to develop their understanding of the economy. Out of these workshops, many people asked us to develop a youth oriented curriculum for formal classrooms settings. In 1999, a UFE board member, Sam Pizzigati, who worked for the National Educators Association (NEA) pushed the idea of this project forward. We are thankful to Tamara Sober Giecek for joining forces with us to design this terrific teaching guide, and to Steve Schnapp, UFE educator par excellence, for updating the guide for this second edition.

Like you, we are optimistic that our students who ask questions today will have the answers to create a better tomorrow.

Introduction

This teacher's guide is our attempt to bring the issue of economic inequality to the high school classroom and to youth organizers. We believe there is a need for economics curricula and supplementary materials that go beyond explaining the theory of competitive markets and take a critical and constructive view of current economic policies. This guide aims to address the human implications of these policies and thereby expand the economic debate. We believe that in order for students to function successfully in our economic system they need to become good critics of economic policy. Also, as our democracy is increasingly threatened with monetary influence over politics, economic critique should garner more attention in government courses.

I was surprised time and again when students entering my 11th and 12th grade Government and Economics courses were unable to differentiate between political and economic systems. They often saw democracy and capitalism as one in the same. However, they were not naïve when it came to understanding the power of money in politics. We hope this guide will help convey to students the importance of debating economic policy issues to sustaining a healthy democracy.

This guide puts a large portion of the research and publications of United for a Fair Economy into 21 sequential yet primarily stand-alone lesson plans. The guide can be used as a unit in an economics course, or used as supplementary materials and activities to enhance standard economics curricula.

Each lesson plan places a high priority on student involvement with the goal of making economics come to life and helping students relate to economics in order to understand its effects on their lives.

— *Tamara Sober Giecek*

Tips for Using These Lesson Plans

United for a Fair Economy's Philosophy of Learning

In general, our approach to education stands under the umbrella of *popular education.* Basically, we try to attend to both the content of what we present as well as the process or form of presentation. Students are not perceived as empty vessels into which we should pour information, but co-creators in the process of learning. Our role is to provide structure, experiences, and material with which students can engage and create meaning. The essence of this approach is to draw on the experience of the students, foster dialogue among students and the teacher, and stimulate action and reflection.

Engaging students in active learning is a primary challenge for the teacher. The lessons in this curriculum pose problems and offer numerous questions to stimulate discussion. Some are open-ended problems and questions and others have specific answers. The more dialogue that occurs in the classroom, we believe, the more opportunities there are to explore and learn about economic issues. Recognizing that students need "space" to talk in class, we encourage them to work in pairs and small groups which will involve more voices without taking too much time.

In our view, an ideal lesson also includes kinetic learning activities — where students physically move around. To this end, we have developed several experiential activities ("live illustrations" of economic trends in income and wealth distribution, for example) that help communicate some of the content in this curriculum.

We believe that a pedagogical approach that emphasizes a collective exploration of economic data, trends, and issues, and invites all the participants to bring their own experience, values, and vision into the dialogue, is essential in preserving democratic traditions and building a sense of civic responsibility and fairness among youth.

Preparation of Materials

Preparation often calls for "placards" meaning simply an 8.5" x 11" sheet of card stock. We often use regular paper then tape it to a piece of cardboard and laminate the board to preserve it for future use. Holes should be punched through the tops of the placards and a string put through them. Students can drape the cards over their necks and free their hands to hold scripts, etc.

You will want to have a supply of large non-toxic markers, in assorted colors with black, blue, red, and green predominating (at least 30).

Large sticky notes (4" x 6", 3" x 3") will also come in handy.

Use of the Charts

The lesson plans frequently refer to the use of a particular pre-printed chart. Copies of all charts (8.5" x 11") are included in each lesson. However, the activities work best if you make a set of overhead transparencies or enlarge the charts to flipchart size. Large format flipchart sets to accompany this book can be purchased from United for a Fair Economy. See the Resources section on page 181 for ordering information.

Objectives:

- *Define economics and discuss how the economy relates to our lives.*
- *Differentiate between democracy as a political system and capitalism as an economic system.*

Concepts and Key Terms:

- *economics*
- *resources*
- *consume / consumer*
- *goods and services*
- *capitalism*
- *democracy*
- *American dream*
- *meritocracy*

Instructional Time:

- *55 minutes*

Preparation:

- *7 large markers*
- *7 large pieces of different colored paper (approximately poster size) taped equal distances apart around the room with the following phrases (all part of the definition of economics) written and hung in the order below (one phrase per piece of paper). The papers are folded up from the bottom and taped so the words are not revealed at first.*

  "Social science,""concerned with the way society chooses,""to employ its limited resources,""which have alternative uses,""to produce goods and services,""for present and future,""consumption"
- *Find out the most recent figures for the unemployment rate in your area. (See the U.S. Bureau of Labor Statistics website: www.bls.gov.)*

Conducting the Lesson

Bellringer Activity 1.1: Defining Economics

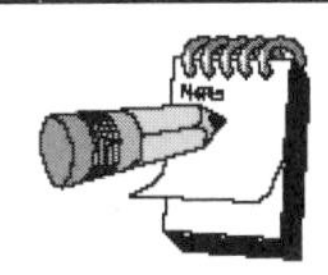

Note to Teacher

This activity may need to be altered according to the ability level of your students. Write definitions on the board of unfamiliar words they will encounter or that you plan to use and discuss these definitions with students before beginning the lesson.

1. Pass out the markers to students and ask students to get in seven equally divided small groups (or have them count off). Each group chooses one of the posters and stands by it. Ask each group of students to unfold their poster in turn and read it. Explain they are each looking at a "part" of the definition of economics. Ask them to brainstorm what their word or phrase means and how it relates to what they know about the word "economics." Ask one student to act as "scribe" and record the group's ideas on the poster under the word/phrase. Assign a set number of minutes to accomplish this task.

2. When the students are done brainstorming explain that when you say "rotate" they should move to the next poster. Have them brainstorm again and add any comments to those already written on the poster. (Walk around and monitor to help jump-start groups that appear stumped.) After a few minutes announce "rotate" and have the students do another brainstorm. Repeat this process until all groups have been to every poster.

3. Next ask the class to gather around the "Social Science" poster. Discuss students' ideas written on the poster. Ask them to explain their ideas. Discussion might center on how "hard" sciences, such as physics, chemistry, or the many fields of biology differ from "soft" sciences, such as sociology or economics. The "hard sciences" are distinguished by strict and rigorous scientific standards, and close attention to formal standards for hypothesis formulation and testing, while the "soft sciences" involve the description and/or observation of the behavior of human beings and take a much more informal approach. This is an opportune time to explain how economics is often infused with a certain set of values to advance particular political viewpoints.

4. Move through the remaining posters, asking students to gather around each poster as it is being discussed. Review students' topics first and then steer the discussion to the ideas that follow for each word or phrase.

"concerned with the way society chooses" – Center discussion on the word "chooses." Explain how economics and the economy do not operate by natural forces, like the weather. There are choices to be made in how the economy operates. People make these choices. (You may want to branch out on just "who" the people are that make these choices, although this subject is covered in Lesson 9 under the topics of monetary and fiscal policy.)

"to employ its limited resources" – Ask students to name resources. Coal, oil, etc., are often named by students. Discuss how "people" are resources and how labor is a resource. You can also touch on unemployment here. (Find out the current level of unemployment in your area before this lesson. Economists debate whether or not there is an "optimum" level of unemployment to keep inflation low, and what that level of unemployment is. Lesson 9 discusses the relationship between unemployment and inflation.)

"which have alternative uses" – Ask students for examples of how resources can be used wisely or unwisely. Examples: clear-cutting versus selective cutting of trees, throwing away paper versus recycling paper, and turning off the water when you brush your teeth. Remind them that there are many examples they may have learned as early as elementary school.

"to produce goods and services" – Ask students for examples of "goods" (shoes, cars, houses, clothes) and examples of "services" (waiting on a table at a restaurant, teaching, performing surgery, and giving legal advice).

"for present and future" – Ask students how we can continue to use resources to produce the goods and services we need now and still plan wisely for the future.

"consumption" – Ask students: What do you think it means to consume? To use? To devour or absorb; to waste; to spend; to destroy? How would you define a consumer? How are we all consumers? Ask students for examples of how *they* consume. Examples: we all buy clothes, shoes to wear, buy food, use gas in cars to go see friends. Other examples?

5. Ask students why they think economics is concerned with consumers.

DEFINITION:

A ***consumer*** is a person that uses products or services, especially for personal needs.

TALKING POINT:

The level of consumption is one indicator of how the economy is functioning. Economists and social scientists also look at which goods and services people are consuming and why and how they consume what they do.

6. This section focuses on differentiating between democracy and capitalism in order to have students discuss: a) how they are connected to the economy; and b) their right, in a democracy, to determine how the economy functions and to have it function for their benefit. Ask students to describe the type of government we have in the U.S. When students respond "democracy" ask them to describe our economic system. Ask them how they would characterize the differences between an economic system and a political system. Spend some time explaining the difference between capitalism and democracy. Make sure students understand them as separate structures: democracy as the political structure of our government and capitalism as the economic structure of our economy.

DEFINITIONS:

Capitalism is the economic system based on the private ownership of the means of production and the distribution of land, factories, mines, railroads, etc., and their operation for the profit of the owners, under predominantly competitive conditions.

Democracy is a political system in which government is by the people, exercised either directly (participatory democracy) or by elected representatives (representative democracy).

7. Ask students to look again at the definition of economics and determine how they might fit into the economy. Ask students to name some ways. Depending on the time available, you may wish to discuss comparative governmental and economic systems — Social Democratic governments in Europe (Sweden & Norway, for example). Also, provide examples of dictatorships where political freedoms are limited yet their economy is largely open to "free" trade and operates under capitalist principles (Indonesia, Myanmar aka Burma, and Saudi Arabia, for example).

8. Ask students to provide examples of how they can "vote" with their dollars.

TALKING POINTS:

Students are consumers. For example, in 2003, young people ages 10-24 bought one third of all CDs, tapes, and digital music downloads sold in the U.S., spending $3.9 billion (Recording Industry Association of America, *2004 Consumer Profile*). In our democracy the right to vote is reserved for those 18 years old and over. However, in our capitalist economy youth can "vote" with their dollars and make their opinions count, even before they have the legal right to vote.

Many students work and pay taxes such as payroll or "FICA" taxes. Also, in most states, sales tax is collected on all purchases, except on items such as food and clothing. Students are also connected to the economy because they are the future workers, producers, owners, etc., and the skills they gain and choices they make can affect the extent to which our economy prospers or falters. Also, the health of the economy may determine what occupation students may choose one day. So students are connected to the economy through their lifetime goals and dreams.

Activity 1.2: The American Dream

1. Invite students to talk about their dreams. Ask them to take out a sheet of paper and write down the type of job they might want to have either after high school or after college. Tell them not to worry about being realistic but to dream and then write about their dream career.

2. Ask for volunteers to share what they wrote.

3. Ask students the following questions. What is the "American Dream"? Some folks say that anyone, including you, can one day become President or can be as rich as Bill Gates, if you work smart and hard enough. What do you think? Students will probably begin to form a discussion around the American Dream being equal opportunity for all. As this discussion evolves, continue to question the students: Is it true that everyone has an equal chance to get ahead with hard work and academic achievement? Is the American Dream true today? Do we have equal opportunity in the U.S.? Is hard work always rewarded with monetary gain? Is everyone who works hard rewarded? How do we define "work hard?" (Many physically-taxing jobs are not well paid.) A system that rewards people who are determined and who work hard to succeed is often referred to as a *meritocracy*. Do we have a meritocracy today?

4. Ask students to keep these questions in mind and continue to think about them during future lessons that will get into the specifics of obtaining the American Dream.

Suggested Homework

1. Drawing on your new knowledge of the definition of economics and our class discussion, answer the following questions for homework:

    a. Name four things you know about economics.

    b. How does economics relate to your life? How does it affect your family?

    c. What role do you play in the economy? What role does your family play?

    d. How does the economy affect your neighborhood?

Additional Resources

The Ad and the Ego (2005 update). A video that demonstrates the critical connection between consumerism, our debased public discourse, environmental degradation, and our blind faith in economic growth at any cost. It is a comprehensive examination of advertising's impact on our culture of consumption. Available from the producers of the film at http://www.TheAdandtheEgo.com or by calling 310-374-2228.

Affluenza. A 60-minute video that explores consumerism and materialism, and their impact on families, communities and the environment. Produced by KCTS/Seattle and Oregon Public Broadcasting. Can be ordered from Bullfrog Films at 800-543-3764 or by e-mail at bullfrog@igc.org and on the web at www.bullfrogfilms.com. Also, see the PBS web site which has additional information about *Affluenza* and its sequel *Escape From Affluenza* <www.pbs.org/kcts/affluenza>.

Lesson 2: What is Income and Why Do Some People Earn So Much More of It Than Others?

Objectives:

- *Define income and identify the sources of income for different people.*
- *Compare income ranges for different occupations and to the poverty and cost of living standards.*
- *Explore a perspective on where various occupations fall on the income scale.*
- *Discuss perspectives on fair and unfair reasons for differences in income levels.*
- *Name and discuss reasons for pay differences.*

Concepts and Key Terms:

- *income*
- *income distribution*
- *cost of living*
- *poverty level*

Instructional Time

- *55 minutes*

Preparation:

For the Bellringer Activity 2.1:

- *Chart 2a, The Dream vs. The Reality*

For Activity 2.2:

- *Place two masking tape lines parallel to one another on the floor (about eight steps apart in width) for half the length of the classroom. Use big signs to label one line "Poverty Line, $16,090 - Family of 3" and the other "Cost of Living Line, $36,000 - Family of 3." (Look up your state's "Self Sufficiency Standard at www.sixstrategies.org.)*
- *Prepare seven 8.5" x 11" occupation placards. Print one of the occupations listed in the chart below on one side of each card. On the other side, print the occupation and the average annual salary as listed in the chart below. (You may want to tailor the average salaries to actual jobs in your community.) Laminate each card, then punch two holes in it and put a circular piece of string through the holes so the card will hang around the student's neck.*

Occupation	Average Annual Wages
Average Full-time Worker	$35,425
High School Teacher	46,120
Professional with advanced degree	61,526
Clothing Store Clerk	15,600
Minimum Wage Worker	10,712
Truck Driver	28,434
Chief Executive Officer (CEO)	11,750,000

For Activity 2.3:

- *Large size sticky notes, rectangles with hook-and-pile fasteners, or index cards with tape underneath, each one labeled with the following words or phrases describing reasons for pay differences: "Race," "Gender," "Age," "Number of hours worked," "Type of work: how difficult or unpleasant," "Type of work: how necessary or important," "Education required," "Private versus public school education," "Experience," "Hard work," "Who you know," "Your family," "Where you live," "Special skills and talents," "Number of other people with the same job."*
- *Create a "Reasons for Pay Differences" chart on paper or on the board with two columns as shown:*

Reasons For Pay Differences	
FAIR	*UNFAIR*

Conducting the Lesson

Bellringer Activity 2.1: Familes You Know

1. Ask students to close their eyes and think about the families they've met in their life. Ask them to identify which family seems to have the least money coming in? Who seems to have the most money coming in?

2. Ask students to open their eyes and, without telling who the family is, discuss why they guessed that someone has a very low income, what about how they're living leads them to that conclusion, why they guessed someone has a high income, and what about how they're living leads them to that conclusion. (Answers are usually car, house, clothes, and other material items.)

3. Explain that the focus for this lesson will be on who earns how much money in the United States and why. Ask students "What is income?" Write students' suggestions on the board. (Examples of sources of income: wages & salary, gifts from a relative, dividends from stocks, child support, savings account interest, social security check, rent collected from owning real estate, the profit you make when you sell something for more than you paid for it.)

4. Announce: "Let's talk about what leads to a successful income in the U.S. Remember the American Dream activity (see Lesson 1 to incorporate this here), where you were asked to write down your dream career? Keep that in mind and let's focus on determining the true meaning of 'The American Dream.'"

5. Display **Chart 2a, The Dream vs. the Reality.** Ask students what they think about the idea that by working hard and getting an education, a person will usually get more money than that same person would have gotten without that effort.

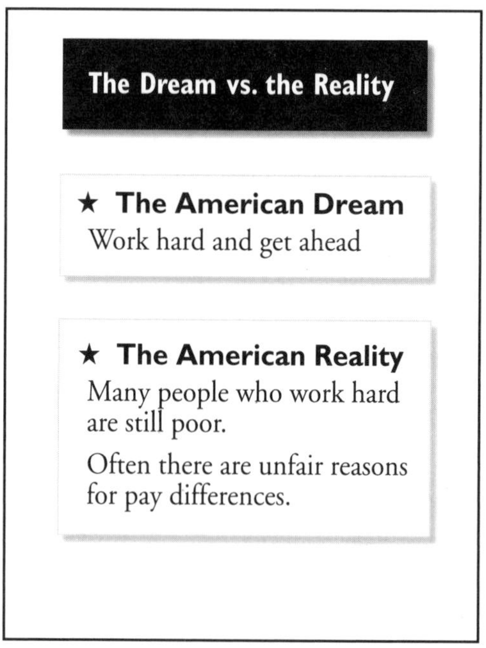

Chart 2a

6. Mention that differences in income between people aren't entirely due to education and effort. Ask students what other factors may affect people's income. (Some examples of factors are race, gender, the quality of schools they attended, parents' income levels, and the city, town, or neighborhood they live in, the availability of well-paying jobs in that area.)

Activity 2.2: Live Illustration of Pay for Different Occupations

1. Ask seven volunteers to stand on the "Cost of Living Line."

2. Explain that the "Cost of Living Line" on which the students are standing is the minimal amount it takes to buy housing, child care, food, transportation, health care, and other necessities, and pay taxes for a family of three. (We have arbitrarily set this line at $36,000 a year, or approximately $17.30 an hour full-time at 40 hours a week. It is based on the "Self Sufficiency Standard," which varies greatly by geographical area. See www.sixstrategies.org to figure out the self sufficiency standard in your area.)

3. Give each of the seven students a card, occupation side showing, and have them line up in the order displayed on the chart.

4. Start with the student holding the card of the "average full-time worker" and ask her to flip over her card to reveal the income level. Explain that for each $5,000 above or below the Cost of Living Line, the student should take one step forward or back. For the "Average Full-time Worker" the $35,425 per year salary is right at the Cost of Living. Ask the student to remain in place.

5. Continue down the line asking the students to show their respective cards and then to move forward (or back) one step for every $5,000 difference between their salaries and the Cost of Living Line.

Occupation	Average Annual Salary	Where to move
Average Full-time Worker	$35,425	Stay in place
High School Teacher	46,120	2 steps forward
Professional with advanced degree	61,526	5 steps forward
Clothing Store Clerk	15,600	4 steps back
Minimum Wage Worker	10,712	5 steps back
Truck Driver	28,434	1 1/2 steps back
Chief Executive Officer (CEO)	11,750,000	2,343 steps forward

DEFINITIONS:

The Self Sufficiency Standard of $36,000 is based on two adults with a preschooler and a school-age child in Alamosa County, CO. The Cost of Living Line would be higher in many large cities and lower in rural areas in the Midwest and South. For this activity, you can estimate your own Cost of Living Line by researching and adding up the typical monthly rent, child-care, food, transportation, and health care costs for a family of three in your area.

Other Self-Sufficiency Standards for a family of three with one adult, one preschooler, and one school-age child:

Adair County, OK	$22,432
Atlanta, GA	$37,982
Chicago, IL	$38,281
Danbury, CT	$58,202
Floyd County, GA	$26,249
Los Angeles, CA	$42,392
Orange County, IN	$20,742
Philadelphia, PA	$38,759
Washington, DC	$47,916

6. As the salary for each occupation is revealed, ask students about the background required for the job (with the exception of the "Average Full-time Worker.")

Teacher: A hard job that requires four years of college education.

Professional: Six to eight years of college; often works long hours.

Store Clerk: Works full-time, eight hours a day, five days a week, 50 weeks a year, yet still earns $10-15,000 less than the Cost of Living!

Minimum Wage Worker: Working full time will still make nearly $6,000 less than the poverty line.

Truck Driver: Works long hours under difficult conditions but may still fall below the self-sufficency standard.

CEO: The top executives of the biggest companies in the U.S. earned an average of $10.8 million in 2005 — more than 1000 times the cost of living.

You may want to stop and talk about the fairness of the incomes, asking for example, "Does it seem fair for the store clerk to work full-time and not be able to support a family of three?"

7. Ask students to suggest typical jobs held by full-time minimum wage workers. (Examples are store clerks, fast-food workers, agricultural workers, teachers' aides, hospital orderlies, etc.)

8. Your discussion may have led to what is fair and unfair regarding income. Thank the volunteers, ask them to take a seat, and begin the next activity where students will review some of the reasons for pay differences and then decide if these reasons are fair or unfair.

Activity 2.3: Separating Reasons for Pay Differences Into Fair and Unfair Reasons

1. Display the "Fair / Unfair Chart." Have the sticky notes with the reasons for pay differences stuck along the side of the chart (not in either column).

2. Ask students to look at the phrases and decide whether they belong in the FAIR or UNFAIR column.

3. Ask for volunteers to come up to the board and place one of the phrases in the column where they believe it fits. You can wait until all of the words are placed in a column to conduct an open discussion, or discuss each word as it is placed. Students will likely disagree with each other on where to place some of the words and this can evolve into a critical review of why people receive large amounts of pay.

4. If you plan to assign the homework below and conduct the lesson that follows this one (Lesson 3), reflect on how the inability for some full-time workers to pay their bills and meet their needs is just one of many "signs of the economic times."

Suggested Homework: Signs of the Economic Times

1. Have students ask their parent, guardian, or an adult neighbor to provide a few "signs of the economic times." Specifically, ask them to identify signs that indicate the condition of the economy. Questions could include:

- How would you describe the differences between the way people live today and the way they lived 20 or 30 years ago? Are people living better today?
- Is there more job stability today?
- Do you feel your real wages (adjusted for inflation) are growing today?
- Are wages keeping pace with inflation?
- Are you feeling pressured to do more work and/or work longer hours for the same amount of money?
- Have retirement and benefit plans been weakened?
- Are health care costs going up?
- Are education costs going up?
- Have you benefited from the stock market boom?
- Do you know people who have been laid off due to corporate downsizing?

2. Students record the answers and bring them to class the next day to share. (See Lesson 3 for putting this homework assignment to use in class.)

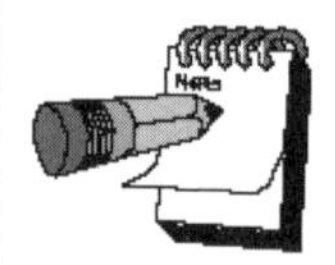

Note to Teacher

Some schools may have policies prohibiting students from taking home questionnaires or anything similar. Check with administrators before assigning this homework.

DEFINITION:

Downsizing is when corporations lay off people and eliminate their positions, asking remaining employees to take on more responsibilities.

The Dream vs. the Reality

★ The American Dream

Work hard and get ahead

★ The American Reality

Many people who work hard are still poor.

Often there are unfair reasons for pay differences.

Chart 2a

Lesson 3: Signs of the Economic Times

Objectives:

- *Review economic trends from 1980 to present.*
- *Explore how these trends have affected our communities, our families, and our daily lives.*
- *Define and compare* ***Gross Domestic Product*** *(GDP) and GDP per capita with* ***Gross National Product*** *(GNP) and GNP per capita.*
- *Compare the merits of GDP and GNP as indicators of economic progress with other social indicators.*
- *Compare full employment versus temporary work.*
- *Discuss trends in availability of worker benefits including health care and retirement plans.*

Concepts and Key Terms:

- *Gross Domestic Product (GDP) and GDP per capita*
- *Gross National Product (GNP) and GNP per capita*
- *pro-family economic agenda*
- *inflation*
- *cooperative*
- *unemployment*
- *economic indicators*

Instructional Time:

- *55 minutes*

Preparation:

For the Bellringer Activity 3.1:

- *15 large black markers*
- *2 large sticky notes per student*
- *Charts 3a, Nation at a Crossroads and 3b, The Trends Since 1980.*

For Activity 3.2:

- *One handout per student of either of the two following articles: "Underemployment" or "Shrinking Benefits." Half the class will work with each article.*
- *Charts 3c, Increase in Number of Total Employees and Temporary Help Employees; 3d, Percentage of Employees with Employer-Provided Benefits, 1986-2004.*

For Activity 3.3:

- *Optional: Obtain data from the latest copy of* State of the World's Children *published annually by UNICEF and available through the United Nations. This document compares GNP with other factors in industrialized and developing countries. (See the Additional Resources section for more information on how to obtain a copy.)*

For Extra Activity 3.5: On Inflation

- *3 candy bars and plenty of play money*

"Yes, this is a two career household. Unfortunately I have both careers."

Conducting the Lesson

Bellringer Activity 3.1: Signs of the Economic Times

1. If you assigned the "Signs of the Economic Times" homework activity from the previous lesson, have students discuss and share their answers in pairs.

2. Otherwise, ask students to identify and discuss in pairs, signs they see around them that indicate how the economy is doing.

3. An alternative to asking students to name some indicators of our economy's economic health is to provide opposing categories listing some "traditional" economic indicators and some "alternative" economic indicators, and ask students to compare the lists. For example:

Traditional Economic Indicators	Alternative Economic Indicators
The Stock Market	Adult literacy rate
GDP and GNP per capita (see below)	Children living in poverty
Unemployment rate	Number of homeless
Inflation rate	Amount of leisure time

4. Hand out large markers and sticky notes. After a few minutes of paired discussion, ask each student to write two of their "signs of the economic times" on a separate post-it for each sign.

5. Ask students to voluntarily come to the front of the room and post their "signs" on the board. Ask them to group similar answers together so themes can be determined.

6. Discuss the themes and make a list of them of them on the board. Then confirm that studies show that economic insecurity is growing for many people and our nation is indeed at a crossroads. Display **Chart 3a, Nation at a Crossroads.** The chart includes "signs" that the students may not have named, such as fear of crime, increase in gated communities, or anger at welfare recipients and immigrants. Discuss these at length if students are interested.

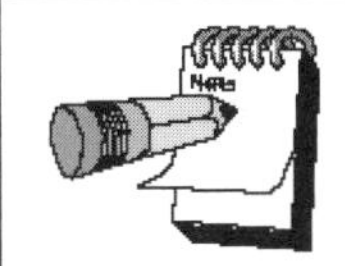

Note to Teacher

Check if your students are aware of how the media portrays the economy. Is it described as "prosperous" or "performing poorly?" How is the performance of the stock market described?

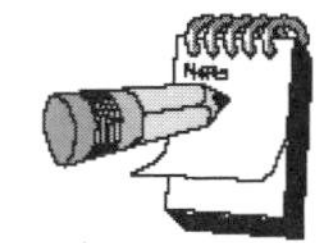

Note to Teacher

Activity 3.3 takes a similar approach as the alternative in Activity 3.1, instruction 2. If you choose to do this activity, you may need to alter the lesson according to students' ability and begin directly with the "Nation at a Crossroads" chart.

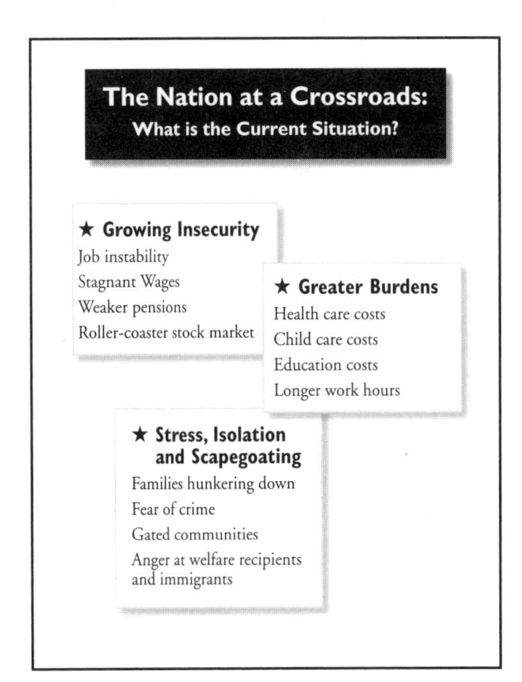

Chart 3a

7. Review the points on **Chart 3b, The Trends Since 1980.**

TALKING POINTS:

These trends are alarming, especially in light of how quickly (less than 20 years) they have occurred.

In most cases, periods of economic growth have resulted in greater equality, as in the 1940s through the 1970s. Over the past 20 years, however, the benefits of the growing economy have been concentrated on a narrow elite at the top. We haven't seen this happen since the 1920s.

Economist Wallace Peterson points out that three out of four U.S. workers have experienced a decline in their standard of living: either a drop in purchasing power, a loss of benefits, or a change in job security. More and more people have the experience of being "temped," "outsourced," "adjuncted," or "downsized" (define these terms, if necessary).

Chart 3b

Activity 3.2: Underemployment and Shrinking Benefits

1. Break students into two groups. Give each member of both groups one of the two articles included with this lesson plan: "Underemployment" or "Shrinking Benefits." Ask the students to silently read their articles and then discuss them with the group. Explain that their task will be to share the information in the article with the other group. Ask one person to serve as "scribe" to summarize the article and record the main points.

2. When sufficient time has passed, ask the group who read "Underemployment" to come to the front of the class and explain what they read.

3. Show the students **Chart 3c, Increase in Number of Total Employees and Temporary Help Employees** and discuss the growth in temporary work. Ask students if they have known anyone or have family members who have accepted temporary work but would prefer full-time work. Explain how temporary and part-time work distorts unemployment statistics. Explain how unemployment statistics in the United States leave out many people, including people who have exhausted their unemplyment insurance benefits, people in prison, and those people who have become discouraged and are no longer seeking employment.

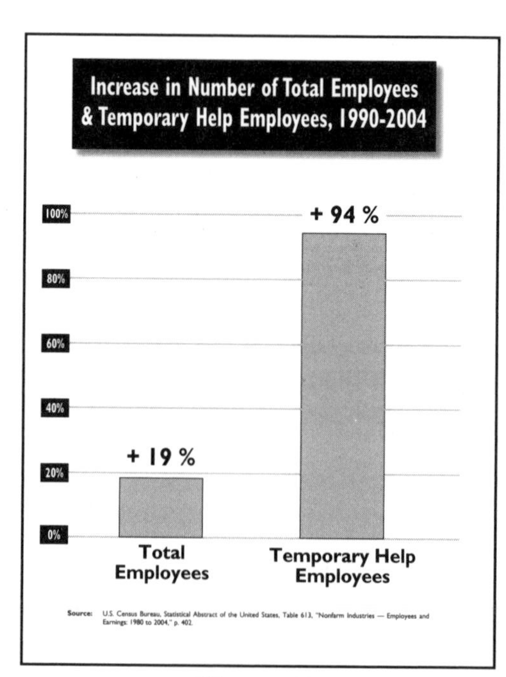

Chart 3c

4. Ask the group who read "Shrinking Benefits" to come to the front of the class and explain the article. Then show students the following charts: **Chart 3d, Percentage of Employees with Employer-Provided Benefits.**

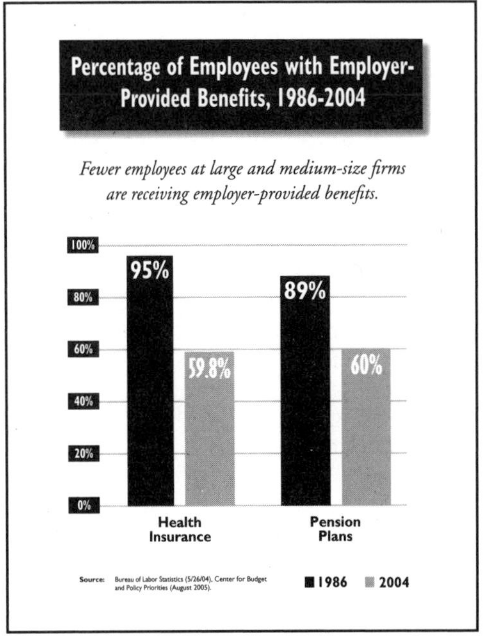

Chart 3d

5. Discuss whether or not students know people without health insurance. You may need to define health insurance and explain the importance of it. Provide students with examples of the high costs of medical care for people without insurance. (A trip to a hospital emergency room for stitches costs several hundred dollars. An operation to remove a burst appendix will probably cost several thousand dollars.)

> **DEFINITION:**
>
> An ***insurance policy*** is a contract entered into to secure against loss, damage, etc. (in this case illness or injury requiring medical treatment) by the payment of a specified sum.
>
> Average health insurance in the U.S. costs nearly $4,000 per person per year ($333 per person per month). Some employers may pay a certain amount of this cost per month to the insurance company for their salaried employees. As the decrease in employer-provided insurance occurs, many people cannot afford the monthly cost of health insurance on their own. Without insurance, these same people are faced with high costs when medical emergencies occur.

6. Summarize: In the 1950s, '60s, and '70s, the jobs people could get with just a high school education often paid enough to support a family, buy a house, pay for college education for their children, and retire with a pension (retirement income) plan. Now, many jobs people obtain with a high school degree don't even pay enough to cover the costs of rent and food. Ask students "Why do you think it is important to pay people a living wage regardless of their educational level? Why not?"

> **TALKING POINT:**
>
> Interestingly, Japan and Sweden, second and third most equal countries in terms of income and wealth, are sixth and seventh highest, respectively, in life expectancy. The U.S., by comparison, is 92nd in income and wealth equality and 48th in life expectancy. — "Healthy, wealthy; even small business can move to make employees healthier, which cuts costs" (Brian Long, *Pittsburgh Post Gazette*, Feb. 28, 2006).

Underemployment

The unemployment rate is more complicated than the percentage of people who are out of work. For example, workers who have part-time or temporary jobs are counted as fully "employed" even though many of them would prefer full-time, permanent work.

In 2005, the annual average unemployment rate was 5.1%. But this doesn't include jobless people who want a job but who have stopped looking for work. These folks are called "discouraged workers." Adding part-timers who want a full time job and discouraged workers to the unemployment rate results in an *underemployment rate* of 9.3% for January 2005.

Pay and benefits are lower for temporary workers, with less than 10% receiving employer-provided medical benefits.

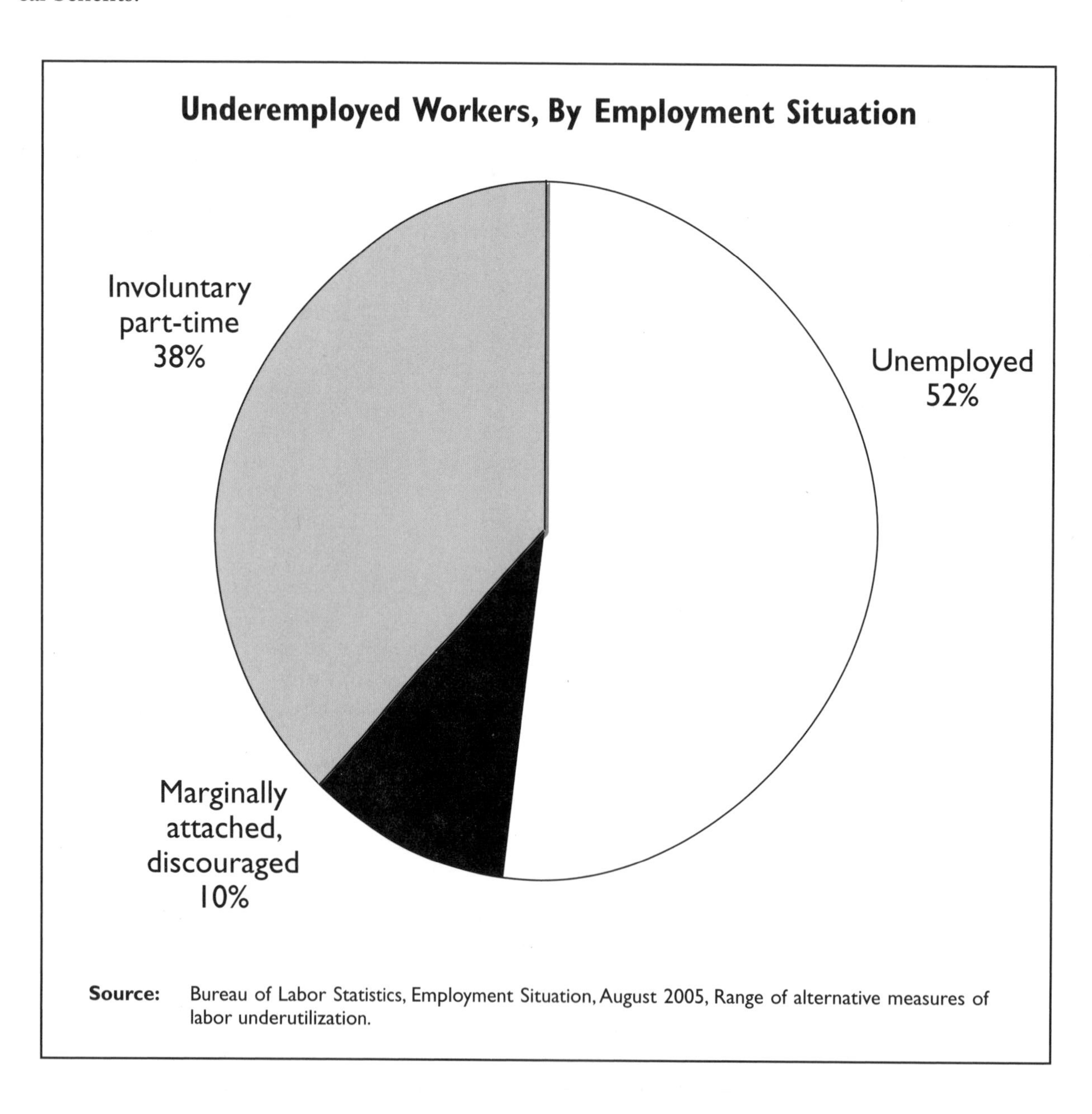

Source: Bureau of Labor Statistics, Employment Situation, August 2005, Range of alternative measures of labor underutilization.

Shrinking Benefits

Employees often get more than a paycheck from their employers. For many workers, health and retirement benefits are just as important as wages or salary. But since the 1980s, fewer employees are covered by these benefits.

The percentage of employees at medium-sized and large firms that had health insurance dropped from 95% in 1986 to 59.8% in 2005. This means that more employees have to pay for health insurance out of their own pockets, or else they have to do without health insurance. The number of people in the U.S. without health insurance rose steadily throughout the 1990s. People lacking health insurance are less likely to get preventitive health care.

Another type of employee benefit is a retirement plan, which sets up payments to the employee for his or her retirement years. The percentage of employees at medium-sized and large firms covered by retirement benefits dropped from 89% in 1986 to 60% in 2005 (36% with defined benefits — employer contribution, the rest are employee contribution plans like 401K.

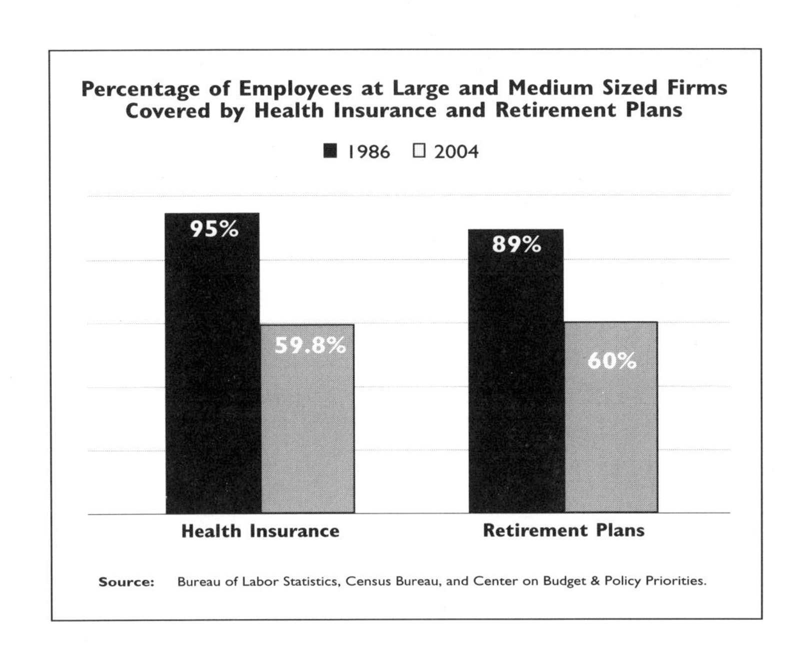

TALKING POINT:

In the wake of the Great Depression of the 1930s and World War II, workers wanted more economic security. In 1950, General Motors (GM), the largest company in the U.S., offered every GM employee health care benefits and a pension, in contract negotiations with the United Auto Workers union (UAW). Walter Reuther, the national president of the UAW, thought that all workers, not just those lucky enough to work for GM, deserved such benefits. The labor movement in general at that time believed that the safest and most efficient way to provide against ill health or old age was to spread the costs and risks of benefits over the biggest and most diverse group possible, i.e., a "universal" program like Social Security. On the other hand, "Engine" Charlie Wilson, CEO of GM, thought that "collectivization" was a threat to the free market and to the autonomy of business owners. Wilson's view prevailed.

Now, the private pension and health care systems in the U.S. are in crisis. Hundreds of thousands of retired steel workers and airline employees, for example, have seen promised health care benefits vanish. Rather than being "over-generous" when it comes to providing benefits, as some say about the big corporations — in fact the U.S. is about average among industrialized countries — the difference is that in most of these countries ***the government*** provides pensions and health insurance.

– "The Risk Pool" by Malcom Gladwell, *The New Yorker*, 9/13/06

Activity 3.3: Family Values and the Gross Domestic Product

1. This "spectrum" activity takes a further step using the "signs of the economic times" to determine how family values have been affected. Explain to students that they will serve as a human social barometer in responding to several statements. After each statement, those who agree stand on one side of the room, those who disagree stand on the other, and those who are in between stand in the middle. Once students have taken their places, ask someone from each group to say why they are there. Ask students questions to clarify their positions and ask them to provide examples. Once the positions have been clarified and some of the arguments made, ask any students who have changed their minds to shift to the part of the room that reflects their new opinion.

Spectrum Statements

"You know a community, or a particular place is healthy and/or successful because...

a. ...it has a low crime rate
b. ...it has a high level of academic achievement
c. ...the houses are big and the cars are new
d. ...the adults have a lot of leisure time
e. ...many of the mothers do not work and spend the day with their children
f. ...there are many stores for shopping

2. After the spectrum activity, ask students to come up with other indicators of a healthy community. Ask if they know the standard indicator used in determining the economic progress of a community and/or country?

3. Ask students to guess what country has the highest GNP per capita in the world. Provide students with the GNP per capita for the United States, which was $29,240 in 2003. Compare the U.S. GNP per capita to that of other countries. Show a range of countries with varying GNP per capita.

GNP per Capita Examples

Country	GNP per capita
Luxembourg	$36,978
Israel	$16,375
China	$1,035
Mexico	$6,059
Sweden	$26,517
Singapore	$20,677

DEFINITIONS:

Gross Domestic Product (GDP): The total market value of all final goods and services produced during a year by resources located within a certain country, regardless of who owns the resources.

GDP per capita: GDP divided by the number of people in a country.

Gross National Product (GNP): The total market value of all final goods and services produced during a year by resources owned within a certain country, regardless of where the resources are located.

(GNP = GDP + net foreign factor income.) Note the difference between GDP and GNP for a given country is whether or not the resources are **located** within the country (GDP) or **owned** within the country (GNP).

4. *Optional:* Add information from the UNICEF report, *State of the World's Children* (2005) here. This report can be downloaded from www.unicef.org. Contrast GNP per capita with other indicators of progress such as economic literacy, infant mortality rates, etc. Students are often surprised to find that countries with lower GNP per capita than the US rank better in categories such as these than the US. This document exposes the GNP and GNP per capita as insufficient indicators of the true progress of a nation.

5. Remind students that some countries provide greater health insurance and more maternity leave for their citizens than the US does. How is it possible that these countries could spend less on health care per capita than the United States and still provide more services?

6. Bring the focus of discussion back to what our economic success looks like for the average family.

TALKING POINTS:

The average vacation time in the United States is two weeks per year, and there is no minimum vacation time mandated by the government. In many European countries, on the other hand, minimum vacation times are written into law. In France the minimum is five weeks paid vacation, in Germany, it is six weeks plus holidays. Workers in Sweden, Spain, Denmark, and Austria all take at least six weeks of vacation per year. The average in Japan is five weeks.

We spend six hours a week shopping and 40 minutes a week playing with our children.

The average person in the U.S. is working 36 more hours per year in 2005 than in 1990 and spends over 100 hours a year commuting to and from work.

Sources: Average vacation time: World Tourism Organization (www.world-tourism.org). Time spent shopping, playing with children, working, and communting: US Dept of Labor, Bureau of Labor Statistics, American Time Use Survey (www.bls.gov/tus/datafiles_2005.htm).

Activity 3.4: Create a Pro-Family Economic Agenda

1. Count students off into small groups of four or five. Give them approximately five minutes to come up with a list (containing at least five items) of what they would do to create a "pro-family economic agenda." Explain that they do not have to go into detail explaining how the agenda will be implemented. They need only to list their ideas. Ask one student in each group to "scribe" the group's answers.

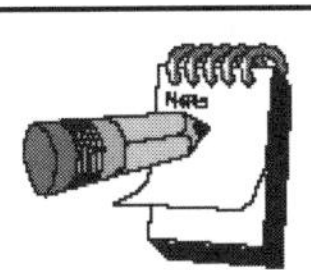

Note to Teacher

If time does not permit this activity, assign it for individual homework and begin by reviewing students' answers the following day. *This is an important part of the lesson. It is vital that students be given a chance to discuss how to implement POSITIVE change and reverse some of the trends they just discussed.*

2. When time is up, ask the scribe to go to the board and write down the ideas the group listed. Use their ideas to come up with an agenda from the entire class. Some of the ideas will likely overlap. (Some suggestions: raise the minimum wage, provide adequate income for families to save money, provide equal access to education and training, provide paid maternity leave, provide equal access to health care.)

3. Take one (or two if time permits) of the students' suggestions and discuss how this change would be implemented. Ideas may range from writing Congress to choosing to boycott products made by companies that don't pay a living wage. (See Lesson 21 for an explanation of The Living Wage Campaign.)

Extra Activity 3.5: Inflation

1. Bring in three candy bars and several pieces of "play" money. (It is easy to make your own.) Hand out a random amount of play money to each student. Start taking bids for the candy bars. Students quickly count their money and complain how some have more than others. Interject that some must have been born into wealthier families than others.

2. Take a few bids and give the candy bar to the highest bidder, taking their money away, and recording the amount paid for the candy bar on the board.

3. Give out even more money this time so there is much more money in circulation. Begin bids for the candy bar again and exchange the candy bar for the money of the highest bidder. Record the amount paid.

4. Repeat the exercise handing out loads of money for the last round. The bids will go much higher this time. Record the amount paid and discuss how the candy bar was the same product but because there was more money in circulation people were willing to pay more for it. They had more money but each individual "dollar" was worth less. Relate this to the definition of inflation.

5. Other subjects that may arise for discussion include whether or not students formed co-operatives or corporations in order to purchase the candy bar together and share it.

Note to Teacher

Depending upon the knowledge base of your students you may need to stop and teach the definition of inflation. This exercise can be done in conjunction with Lesson 1 (while explaining the relationship between unemployment and inflation), with Lesson 2 (in assigning the homework questions for "Signs of the Economic Times,") or in Lesson 3 with the Bellringer activity.

DEFINITION:

Inflation is a rise in the price level (or average level of prices) of all goods and services over a period of time. Equivalently, it is a decline in the purchasing power of a unit of money (such as the dollar) over a period of time.

Additional Resources

- *The State of the World's Children*, published annually by the United Nations Children Fund (UNICEF), available online at www.unicef.org.

- *Genuine Progress Indicator.* Each year, **Redefining Progress** releases the *Genuine Progress Indicator,* an alternative to determining economic health using the Gross Domestic Product <www.rprogress.org>. The gross domestic product simply adds up all the money we spend and calls the results economic growth. In 1995, Redefining Progress created a more accurate measure of progress, called the Genuine Progress Indicator (GPI), which adds in the economic contributions of household and volunteer work, and subtracts factors such as crime, pollution, and family breakdown.

- *Who's Counting, Marilyn Waring on Sex, Lies and Global Economics.* A film produced by The National Film Board of Canada; available from Bullfrog Films <www.bullfrogfilms.com>. This film takes a closer look at GDP figures and how they form the basis of macroeconomic policy throughout the world without relation to the well-being of people and communities.

- *Life-Centered Economic Indicators* is a study packet of alternative ways of measuring our quality of life at national and local levels, to supplement or replace the GDP. Purchase from the Who's Counting? Project c/o Lebensold, 7575 Sunkist Drive, Oakland, CA 94605. E-mail: loisjoines@igc.apc.org.

The Nation at a Crossroads:
What is the Current Situation?

★ Growing Insecurity
Job instability
Stagnant Wages
Weaker pensions
Roller-coaster stock market

★ Greater Burdens
Health care costs
Child care costs
Education costs
Longer work hours

★ Stress, Isolation and Scapegoating
Families hunkering down
Fear of crime
Gated communities
Anger at welfare recipients and immigrants

Chart 3a

The Trends Since 1980

★ The Good News

Inflation down

Unemployment down

★ The Bad News

Most growth in income has gone to the top 1%

Wealth is even more concentrated at the top

Wages have not recovered to early-1970s level

Gap between highest and lowest paid workers has widened

★ By some measures, the U.S. economy has done well.

★ But the rising tide has only lifted a few boats.

Chart 3b

Increase in Number of Total Employees & Temporary Help Employees, 1990-2004

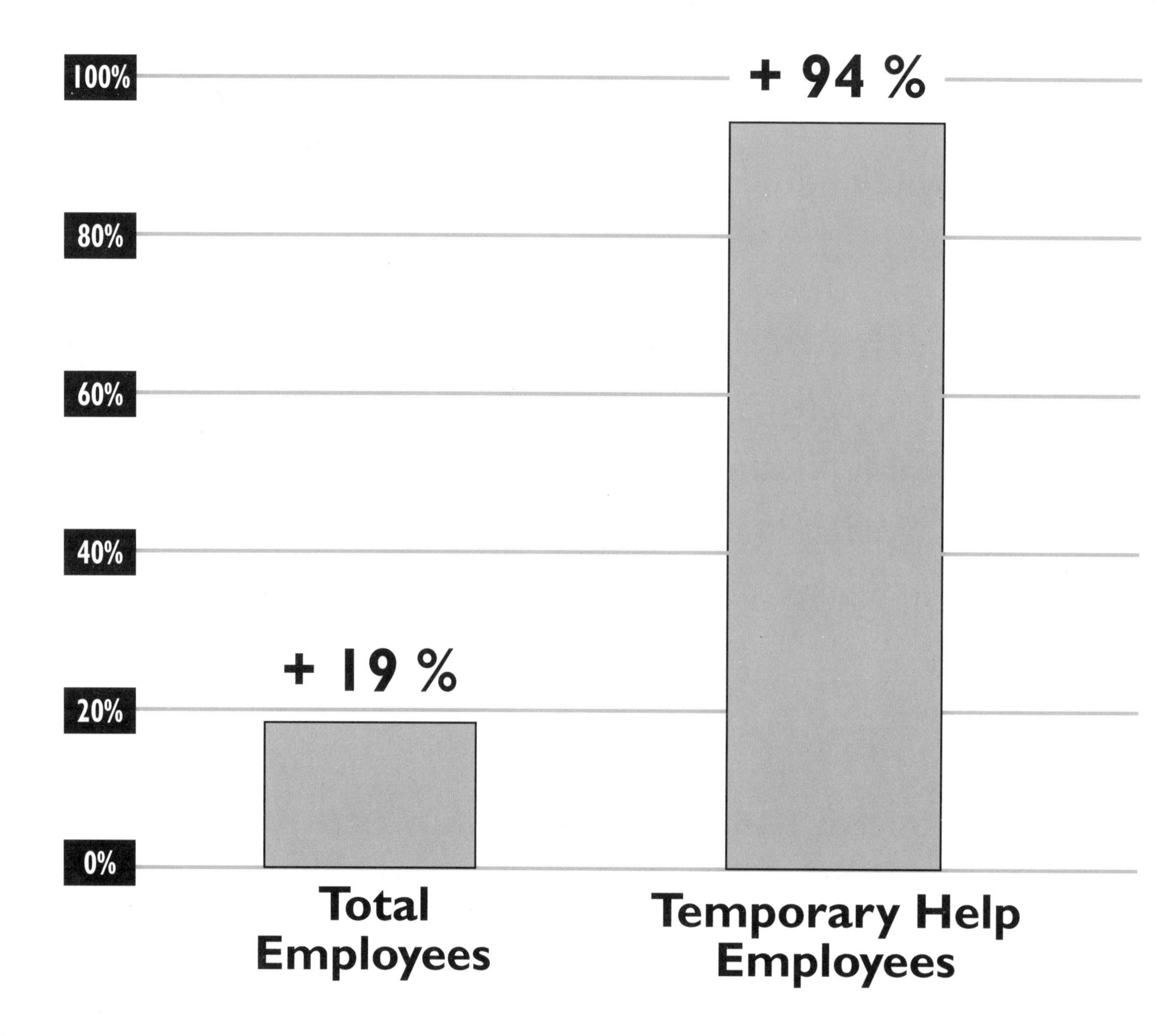

Source: U.S. Census Bureau, Statistical Abstract of the United States, Table 613, "Nonfarm Industries — Employees and Earnings: 1980 to 2004," p. 402.

Chart 3c

Percentage of Employees with Employer-Provided Benefits, 1986-2004

Fewer employees at large and medium-size firms are receiving employer-provided benefits.

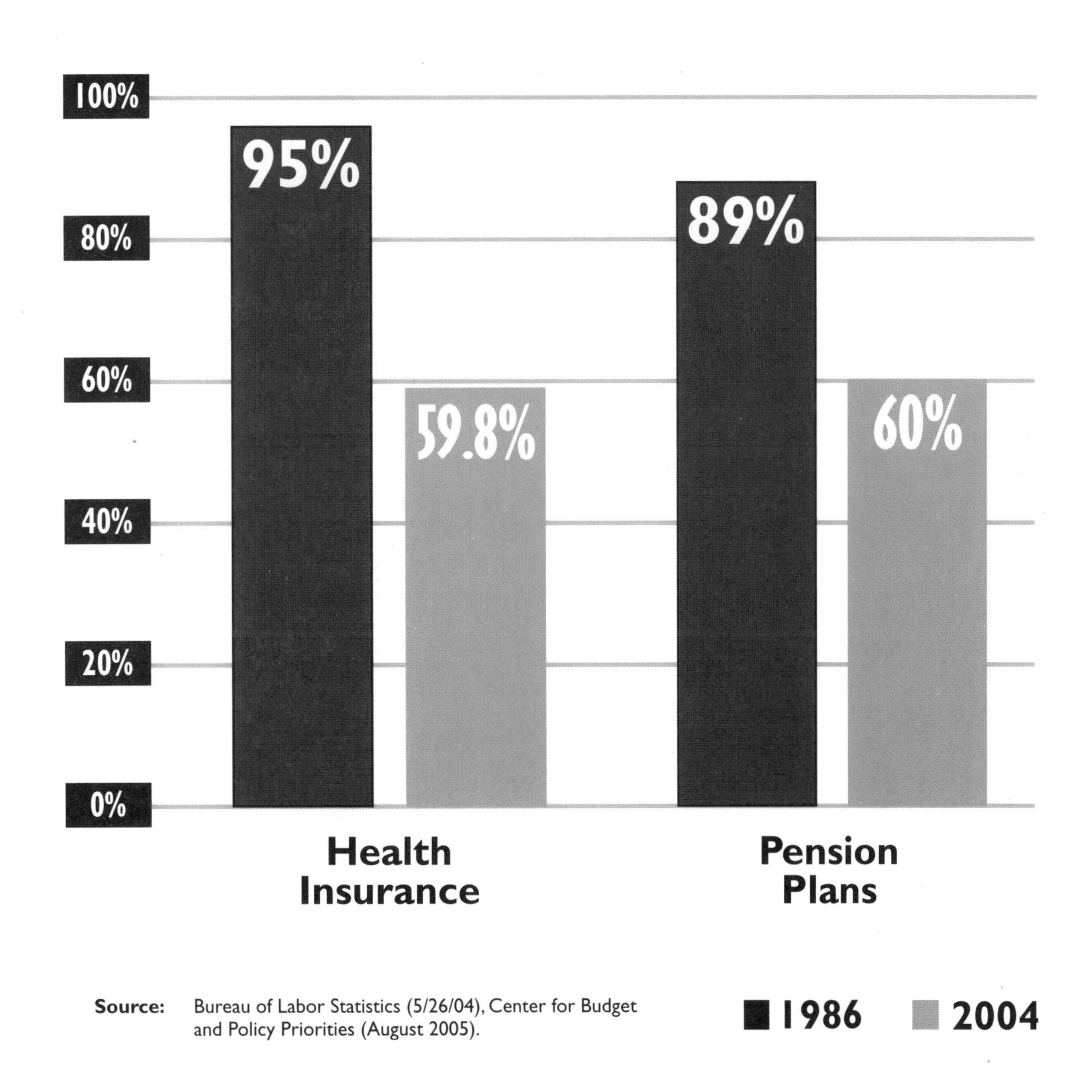

Source: Bureau of Labor Statistics (5/26/04), Center for Budget and Policy Priorities (August 2005).

■ 1986 ■ 2004

Chart 3d

Lesson 4: Distributing Income: You Be the Judge

Objectives:

- *Experience the realistic decision-making process of determining who should have an increase or decrease in income.*
- *Explore how most decisions are made in the business world regarding increases and decreases in income.*

Concepts and Key Terms:

- *distribution of income*
- *how businesses often decide to distribute income*
- *the merits of belonging to a union*

Instructional Time:

- *55 minutes*

Preparation:

For the Bellringer Activity 4.1:

- *Five chocolate bars ("$100 Grand" bars if available)*
- *Seven sets of five post-its marked $100,000. Mark one of the seven sets with B on the bottom of each $100,000 bill. Hand these to the Bosses when you are handing out the $100,000 post-it bills.*
- *Seven 8.5"x11" placards, each displaying one of the job titles in the following chart. Put strings through each sign so students can hang them over their necks.*
- *The following chart made into poster size, and hung at the front of the classroom.*

Bosses	$450,000/year
Doctors	$125,000/year
Nurses	$40,000/year
Kitchen Workers & Nurses Aides	$13,000/year
Gardeners/Security Guards/Janitors	$16-21,000/year
Patients	fixed income, social security
Low-income Elderly on Waiting List	$10,000/year

- *Place the profiles below and on page 25 onto seven separate index cards (and then paired with the corresponding placard explained above).*

---

*You are the **Bosses**: the management of Sunnyvale and of the nursing home chain that owns Sunnyvale.*

Possible Arguments:

- *Senior managers here make less money than at other nursing homes. At another chain, executives make $500,000 to $700,000!*
- *Because of this, turnover is high. There have been three financial managers in five years!*
- *We deserve a raise! We only received a $5,000 raise last year. We cut costs by reducing the number of nurses and gardeners last year. We should be rewarded for this cost cutting.*
- *With just three of the $100,000 bills, all five of the top managers could make as much as we would at other nursing homes.*

---

*You are the **Doctors** at Sunnyvale.*

Possible Arguments:

- *If we went into private practice, we'd all make $200,000 a year or more — double the measly amount we make here.*
- *The patients we treat are getting older and sicker, so our work is getting more complicated.*
- *We have the longest training and the most advanced skills of anyone here. We deserve to get the biggest raise. Two of the five $100,000 should go to us.*

You are the **Nurses** at Sunnyvale.

Possible Arguments:

- *There are fewer nurses taking care of more patients than last year. We are working harder and so should get paid more — but we only received a $400 raise last year! For some of us, our rent went up more than that!*
- *It's ridiculous that we go to four years of specialized school and our pay ceiling is $45,000. It's because most of us are women!*
- *Just two of the five $100,000 bills would give us raises we think would be fair.*

You are the ***Janitors, Security Guards, and Gardeners*** at Sunnyvale.

Possible Arguments:

- *Our work is dirty and sometimes dangerous. We have to work outside in all weather. Two gardeners now do all the work that four gardeners used to do.*
- *We can hardly support our families on this pay. We can't save money or buy health insurance, or send our kids to college.*
- *Some of us have worked here since Sunnyvale started 15 years ago, and we've hardly gotten any raises in all that time!*
- *With two of the $100,000 bills, we could get health insurance and a raise to a living wage.*

You are the **Patients** at Sunnyvale.

Possible Arguments:

- *The fees for our nursing home are so high that they harm our families. The fees take money that they need for other things.*
- *Some nursing homes charge less and have nice facilities that we don't have, like a swimming pool, and activities every day instead of every other day.*
- *With just two of the $100,000 bills, we could get a cut in the fees we pay AND some new and improved facilities and activities.*

You are ***the Kitchen Workers and Nurses' Aides*** at Sunnyvale.

Possible Arguments:

- *We can't support our families on the pay here. Many of us don't have cars, phones or health insurance.*
- *We think it's because we're all women – mostly women of color or recent immigrants, – that we're paid less than anyone else here.*
- *We are the ones who actually care for the patients.*
- *Our work is dirty and difficult. We change diapers and bathe patients. We stay an average of only five months because we are continually looking elsewhere for higher pay. This high turnover is bad for the patients who see new faces constantly.*
- *With two of the $100,000 bills, we could get raises to a wage where we could meet our expenses and pay our monthly bills. With a third one, we could have health insurance.*

You are the ***Low-income Elderly People on a Waiting List*** to get into one of the 10 government subsidized* slots at Sunnyvale.

Possible Arguments:

- *We really need a nursing home. We can't live at home any more, because we can't feed or dress ourselves and we need daily medical care. It might be many months before a Medicaid (subsidized*) slot opens up.*
- *On our incomes of $10,000 or so, how could we afford the standard $30,000 a year price for Sunnyvale?*
- *Our families can't afford it either.*
- *Sunnyvale should spend three of the $100,000 bills subsidizing slots for us, so we can move in now.*

** Subsidize: to grant public aid (money) to an individual or a private enterprise (corporation) for public benefits.*

Conducting the Lesson

Bellringer Activity 4.1: Income Distribution Role Play

1. Tell the class, "We have been talking about how American workers are losing ground. We will now look at "why" this happens by conducting a role-play based on a real life situation where we will look at the fairness in the distribution of incomes."

2. Announce: "Sunnyvale Nursing Home has an extra $500,000. We are going to decide who should get this extra money. These five candy bars represent five $100,000 bills, and at the end of the role-play I will divide the candy up the way the money is allocated in the role-play. Each of you get five $100,000 bills to vote on who you think should get the money. There are seven different groups at Sunnyvale Nursing home, so I need seven volunteers (to sit in the middle of the circle or at the front of the room). You will be given teams and you will be the spokesperson for your team."

3. Divide the rest of the students evenly among the seven volunteers and ask them to sit together as seven separate teams. Give each team's spokesperson the bills (give marked bills to the bosses), index cards, and signs (to hang around their necks).

4. Announce: "Your job is to persuade the other groups that your group should get some of the money. Read and discuss your card with your group, then decide where you think the five $100,000 bills should go. Each spokesperson (and members of their group) will have a turn to state their opinion. You can propose something different than what is on the card; these are just suggestions."

5. After seven people speak in turn, conduct discussion as time allows, then conduct a "vote" by asking the spokesperson from each group to place the $100,000 bills on the chart at the front of the room, allocating the funds as they feel they should be distributed.

6. Announce the tallies of how everyone voted. Then hand out the candy bars according to the bosses' vote (marked on the back of their $100,000 bills). See if people object or offer to share, then hold a discussion. Make the point that in a unionized workplace, workers would be represented in this discussion; at a worker coop, everyone would have a vote; at non-union workplaces, the bosses would decide behind closed doors.

Objectives:

- *Review a historical perspective of U.S. income distribution.*
- *Explore current trends of U.S. income distribution.*
- *Examine influential factors in income distribution.*

Concepts and Key Terms:

- *income distribution, historical perspective*
- *income levels, comparing increases during various time periods*
- *income distribution, influential factors*
- *quintile*

Instructional Time:

- *55 minutes*

Preparation:

For the Bellringer Activity 5.1:

A. "Rat Race" Method:

- *60ft x 10ft space*
- *eleven scripts of the "The Rat Race" (included on the following pages); highlight each character's lines on a different script and label the script "ANNOUNCER," "REFEREE," etc., so it will be easy to follow during the performance*
- *seven rat noses (made from the bottom of an egg carton)*
- *two ties (suit jackets optional; find an old suit jacket at home or purchase one or two from a thrift store and keep them at school for other activities.)*
- *two fake microphones (use a walkmate's headphones and two rulers for the commentator look)*
- *one referee shirt (optional)*
- *one whistle*
- *Charts 5a, 1947 to 1979 - Real Family Income Growth by Quintile & for Top 5% and 5b, 1979 to 2003 - Real Family Income Growth by Quintile and for Top 5%.*
- *8.5" x 11" nametags with salary numbers (see below); laminate for future use and put a string through them so students can place them over their necks*
- *three or four copies of cheers for cheerleaders*
- *banners reading "Start line" and "Finish line" (ask for student volunteers to hold the banners)*

B. "Giant Steps" Method:

- *Six, two-sided, 8.5"x11" laminated placards, identifying the income quintiles and income ranges shown in the two tables on page 28. (Put only "income quintile" and "yearly income range" on the cards. The other information is for teacher use. Income is listed in 1979 and 2003 real — adjusted for inflation — dollars.)*

Example of text on one nametag:

Front side: *1947-79 Lowest Income Quintile = $0-9,861*

Flip side: *1979-03 Lowest Income Quintile = $0-24,117.*

- *Charts 5a, 1947 to 1979 - Real Family Income Growth by Quintile & for Top 5% and 5b, 1979 to 2003 - Real Family Income Growth by Quintile and for Top 5%.*

1947-1979 Income Ranges and Change by Quintile

Income Quintile	Yearly Income Range ($1979) (family income before tax)	% Change	Steps (For teacher use only, do not put on the card)
Lowest	$0-9,861	+116%	11 1/2 steps forward
Second	$9,861-16,215	+100%	10 steps forward
Middle	$16,215-22,972	+111%	11 steps forward
Fourth	$22,972-31,632	+114%	11 1/2 steps forward
Highest	$31,632 and up	+ 99%	10 steps forward
Top 5%	$50,746 and up	+ 86%	8 1/2 steps forward

1979-2003 Income Ranges and Change by Quintile

Income Quintile	Yearly Income Range ($2003) (family income before tax)	% Change	Steps (For teacher use only, do not put on the card)
Lowest	$0-24,117	- 2%	1/2 step back
Second	$ 24,117-42,057	+ 8%	1 1/2 steps forward
Middle	$42,057-65,000	+ 15%	3 steps forward
Fourth	$65,000-98,200	+ 26%	5 steps forward
Highest	$98,200 and up	+ 51%	10 steps forward
Top 5%	$170,082 and up	+75%	15 steps forward

Conducting the Lesson

Bellringer Activity 5.1: Income Quintiles

This activity compares income distribution in two recent periods of economic growth in the U.S. 1945-1979 and 1979-2003 using **Chart 5a, 1947-79: Real Family Income Growth by Quintile** and **Chart 5b, 1979-2003: Real Family Income Growth by Quintile.**

These charts show income broken into "quintiles," with a separate bracket for the top five percent. Economists often talk about the U.S.

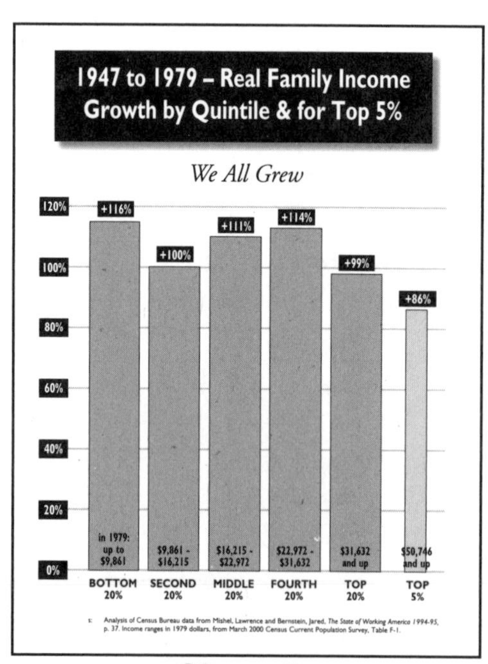

Chart 5a

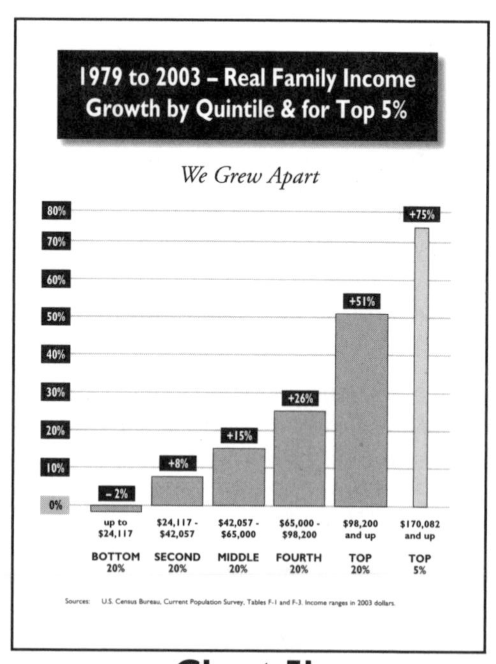

Chart 5b

population in "quintiles" or "fifths" of the population. They imagine the entire population of the U.S. lined up in order, from the lowest income to the highest. They then divide that line into five equal parts.

A. The Rat Race Method

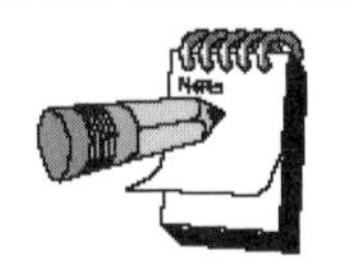

Note to Teacher

This lesson plan provides two methods for demonstrating the growth and decline of incomes in the two time periods — the more detailed "Rat Race" or the more straightforward "Giant Steps." Choose one method and follow the instructions.

1. The Rat Race script humorously portrays the unequal income growth that has occurred among these different economic levels (quintiles) over the last fifteen years. It is a sporting-event spoof with play-by-play TV announcers, cheerleaders, and so on. Different runners in the "rat race" represent different economic strata, and the number of steps they take forward (or backward) during the race accurately represents the growth (or loss) of income during the recent period. The results of the race paint a brutal picture of economic disparity that the skit cuts with humor. Before starting the skit, explain income quintiles and the phrase "rat race" to students. Review the definition of income (from Lesson 3).

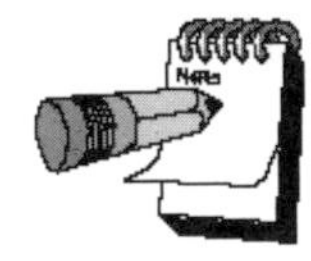

Note to Teacher

This "Rat Race" activity is well worth the preparation needed and leaves a lasting impression on students, who find it enjoyable and informative. It may be easier to assign roles in advance to students you know will be willing to ham it up. For a change of pace, take students outside for "The Race!"

2. Ask for volunteers and assign roles, then take students outside to get in their positions. If you prefer to have students read the script in advance, you may want to ask for volunteers and assign roles the day before you conduct this activity. Or if you want to rehearse the skit before performing it, arrange to have a colleague sit for approximately ten minutes with the students not in the skit and have an alternative activity for them. Then take the students involved in the skit outside. It is possible to include many students in the skit. There are thirteen scripted parts. You can add four students to hold the banners and as many cheerleaders as desired to include the entire class in the skit. The skit takes approximately ten minutes to perform, not including additional time spent discussing the "Talking Points" listed below.

3. Each step a runner takes forward (or backward) represents a 10% change in income for 1947-1979 and a 5% change in income for 1979-2003. Thus the exact number of steps each runner takes is a very important detail. Draw students' attention to their number of steps before beginning the performance.

4. An equally important part of the performance are the runners' salary numbers. These show the actual beginning and ending income statistics for each runner and should be used, if possible. Place one set of numbers (1979 income) on one side of the 8.5"x11" laminated card and the other set (2003 income) on the back side of the card. (See point in script where announcer indicates changes in the runners' salaries.)

5. Further develop the Cheerleaders' role. Create lots of your own chants, using names students will recognize. Develop the text of the TV announcers. Add local flavor to the runners' characters and personal stories. Involve the audience. Near the end of the skit, when announcer is saying, "Many fans are saying that the race is rigged...", have the announcer actually go up to students on the sidelines and interview them, polling their feelings on the topic. To do this well, the announcer must stay in character and keep things moving.

6. Keep students on task. To encourage participation and attentiveness, announce that students will be graded on their content knowledge of the skit at the end of class.

Rat Race Script:

Scene 1:	Pre-Race Warm-Up
Scene 2:	Race
Scene 3:	Post-Race Wrap Up

Character	Costume
ANNOUNCER	Suit, mike
COLOR COMMENTATOR	Suit, ear piece, mike
RACERS: BOTTOM 20% ("**Bottom Dollar**") SECOND 20% MIDDLE 20% ("**Middle Man**") FOURTH 20% TOP 20% TOP 5% ("**Top Dog**")	Shirt & tie above waist, running gear below waist, rat noses, race numbers front & back
REFEREE	Black and white stripes
CHEERLEADERS	Matching outfits: pleated skirt and turtle neck decorated with dollar signs
MUSIC/TRUMPETEER	Cool jazz look

Scene 1: Pre-Race Warm-Up

(Cheerleaders do their pre-game set of cheers. These cheers can be repeated throughout the skit.)

CHEERLEADERS:

2, 4, 6, 8, how do stocks appreciate

Wall Street, Wall Street, Yeaaaaa!!! Wall Street!

Corporate power, corporate power!

Send the losers to the shower!

The wealthy, the wealthy, we gotta keep 'em healthy!

The poor, the poor, kick 'em out the door!

Donald Trump, he's our man!

If he can't do it, no one can!

(Runners are warming up, running in place, stretching... etc.)

ANNOUNCER: Welcome back to WIOU's Widening World of Sports. I'm here with Bob-Cost-Us-A-Lot. We now pause in our coverage of the 100th anniversary of the Boston Marathon...and turn our attention to the race all of us are running, yes, the one we run every day of our lives: the Rat Race.

As with all rat races, the runners here today are competing for income. They have come from every corner of the economy, from the bottom 20% to the top 5%, to compete here today. The runners will begin in their 1979 positions. Each stride they advance represents a 5% growth in income. How far will they get? We'll see in just a few minutes....

So, Bob, what can past races tell us about the results we might see today....

COLOR COMMENTATOR: Not very much, Dave, not much. You see, Dave, it's just not the same sport it used to be. *(Flips up **Chart 5a, Real Family Income Growth by Quintile and for Top 5% - 1947-1979.**)* Looking here, you can see the results from the last time these athletes all competed against each other. The period was 1947 to 1979, and as you can see it was a pretty even contest. Income for all of the competitors rose steadily. But you know, Dave, most commentators feel the sport has changed a lot since then. No one knows what to expect today.

ANNOUNCER: Thanks, Bob. And now tell us...who should we be looking out for today?

COLOR COMMENTATOR: First up, in lane 6, from Dorchester, Mass, we have ***Bottom Dollar*** *(runner raises hands).* Carrying the banner for the bottom 20% of the population today, the hopes and dreams of new immigrants, fast food workers and the underemployed are all riding on her economic performance today.

And at the other end of the track, in lane 1, from Beacon Hill, we have the venerable ***Top Dog*** running for the richest 5% of the population today. He's the favorite of corporate lobbyists, overpaid media stars, and the idle rich everywhere. In the last few years, he's become a truly multi-national powerhouse.

And finally, rounding out the field in lane 4, from Quincy, Mass., our very own ***Middle Man***, representing the middle 20% of the population. Once the defining presence of the sport, this tough competitor has been hamstrung by a series of injuries, forcing her to run tag-team with her spouse on the off-season. And that's about it, Dave, back to you.

ANNOUNCER: Thanks, Bob. All of these athletes have incredible stories. We'll just have to see how these various factors play themselves out....

And looking over at the Referee, it seems we're about to get under way... the runners are now taking their 1979 starting positions...and, remember fans: each stride forward is a 5% growth in income....

Scene 2: The Race

REFEREE: On your marks. Get set. Go! (Fires cap gun or blows whistle.)

ANNOUNCER: And they're off!

(Scene goes into another space: a more inward, dramatic, slow-motion pace.)

(Runners move simultaneously in exaggerated slow motion.)

(Bottom Dollar moves as if running into an incredibly strong head wind, for a brief moment leaning over the starting line but then being blown backwards one-half step.)

(Second 20% inches ahead a step and a half)

(Middle Man runs in place very rapidly and then at the very end, takes three steps forward.)

(Fourth 20% moves ahead five steps.)

(Top 20% moves forward ten steps.)

(Top Dog moves forward fifteen steps in long, loping, caricatured, high-stepping strides.)

(All runners stay in their final positions until skit is over.)

(During race, EITHER:

1) Musician plays theme from Chariots of Fire

OR

2) ***ANNOUNCER & COLOR COMMENTATOR*** *keep up an improvised, very rapid, run-together, play-by-play commentary, based on the following:*

ANNOUNCER/
COLOR COMMENTATOR: In lane 1, we've got…trickle down, real-estate speculation, initial public offerings….

In lane 4, we've got downsizing, permanent displacement, and loss of benefits….

In lane 6, we've got plant shutdowns, low wages, temp work, and run-away shops….

Labor unions are under attack….

Big money is gaining control of politics….

Tax cuts seem to be favoring the wealthy….

Government services are being cut across the board….

Salaries of top corporate executives are multiplying exponentially….

Housing, college, and health care costs are exploding….

The minimum wage is falling behind inflation….

ANNOUNCER: And it's all over folks. That's it. The race is run. And we've got clear winners and losers today. A staggering triumph for privilege. A crushing defeat for the less fortunate. The fans are stunned.

Scene 3: Post-Race Wrap Up

ANNOUNCER: We go now to the field, to get some perspective on this truly polarizing outcome.... *(Flips up **Chart 5b, Real Family Income Growth by Quintile and for Top 5% - 1979-2005.**)*

...Bottom Dollar, running today for the bottom 20%, you experienced a truly punishing loss...what happened out there...?

BOTTOM 20%: I was working hard out there Dave, I was struggling the whole time, but it was brutal. Right from the start, I just seemed to be slipping further and further behind...there wasn't even a safety net to catch me....

ANNOUNCER: ...Bottom Dollar, what is going through your head right at this very moment?

BOTTOM 20%: In part I blame myself, Dave, but it also makes me ANGRY...it's just not the same sport anymore, Dave. Making minimum wage, with no health care, I just can't keep up. Some of us rats just don't have a chance anymore....

ANNOUNCER: It's been a tough couple of decades for you, Bottom Dollar, but I'm sure the fans are hurting right along with you. Maybe you need to pick up another job or two between seasons. Well, hang tough and good luck to you....

ANNOUNCER: ...and Middle Man, representing the middle 20%, you were stagnating out there today, moving ahead only three steps. How do you feel...?

MIDDLE 20%: Frankly, Dave, I'm still stunned... *(panting)*.... I was running hard, really hard, but I just couldn't seem to make much headway at all. With wave after wave of corporate downsizing, I never feel secure. I just don't see how I'll ever get out from under debt or put my kids through college, even if I retrain all season....

ANNOUNCER: I'm sure a lot of fans share your concerns today, Middle Man. With so many middle-class hopes and American dreams pinned on Middle Man's performance, it's surely a dark day for the American rat race....

ANNOUNCER: But even though more than 60% of the population didn't make it more than three steps out of the starting gate today, it's not all bad news...on the bright side, and the surprise of the afternoon, and racking up a triumph unprecedented in the history of the sport, we have Top Dog. Running today for the richest 5%, you swept the field, nearly doubling your income! Congratulations!

TOP 1%: *(Compared to the other runners, an air of victory and proud calm.)* Thanks, Dave, thanks. Yeah, I have to say, it's a really sweet victory, sweeter than I ever expected. Of course, the conditions were all in my favor; I just went out there and did my privileged best. But you know, Dave, I never could have done it alone; I had the whole team behind me. I want to take this opportunity to thank my lobbyists and government inside players. They made it possible for me to cut my taxes, ship jobs overseas, and bust unions. Together we've put in a lot of hard years and today it just paid off.

ANNOUNCER: Congratulations, Top Dog, and the fans seem to think you earned every million of it! Your victory today surely marks the transition to a whole new economy.... Where to now?

TOP 1%: I'm going to Disney World!! And maybe I'll buy it!

ANNOUNCER: Well, we've just heard from the runners and clearly today's results dramatically confirm something we've been hearing a lot about lately: the vast and growing divide between the very, very richest rats and the rest of us. In fact, all this year we've heard grumblings from the fans that the race is rigged. Bob, how true is this? And what's being done?

COLOR COMMENTATOR: Well, Dave, down here in the field I can tell you it's true all right: a lot of fans are telling us that the race isn't fair. They're saying that to bring this sport back to respectability, we need a major policy overhaul. We need a radical change in the rules of the game in order to level the playing field. And these fans already have a lot of ideas about what kinds of changes we need. We've heard calls for an end to corporate give-aways, an increase in the minimum wage, and electoral reform to get big money out of politics.

ANNOUNCER: Thanks, Bob. Clearly there is a strong sentiment for change out there. But the big question, Dave, is whether those fans who want change will talk it up, organize and press home their demands. It's really up to them. The future of the sport is in their hands.

ANNOUNCER: And that's it for today. Thank you for tuning into WIOU's Widening World of Sports. We now return you to live coverage of the Boston Marathon.

B. Giant Steps Method

This activity will compare the income distribution in the two recent time periods shown in **Chart 5a, Real Family Income Growth by Quintile and for Top 5% - 1947-1979** and **Chart 5b, Real Family Income Growth by Quintile and for Top 5% - 1979-2003.**

1. Review the definition of income (from Lesson 3).

2. Explain the definition of income "quintiles" to students.

3. Ask for six volunteers. Ask the volunteers to stand in a line facing the "audience." For this activity to work well, volunteers will need plenty of space to move forward and some space to move back. Hand each of the volunteers an Income Quintile Card: lowest, second lowest, middle, fourth, highest and then the top five percent.

4. Looking at the 2003 income ranges, ask students to name some of the occupations or economic situations they imagine would fall into each quintile. Go through the quintiles one by one, asking the volunteer to hold up the sign so students can see the income range. Remind students this is "household" income. For example, the middle income of $42,057-$65,000 may be a family where Dad is an accountant and Mom stays at home with the two children. Or it may be a family with two people employed as first year teachers.

An alternative is for you to name the occupation and ask the students in which income range the occupation should be placed.

5. Announce that we will review what happened to the incomes of the various quintiles during two periods of economic growth: 1947-79 and 1979-2003. Start with the 1947-79 time period (volunteers flip their card to show this side). Each volunteer, representing a quintile or fifth of the US population, will step forward or back according to whether their income gained or declined. Each step equals a 10-percent change for 1947-1979 and a 5-percent change for 1979-2003. (Use the table shown in the preparation section on page 28 to instruct the volunteers, one by one, to take the appropriate number of steps forward or backward.)

6. Refer students to **Chart 5a.** This chart shows what students just represented with their steps. Interject appropriate talking points listed above at this point, first asking students to speculate on why they think *all income groups were growing at relatively equal percentage rates.* Remind them of U.S. history and ask them to think of what they know was going on in the 1950s. (The idea is to bring out their knowledge of post-war incentives such as the GI Bill of Rights, government home ownership programs, etc.)

7. Announce that we will next look at what happened between 1979 and 2003. Using **Chart 5b,** ask the volunteers, one by one, to take the appropriate number of steps forward or backward.

8. Ask students what they feel is different about the two time periods.

Follow-up Activity:

It is important to allow class time after the activity to elaborate further on the talking points and to ask students to summarize what they learned from the activity. The goal is for them to have a clear understanding of what happened to real (adjusted for inflation) household income during the two different time periods. Clarify any points of confusion for students and then ask them to write a paragraph summarizing the activity. Grade the paragraphs on content.

1947 to 1979 – Real Family Income Growth by Quintile & for Top 5%

We All Grew

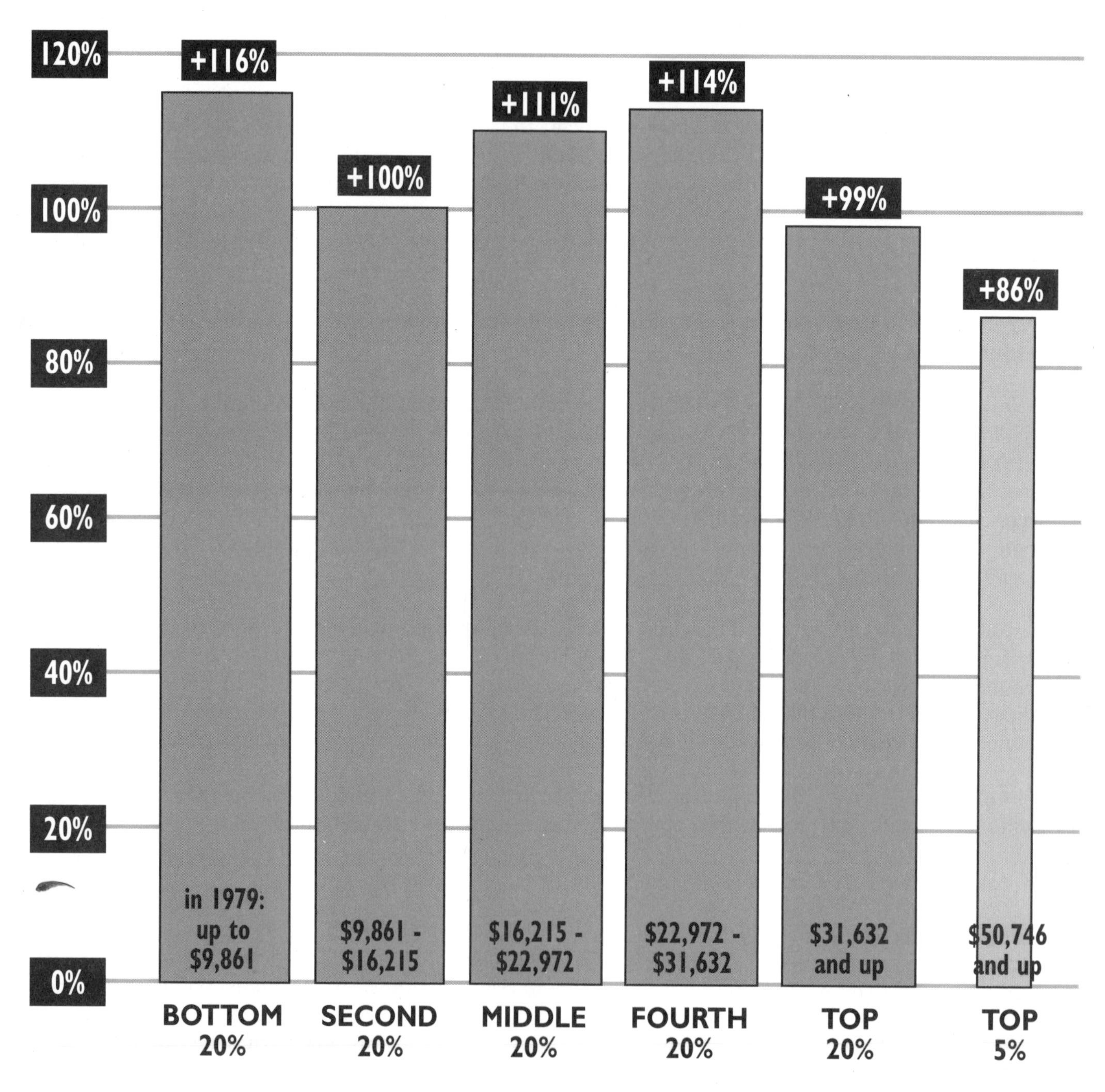

Sources: Analysis of Census Bureau data from Mishel, Lawrence and Bernstein, Jared, *The State of Working America 1994-95*, p. 37. Income ranges in 1979 dollars, from March 2000 Census Current Population Survey, Table F-1.

Chart 5a

1979 to 2003 – Real Family Income Growth by Quintile & for Top 5%

We Grew Apart

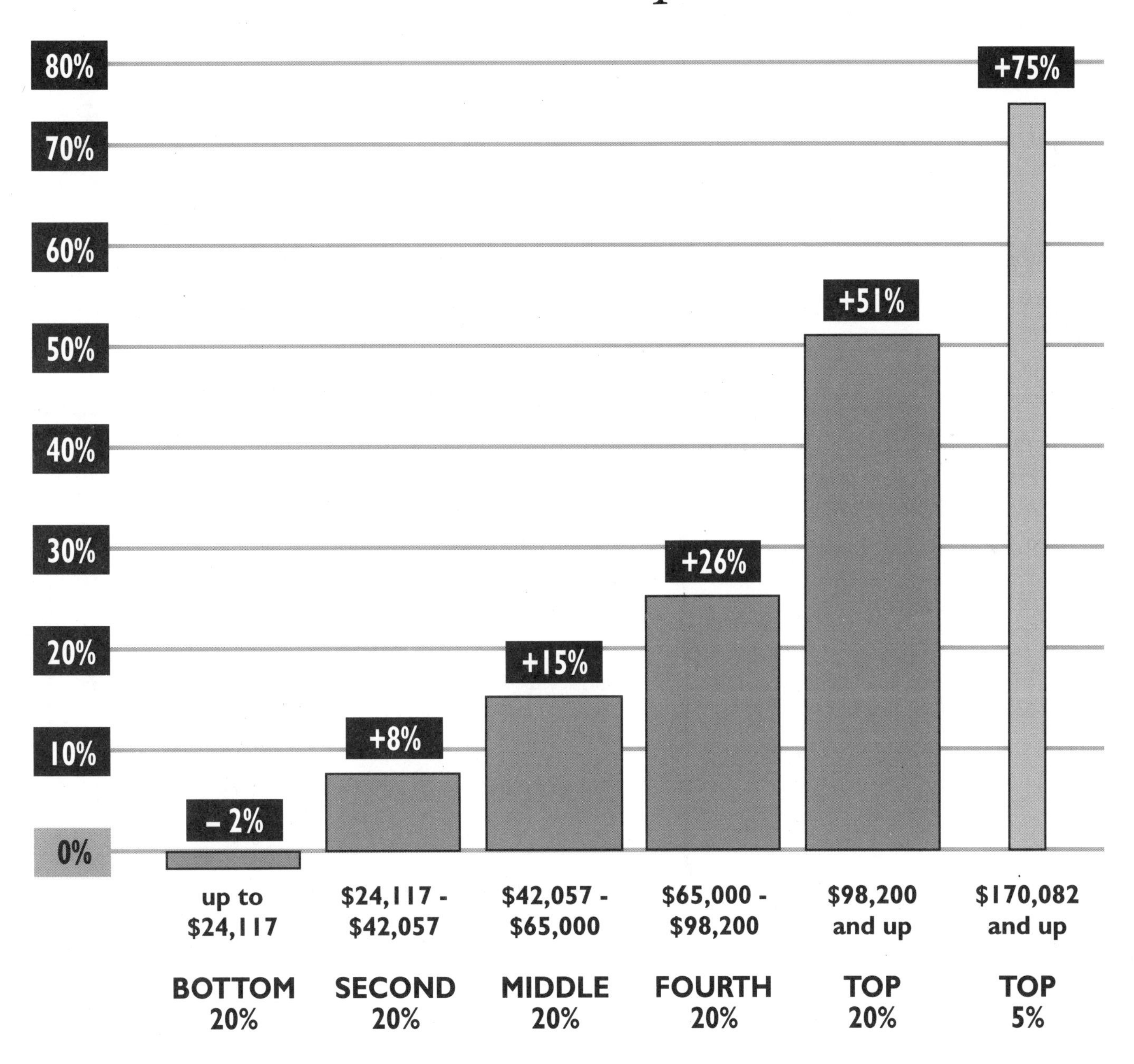

Sources: U.S. Census Bureau, Current Population Survey, Tables F-1 and F-3. Income ranges in 2003 dollars.

Chart 5b

Objectives:

- *Compare income statistics by race*
- *Compare wage statistics by gender*

Concepts and Key Terms:

- *racial income inequality*
- *gender wage inequality*

Instructional Time:

- *55 minutes*

Preparation:

For the Bellringer Activity 6.1:

- *Chart 6a, Median Family Income by Racial Category 1947 - 2004*

For Activity 6.2:

- *Chart: 6b Median Wages for Men and Women, 1973 - 2004*
- *Placards reading "Median Male Wage-Earner" and "Median Female Wage-Earner"*

Conducting the Lesson

Bellringer Activity 6.1: Median Income by Race

1. Display **Chart 6a, Median Family Income by Racial Category, 1947 - 2004.**

2. Ask students, "What strikes you about this information? What do you feel is most significant? How would you explain the data?"

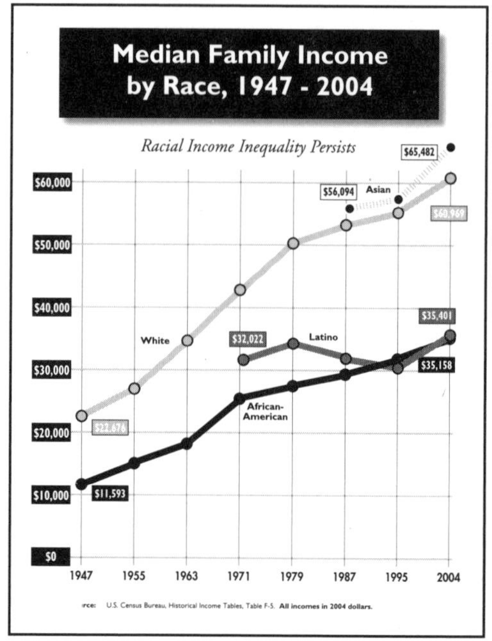

Chart 6a

> **TALKING POINTS:**
>
> In spite of claims made by opponents of affirmative action, there remains a huge chasm among racial groups in terms of income. The income gap between whites on the one hand and African Americans and Latinos on the other has actually increased since 1947. Neither of the two periods we looked at in the Income Quintiles activity (Lesson 5) were times of increasing *racial* equality.

Activity 6.2 The Gender Pay Gap

1. Ask students to talk about the history of work in the U.S. as it relates to gender differences. How have men and women been "tracked" into different occupations? What occupations have been generally closed to women? What did these barriers look like? How are these conditions changing?

2. "The thing we don't often hear about is what is really driving this narrowing gap between men's and women's wages. Let's do an activity to find out. We'll need two volunteers.

3. Line up the two volunteers shoulder to shoulder. One will play the median male wage-earner, the other the median female wage-earner. Give them the appropriate placards.

4. Say, "Let's look at the wage gap in 1973. For men, the median yearly income in 1973 was $29,668 (in 2004 dollars). Male wage-earner, take 15 steps forward (1 step for every $2,000). For women, the median yearly income in 1973 was $10,297. Female wage-earner, take five steps forward. The median wage for women was a little more than 1/3 of the median male wage."

> **TALKING POINTS:**
>
> Historically, women and men have done different types of work. Women generally did work inside the home, and men generally did work outside the home.
>
> Back in the early 1800s, the work that women did in the home was regarded as economically valuable. But since the late 1800s, economists have come to view housework as having no economic value at all. Economics textbooks often explain gross domestic product with the following illustration: "If a man marries his housekeeper, the nation's gross domestic product drops." Even though she's doing the exact same work, it is no longer considered "productive" simply because she is not being paid for it.
>
> Although the occupational barriers to women are slowly breaking down, the historical division of labor into "men's work" (building trades, manufacturing, business, and the professions — doctors, lawyers, college professors) and "women's work" (housework, child care, teaching, clerical, and nursing) has formed the basis for much of the inequality in wages between men and women.

5. Say, "Now let's look at 2004. The median income for women has grown 71% — not bad, right? Let's look a little closer."

"Female wage earner, take one step forward. Now in 2004, you have a yearly income of $17,629. Take 4 steps forward. Male wage-earner, with a median yearly slary of $30,513 in 2004, take only a half step forward. The stagnating wage for men is as responsible for narrowing the income gap between men and women as is the increase in women's earnings. What are the implications of this?"

> **TALKING POINTS:**
>
> **Implications of stagnating incomes for men while incomes for women grows slowly:**
>
> - Greater burden on families with male wage-earners.
> - Frustration among male wage-earners who see their wages stagnating; leads to scapegoating and anger towards women.
> - Confusion and frustration among many two-earner families who see the wage gap narrowing but their family's standard of living hardly changing.
> - Longer hours of work often needed to maintain a given standard of living.

6. Have students look at **Chart 6b: Median Income for Men and Women, 1973-2004.** Encourage them to try to name some of the factors that have enabled women to make the modest gains reflected in the data? Why do you think the median men's wage has stagnated since the early 1970s?

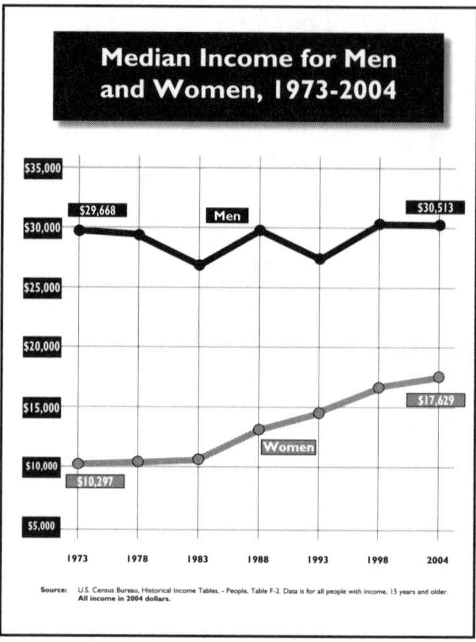

Chart 6b

TALKING POINTS:

A substantial portion of the narrowing of the gender gap over the past 30 years has been due to the stagnation of men's wages.

While there are more well-paid women in the professions than twenty years ago, there are many more women who have been forced to enter the low-paid service sector.

Most of these low-paid service jobs are low-paid precisely because they have traditionally been classified as women's work.

Based on median earnings for full-time workers, women earn 76¢ to a man's $1.00 (U.S. Census Bureau, *Income, Earnings, and Poverty from the 2004 American Community Survey*, August 2005, p.7) .

Median Family Income by Race, 1947 - 2004

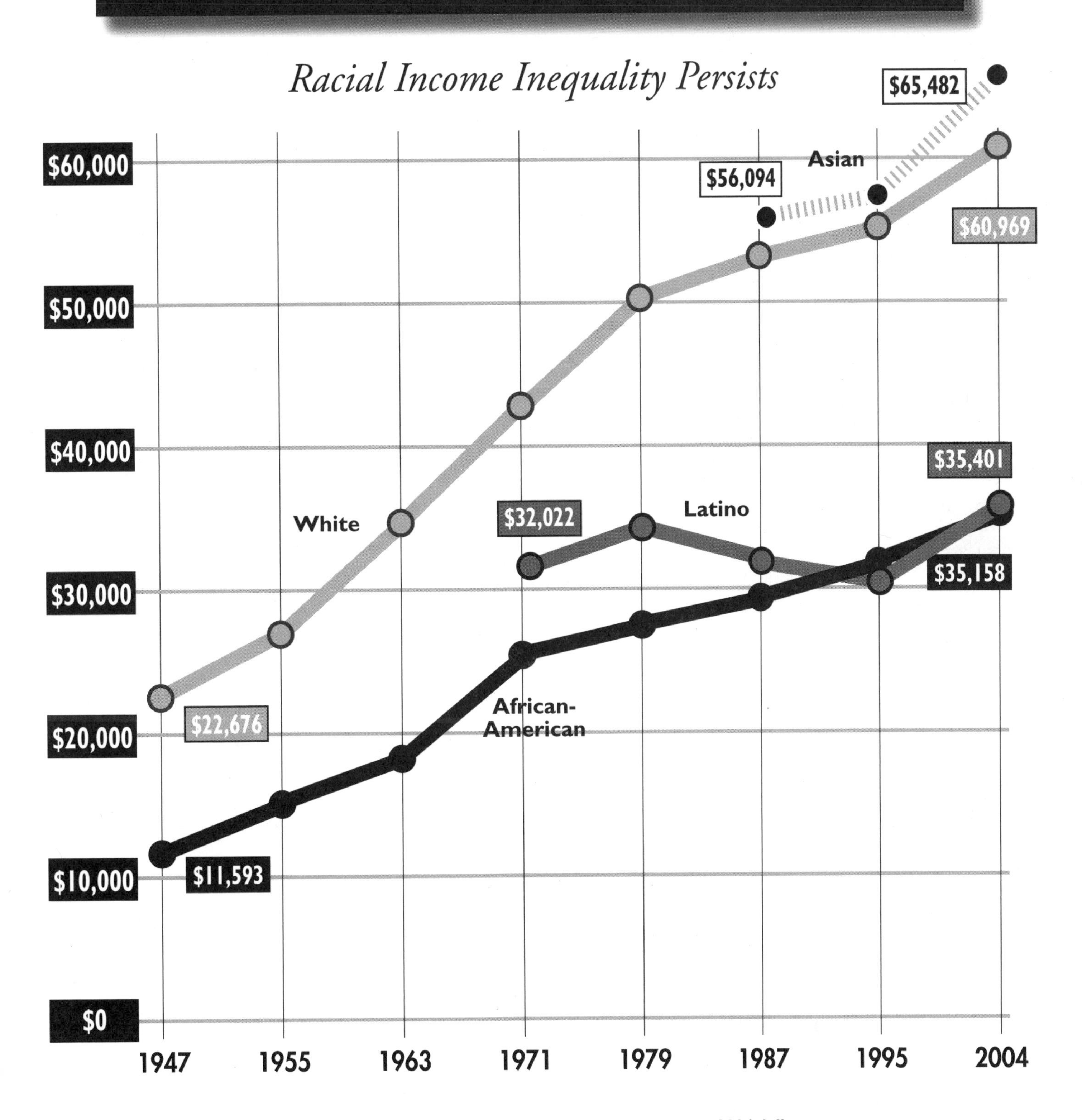

Source: U.S. Census Bureau, Historical Income Tables, Table F-5. **All incomes in 2004 dollars.**

Chart 6a

Median Income for Men and Women, 1973-2004

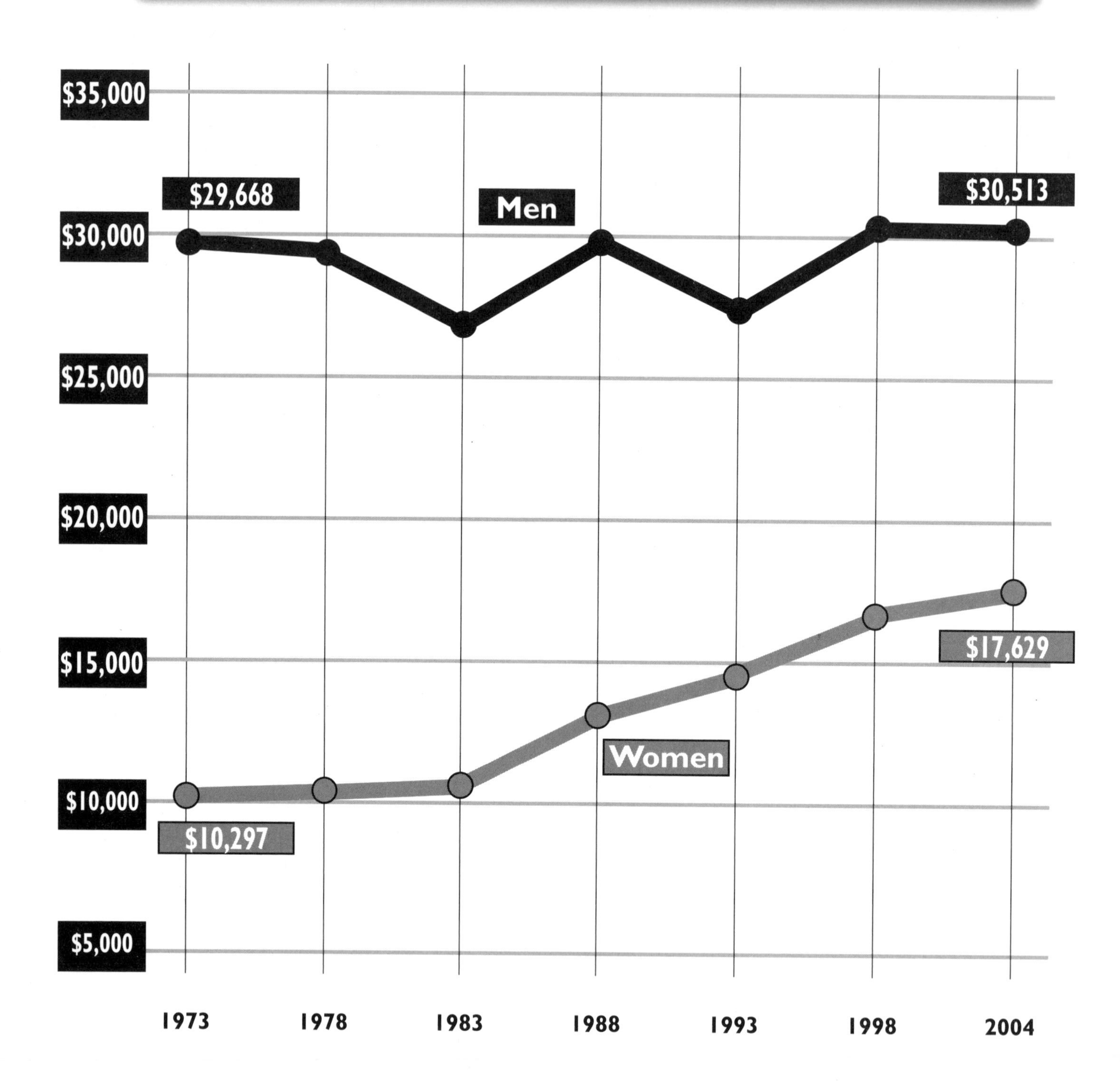

Source: U.S. Census Bureau, Historical Income Tables, - People, Table F-2. Data is for all people with income, 15 years and older. **All income in 2004 dollars.**

Chart 6b

Objectives:

- *Experience a dramatization of the widening gap between the highest and the average paid workers in the U.S.*
- *Explore why the wage gap in the U.S. is wider than in other industrialized nations.*

Concepts and Key Terms:

- *CEO pay gap*

Instructional Time:

- *55 minutes*

Preparation:

For the Bellringer Activity 7.1:

- *Chart 7a, Top 10 CEOs Total Compensation - 2004*

For Activity 7.2:

- *Charts 7b, CEO Pay as a Multiple of Average Worker Pay, 1960-2004 and 7c, The Economy of the 1980s and 1990s: Who Really Benefited?*
- *Placards that read: "U.S. Worker - 1980," "U.S. CEO - 1980," "U.S. Worker - 1990," "U.S. CEO - 1990," "U.S. Worker - 2004," "U.S. CEO - 2004"*

For Activity 7.3:

- *Chart 7d, The Wage Gap Around the World in 2003-04*
- *Placards that read: "Japanese Manufacturing Worker - $44,000," "Japanese CEO - $487,000," "German Manufacturing Worker- $41,000," "German CEO - $534,000," "U.S. Manufacturing Worker - $40,000," "U.S. CEO - $1,351,000"*

Conducting the Lesson

Bellringer Activity 7.1: Executive Pay

1. Hand out a copy of **Chart 7a, Top 10 CEOs Total Compensation - 2004.** Ask students to discern by looking at the pictures what the CEO's all have in common. (They are all white men.)

Chart 7a

2. The highest-paid CEO is Terry S. Semel, of Yahoo. He was paid $230.6 million in 2004. You could ask students to figure out what he made every week, day, hour, minute, and second, assuming a 52-week year and a 40-hour workweek.

The results:

$4,434,615.38	per week
886,923.08	per day
110,865.38	per hour
1,847.76	per minute and
30.80	per second

TALKING POINTS:

Because of the cap on wages that are subject to the Social Security tax, Terry Semel was done paying into Social Security about 49 minutes after he started work on the first day of the year. Most taxpayers have Social Security tax taken out of every one of their paychecks.

In 1997, George Fisher, CEO of Kodak laid off 20,100 workers. In that year, he was paid $17 million! ($136 a minute).

3. Ask students to pair off and summarize in a sentence or two how they feel about this high compensation for CEOs and then ask volunteers to share their sentences. Our view: CEO over-compensation is neither fair nor good for the economy. It transfers wealth upward from employees and shareholders to already affluent top executives and distorts the democratic process.

Activity 7.2: CEO Pay Gap Over Time

This activity is a role-play that illustrates the ratio between those who are paid the most — Chief Executive Officers (CEOs) — and average workers. Six volunteers, each carrying an identifying sign, will role-play CEOs and average workers from three different time periods. The volunteers representing CEOs will move across the room in proportion to the difference between their compensation and their worker's pay.

1. Six volunteers represent U.S. workers or CEOs from three different time periods. One column represents the CEOs and the other column represents average workers. Each student volunteer holds a sign identifying who they represent so all can see.

2. The 1980, 1990, and 2004 CEOs move sideways step by step with each step equal to a 10 : 1 ratio. (Therefore, if the average worker is paid $40,000 and the highest paid executive receives ten times that amount — $400,000 — they would be one step apart).

3. The income ratio between the 1980 CEO and the 1980 American worker is 42 to 1. The 1980 CEO takes two sideways steps. The income ratio between the 1990 CEO and the 1990 Worker is 107 to 1. The 1990 CEO takes ten and a half sideways steps.

4. Finally, let's look at the wage gap in the U.S. in 2004. By 2004, the ratio was 431 to 1, so the 2004 CEO takes 43 sideways steps.

1980 U.S. worker —(4 steps)— 1980 U.S. CEO
1990 U.S. Worker ——— (11 1/2 steps) ——— 1990 U.S. CEO
2004 U.S. Worker ——————— (43 steps)——————— 2004 U.S. CEO

5. Ask students, "What strikes you about the income ratio comparison? How would you explain the difference in income ratio for the three years?" Display **Chart 7b, CEO Pay as a Multiple of Average Worker Pay** and **Chart 7c, The Economy since 1980: Who Really Benefited?**

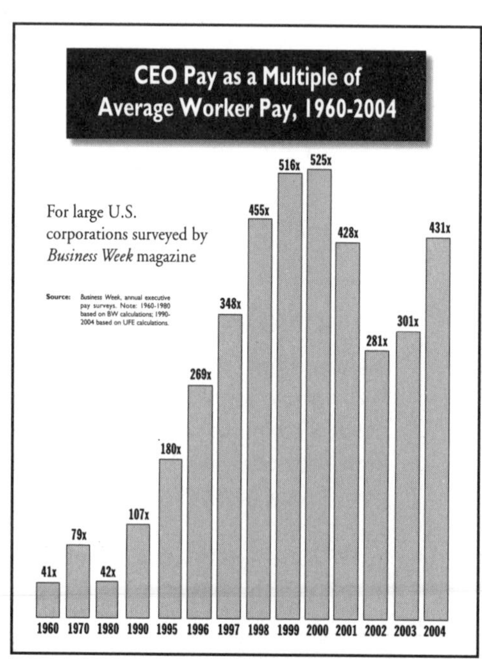

Chart 7b

Chart 7c

TALKING POINTS:

Chart 7b shows the average wage ratio of CEOs to average workers at large corporations, according to *Business Week*. Many large firms in the U.S. have even larger ratios. For example, in 2005, the CEO of investment firm Goldman Sachs, Henry Paulson, now the U.S. Treasury Secretary, pulled in $43 million, over 1,000 times the average worker's compensation — a gap of 100 steps.

Successful organizational management consultants, such as Peter Drucker, believe that corporations must flatten out their structures — which exist primarily to justify excessive salary differentials. He speaks specifically of establishing a wage ratio between top and bottom. In recent years, shareholder activists have begun to draw attention to the issue of the huge gaps between CEO and worker pay by demanding that the corporations set wage ratios.

We've really seen "A Tale of Two Economies" in America since the 1980s. CEOs and people with lots of money invested in the stock market have done quite well.
Meanwhile, average workers have had to contend with declining wages and rising job insecurity, touched off by the phenomena of outsourcing and downsizing.

Some people might look at these figures and argue that American businesses had to "restructure" in the 1980s in order to get back on their feet. But the question remains: why did all the pain of the restructuring — layoffs, cuts in benefits, stagnant pay, job insecurity — have to be borne by working families? Is it right that CEOs and Wall Street should reap all of the economic benefits of the "leaner, meaner" American economy? Some people view the economy since the 1980s as the breaking of an informal "social contract" that had worked to spread prosperity more evenly in the 1950s and '60s. Others point out that this "contract" was never fully open to everyone, including women and people of color.

As citizens, it is up to us to think about what kind of economy we want to have. That involves finding out who benefits and who pays for the various policies and rule changes that affect our economy.

Activity 7.3: CEO Pay Gap In Other Countries

This activity is a role-play that illustrates the ratio between those who are paid the most — Chief Executive Officers (CEOs) — and average manufacturing workers. Six volunteers, each carrying an identifying sign, will role-play CEOs and average workers from three different countries. The volunteers representing CEOs will move across the room in proportion to the difference between their compensation and their worker's pay.

Unlike the large U.S. companies that formed the basis for Activity 7.2, this demonstration uses data for medium-sized companies — those with sales of approximately $500 million — which is the only recent data that could be located for international CEO pay comparisons. Another factor making the U.S. pay gap smaller in this exercise is that the CEO pay is compared to average manufacturing pay rather than average worker pay. Manufacturing workers have higher-than-average wages.

1. Six volunteers representing workers or CEOs of medium-sized companies from the U.S., Japan, and Germany line up in two columns facing the audience. One column represents the average CEO and the other column represents the average manufacturing worker in that country. Each student volunteer holds a sign identifying who she/he represents so all can see.

2. The U.S., Japanese, and German CEOs move sideways step by step with each step equal to a 10 : 1 ratio. (Therefore, if an average worker is paid $40,000 and the highest paid executive receives ten times that amount — $400,000 — they would be one step apart).

3. The income ratio between the German CEO and the German manufacturing worker is 21 to one. The German CEO takes two sideways steps. Next, the Japanese CEO, who makes about 9 times what the average Japanese manufacturing worker makes: he takes one sideways step.

4. Finally, let's look at the wage gap in the U.S. In 2003-04, the ratio was about 44 to 1 for medium-sized companies. The U.S. CEO takes four and a half sideways steps.

U.S. manufacturing worker ———————————— (4 1/2 steps)———————————— U.S. CEO
Japanese manufacturing worker —— (1 step) —— Japanese CEO
German manufacturing worker ——— (2 steps) ——— German CEO

5. Ask students, "What strikes you about the income ratio comparison? How would you explain the fact that the pay gap is over twice as large in the U.S. as it is in Germany and Japan?" Display **Chart 7d, The Wage Gap Around the World, 2003-2004.**

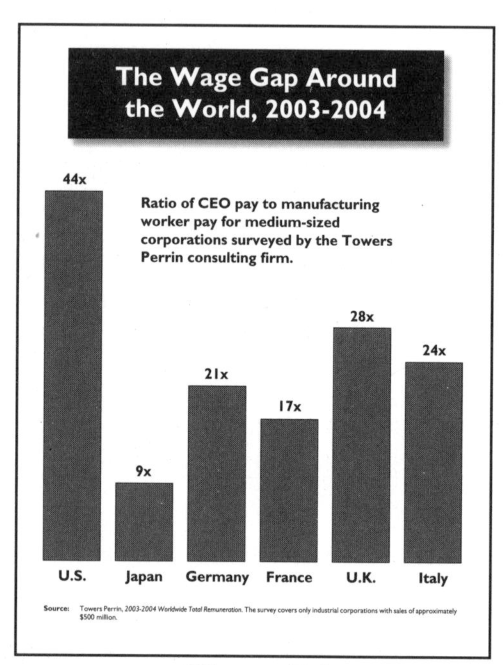

Chart 7d

"Thanks to the economic boom... we only have to cut your wages 10% this year."

TALKING POINTS:

U.S. CEOs do not seem to face the kind of wage competition that has held down the wages of U.S. manufacturing workers. For example, the CEO of the British pharmaceutical company Glaxo Wellcome makes just $2.8 million a year, much less than his counterparts at U.S. drug companies such as Schering-Plough ($29 million), Warner-Lambert ($15.8 million), Amgen ($39.2 million) and Bristol-Myers Squibb ($56.3 million).*

In Japan the ratio is 9 times; in Germany, 21 times. Yet there are no laws in Germany restricting or capping compensation.

In Germany a strong trade union movement helps enforce a "social contract" which ensures that top and bottom wages don't get too far apart. German workers are represented on over half of the corporate boards which allows them input in setting CEO compensation.

In Japan, there is a strong value (some folks call it a "cultural compact") that views an excessive pay gap as undermining the "team." Top managers recognize that too large a gap is unhealthy for the sense of teamwork and shared commitment necessary to run a productive firm. Also, in Japan many top managers share the value that an excessive pay gap would be a cause for shame.

In the U.S. we have neither a social contract nor a cultural compact. Trade unions are weaker here and employees are unable to enforce smaller wage ratios. CEOs frequently ignore the "team culture" within firms or the ways in which huge differences in pay scales undermine employee solidarity. And there is no culture of shame about excess in the U.S.

Successful organizational management consultants, such as Peter Drucker, believe that corporations must flatten out their structures — which exist primarily to justify excessive salary differentials. He speaks specifically of establishing a wage ratio between top and bottom.

In recent years, shareholder activists have begun to draw attention to the issue of the huge gaps between CEO and worker pay by demanding that the corporations set wage ratios.

* United for a Fair Economy and Institute for Policy Studies, *A Decade of Executive Excess: The 1990s* (UFE: 1999).

Top 10 CEOs
Total Compensation - 2004

Special Report: CEO Compensation
Edited by Scott DeCarlo, 4/21/05

#1. Terry S. Semel
Yahoo
$230.6 million

#2. Barry Diller
IAC/InterActive Corp
$156.2 million

#3. William W. McGuire
UnitedHealth Group
$124.8 million

#4. Howard Solomon
Forest Labs
$92.1 million

#5. George David
United Technologies
$88.7 million

#6. Lew Frankfort
Coach
$86.5 million

#7. Edwin M. Crawford
Caremark Rx
$77.9 million

#8. Ray R. Irani
Occidental Petroleum
$64.1 million

#9. Angelo R. Mozilo
Countrywide Financial
$57 million

#10. Richard D. Fairbank
Capital One Financial
$56.7 million

Chart 7a

CEO Pay as a Multiple of Average Worker Pay, 1960-2004

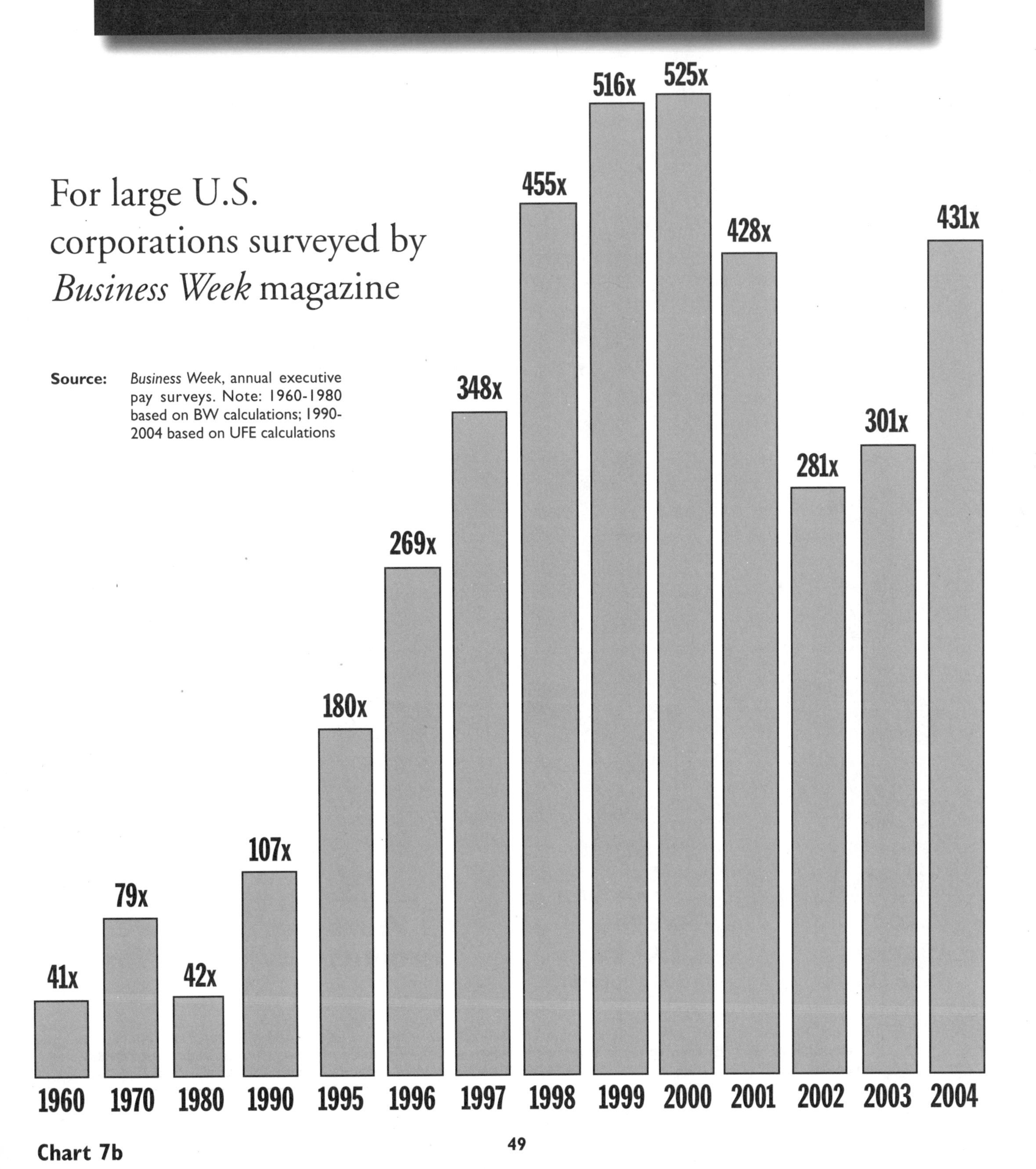

Chart 7b

The Economy since 1980: Who Really Benefited?

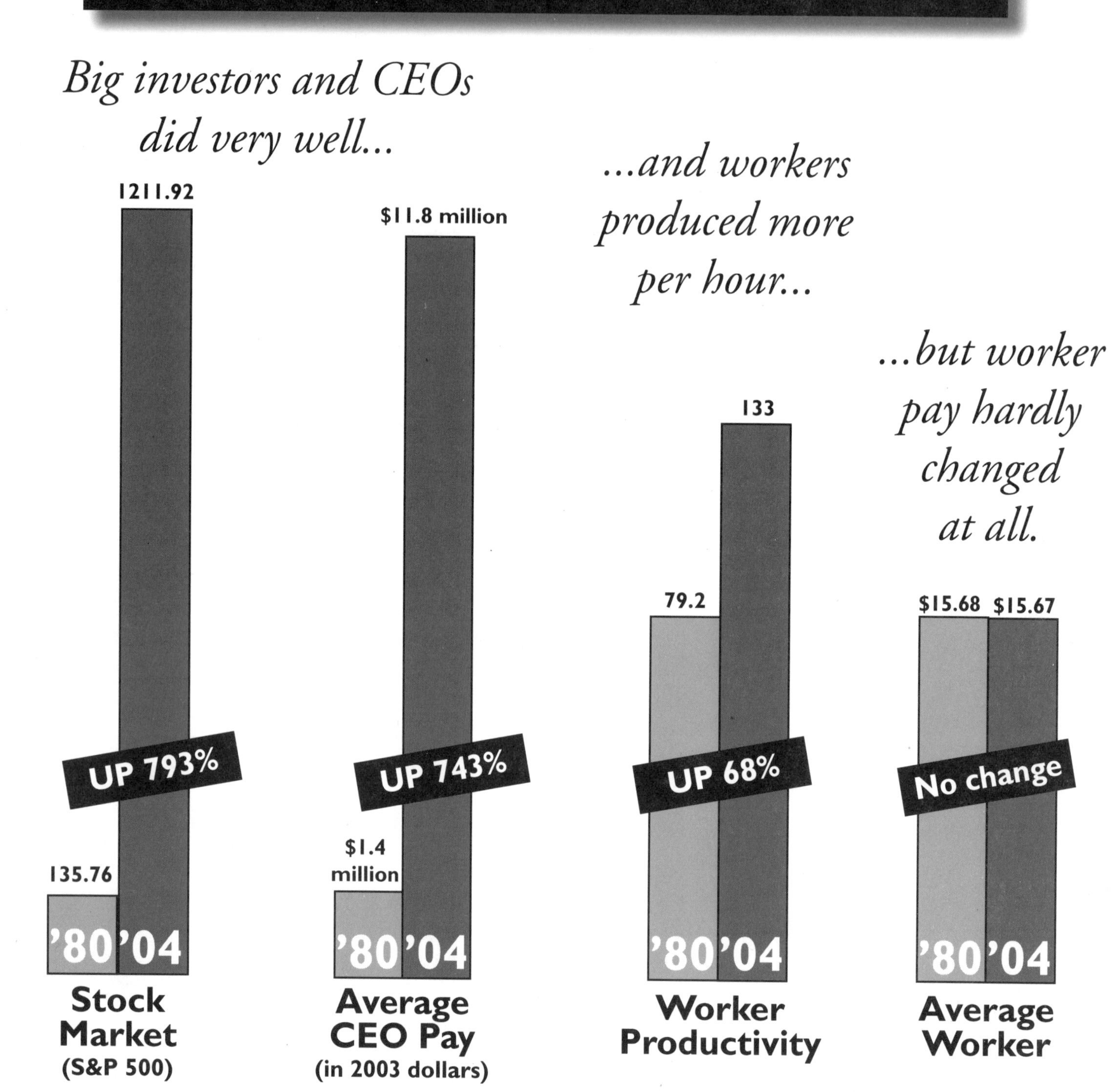

Sources: For the **Stock Market:** Standard & Poor's Corporation, S&P 500 Index at end of year. **For CEO-Worker Pay Gap:** *Business Week,* May 1,1989 and April 18, 2005. Adjusted for inflation by UFE. **For Worker Productivity:** Bureau of Labor Statistics data. Business Output per Hour Index (1992=100), Series ID: PRS84006093. **For Hourly Wage:** Bureau of Labor Statistics data. Average Earnings of Production Workers, Series ID: CEU0500000006. Adjusted for inflation by UFE.

Chart 7c

The Wage Gap Around the World, 2003-2004

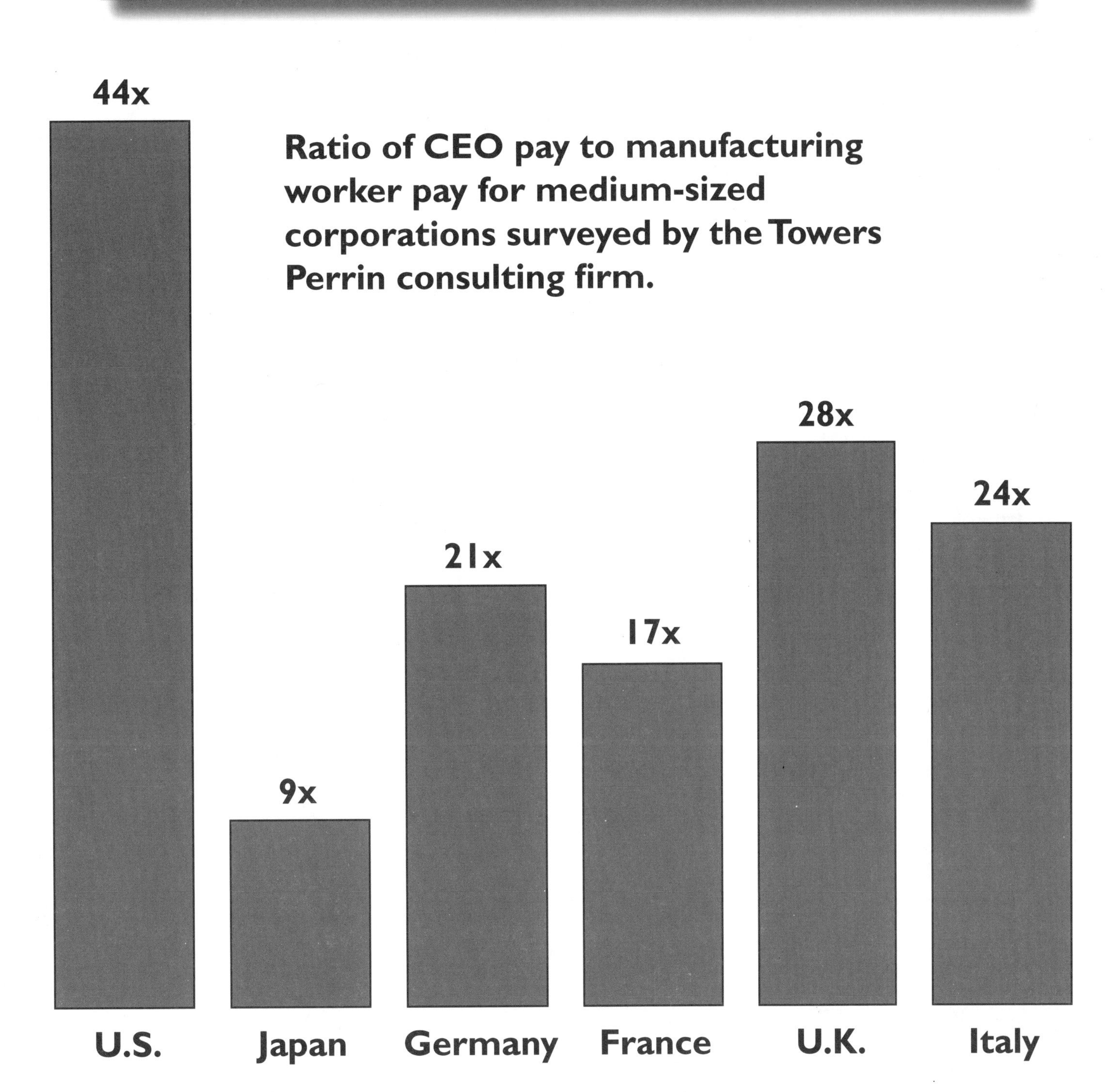

Source: Towers Perrin, *2003-2004 Worldwide Total Remuneration*. The survey covers only industrial corporations with sales of approximately $500 million.

Chart 7d

Lesson 8: The Widening Pay Gap, What the Experts Say, What Government Can Do About It, and How it Affects the Business Cycle

Objectives:

- *Hear experts' opinion on the widening pay gap.*
- *Review actions that government can take to limit excessive CEO pay.*
- *Examine the phases of the business cycle.*
- *Identify the factors (variables) that influence the business cycle and examine how they influence it.*
- *Explore how excessive CEO pay affects the business cycle.*

Concepts and Key Terms:

- *business cycle*
- *CEO pay gap*
- *Income Equity Act*
- *corporate salary deductions*
- *recession*
- *depression*

Instructional Time:

- *55 minutes*

Preparation:

For the Bellringer Activity 8.1:

- *Chart 8a, The Minimum Wage and CEO Pay 1968-2003*

For Activity 8.2

- *Chart 8b, The Business Cycle*
- *Make a large circle with masking tape on the floor (as round as the classroom will allow) with the following nine phrases on signs (8.5" x 11" laminated) taped to the floor and spaced an equal distance apart, in the following order along the circle.*
    - *Automation, runaways, layoffs*
    - *Fewer Workers Hired*
    - *Wages Fall*
    - *Higher Profits*
    - *More Workers Hired*
    - *Wages Rise*
    - *Profits Fall*

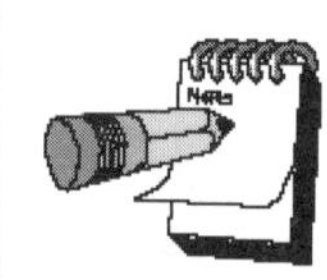

Note to Teacher

Lesson 7 focused on the enormous pay gap between CEOs and the average worker in the U.S. The following mini-lecture includes important points regarding what experts say about this subject and what government can do about it. You may want to break the class into groups and have each group review a portion of the material and then present it to the rest of the class. Or if you haven't used it in a while, employ the "Human Social Barometer" technique after each talking point. (See Lesson 3, Activity 3.3 for an explanation of this technique.)

Conducting the Lesson

Bellringer Activity 8.1: What the Experts Say and What Can be Done About Excessive CEO Pay

1. Display **Chart 8a, The Minimum Wage and CEO Pay 1968-1979-2005.** Present the information in the talking points below as a mini-lecture on excessive CEO compensation.

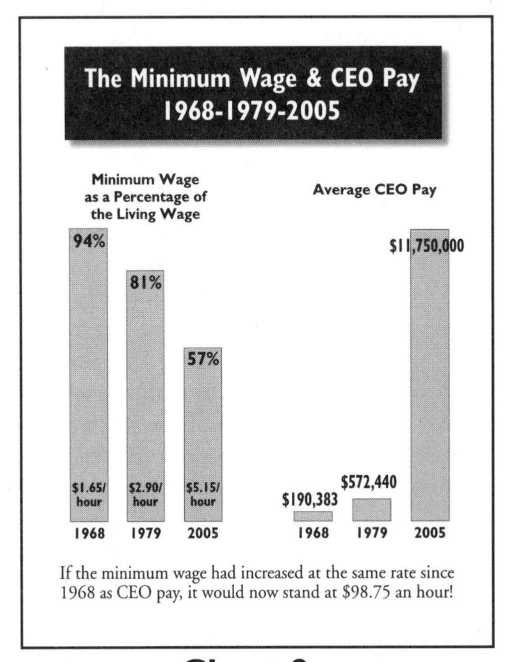

Chart 8a

TALKING POINTS:

If the minimum wage increased as fast as CEO pay did since 1968, it would now stand at $98.75 an hour.

The average CEO now makes 1,097 times more than a full-time minimum-wage worker in the U.S. In 2004, the heads of the Standard & Poor 500 largest companies received an aggregate 54% pay raise, while *per capita* income fell slightly for the second year in a row.

According to the April 2005 Executive Excess report by the Institute for Policy Studies and United for a Fair Economy, CEOs of those firms with the most underfunded pensions, on average, received 72% more than the average large company CEO. Exxon Mobil's CEO, Lee Raymond, took home $81.7 million in 2004, while Exxon-Mobil's pension shortfall is so large it will take 24 years to close the gap.

Also in 2003, 46 large companies paid no federal income tax, despite collectively earning $30 billion in profits. Some of the savings wound up in the pockets of their CEOs; Pfizer's CEO, Hank McKinnell, for example, earned $28 million in 2004 and Pfizer earned $6 billion in profits, but they still received a $168 million tax refund from the federal government.

In the last ten years, CEOs of firms with shady accounting appeared 18 times on the top ten lists of highest paid executives. This includes leaders whose companies were either later found to have committed fraud or were forced to make material restatements of earnings to correct previous overstatements of profits.

2. Ask the students to listen to what some of the experts say about the widening pay gap.

TALKING POINTS:

Business management guru Peter Drucker warned companies against widening pay gaps, arguing that they undermine teamwork and productivity.

"Since no other industrialized nation has CEO pay ratios even close to ours, it is nonsense to claim we have to do it to stay competitive in the new global economy."
— Peter Barnes, founder of the mutual fund company Working Assets

"We believe that business leaders should share in the sacrifices of corporate restructuring and mergers by freezing their own pay during periods of massive downsizing. This would help rebuild the kind of moral leadership that U.S. businesses need to compete in the next century. And it would go a long way toward rebuilding a sense of social contract in our nation."
— Frank Butler, retired CEO of Eastman Gelatine, a subsidiary of Eastman Kodak

"There's a point where a board should tell the CEO, 'You have enough to incentivize you,' but it's still business as usual at most companies. It's all about keeping up with the Joneses. There's still a disconnect between paying for performance and actually delivering it. There's no shame factor."
— Paul Hodgson, pay analyst for The Corporate Library (as quoted in *USA Today*, 4/11/06).

According to a *Bloomberg-Los Angeles Times* poll conducted in February/March 2005 (*Bloomberg News*, 3/22/06), 81% of the respondents believe that CEOs are making too much money. Remarkably, among a well-to-do subset of those polled — investors with incomes exceeding $100,000 — 84% agreed that CEOs are paid too much!

DEFINITION:

A ***shareholder*** is a person who owns shares of stock in a corporation.

3. Ask students what they think should and can be done about excessive CEO pay. Explain what is being done about excessive CEO pay.

TALKING POINTS:

Solution #1: Enacting legislation that would cap salary deductions
Many people in the U.S. are unaware that corporations are allowed to deduct executive salaries, benefits, and perks as a routine business expense. In 1993, Congress limited the deduction for executive compensation to $1 million per executive. Rep. Martin Sabo (D-Minnestoa) has introduced legislation that would take the next common sense step to limit deductibility to an amount that correlates to a company's existing pay scale.

> "The income gap that has been growing since the late 1970s remains with us, threatening dire consequences for our society. If economic opportunity is not extended to all Americans, we face the possibility of becoming a nation sharply divided between winners and losers. Such a development would threaten the very fabric of our economy and society. It is therefore in our common interest for the government to address economic inequality in America.
>
> "I have proposed one way to address the income gap: using the tax code to eliminate what is essentially a subsidy for excessive executive pay. My legislation, the Income Equity Act of 2005, does this by limiting the tax deductibility for compensation to 25 times the salary of the lowest-paid worker in a firm. In other words, if the lowest-paid worker is a clerk who makes $20,000 a year, the company could deduct only $500,000 of its CEO's salary."
>
> — U.S. Representative Martin Sabo (5th District of Minnesota)

Using 1997 data, the 365 U.S. firms listed in the Business Week salary survey would pay an extra $493 million in increased income taxes if the deduction was reformed in a way that capped the corporate deductibility of the salary and bonus of just their top two executives.

Solution #2: Enacting legislation that would raise the Federal Minimum Wage.
The minimum wage has historically played an important role in raising the earnings of low-wage workers. Unfortunately, the policy debate over the issue has focused almost exclusively on the risk of job loss, despite the fact that recent research demonstrates that such employment effects are either nonexistent or negligible. The Federal minimum wage has not been raised since 1997. As of January 2006, the minimum wage was 33% of the average hourly wage of American workers, the lowest level since 1949.

S. 2725, "Standing with Minimum Wage Earners Act of 2006," introduced in the Senate in May, if passed would raise the minimum wage in several stages to $7.25 in 2009.

Activity 8.2: The Business Cycle

After discussing the CEO pay gap it is helpful to examine the business cycle. Students often provide simplistic views of the marketplace ("CEOs are paid more in America because our economy is doing better" or "If we lower CEO pay, profits will fall and the economy will be in worse condition").

> **DEFINITION:**
> ***Recession*** is the downward phase of a business cycle, in which the economy's income, output and employment are decreasing. This is reflected with a declining rate of consumption (people don't buy goods or services) and investment (people don't invest their money in companies). A recession year is one in which the GNP is lower than it was in the previous year. A ***depression*** is a recession that last a long time.

Gaining a grasp of the business cycle will help them understand the key variables that accelerate or retard economic growth.

1. Explain to students that in order to understand the business cycle, we will look at the relationship between wages, profits and unemployment.

2. Place all the laminated signs in a line on the board (or a circle on the floor) in random order.

3. Ask students to work in small groups of three or four. Explain that the goal for each group is to put the signs (phases of the business cycle) in the order that they believe the phases occur. Have one student record the group's suggested order. Whenever a group is ready, have them come to the front of the room and physically place the signs in their suggested order while they explain each phase. When the group is finished, ask the class their opinions of the order. Allow other groups to make changes in their proposed order. Take this opportunity to teach about the various phases of the cycle. For example: explain how automation causes workers to be laid off.

4. Wrap up by displaying **Chart 8b, The Business Cycle.**

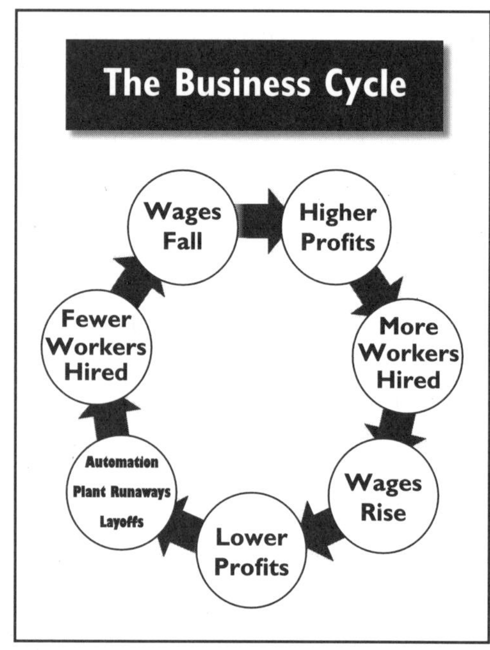

Chart 8b

Follow-up Activity 8.3

1. A recession can occur when wages are so low that workers cannot afford to buy what is produced. Where might a recession occur on the business cycle? (Answer: after "Wages fall" and before "Profits rise.")

2. Ask students if they think that in the U.S. increased profits always lead to increased economic growth? Why or Why not? (Answer: No, because sometimes a company will increase its profits, but still move their factories overseas to increase profits even more, thus laying off U.S. workers.)

3. Ask students what other reasons they can think of why increased profits may not always lead to increased economic growth? (Answer: CEOs are paid enormous salaries, therefore growth is concentrated in a few hands.)

4. Ask students to reflect on the economy's current economic growth and corporate profits (recent stock market boom, etc.). How would they describe changes in the business cycle from how it has traditionally functioned? (Answer: Companies are receiving higher profits but are not hiring more workers.)

Additional Resources:

- The AFL-CIO launched its *Executive Paywatch* website <www.aflcio.org/corporatewatch/paywatch> in April of 1997. The website allows workers to send an e-mail to government officials and to calculate how many years it would take to earn what their company's CEO makes in a year. The website is also a source of good general information on trends in executive pay over the past few years.
- *Business Week* at www.businessweek.com.
- Representative Martin O. Sabo's website: <http://sabo.house.gov/>.
- Research CEO pay in company proxy statements using the EDGAR database at the Securities and Exchange Commission website: <www.sec.gov/edgar.shtml>. See the Executive Paywatch website (above) for instructions on how to access and read a company proxy statement.
- The Interfaith Center on Corporate Responsibility <www.iccr.org>, 475 Riverside Drive, Room 550, New York, NY 10115. Phone: 212-870-2293. Fax: 212-870-2023.

BARRIE MAGUIRE ILLUSTRATION

The Minimum Wage & CEO Pay 1968-1979-2005

If the minimum wage had increased at the same rate since 1968 as CEO pay, it would now stand at $98.75 an hour!

Source: *Business Week*, annual executive pay surveys. U.S. Census Bureau.

Chart 8a

The Business Cycle

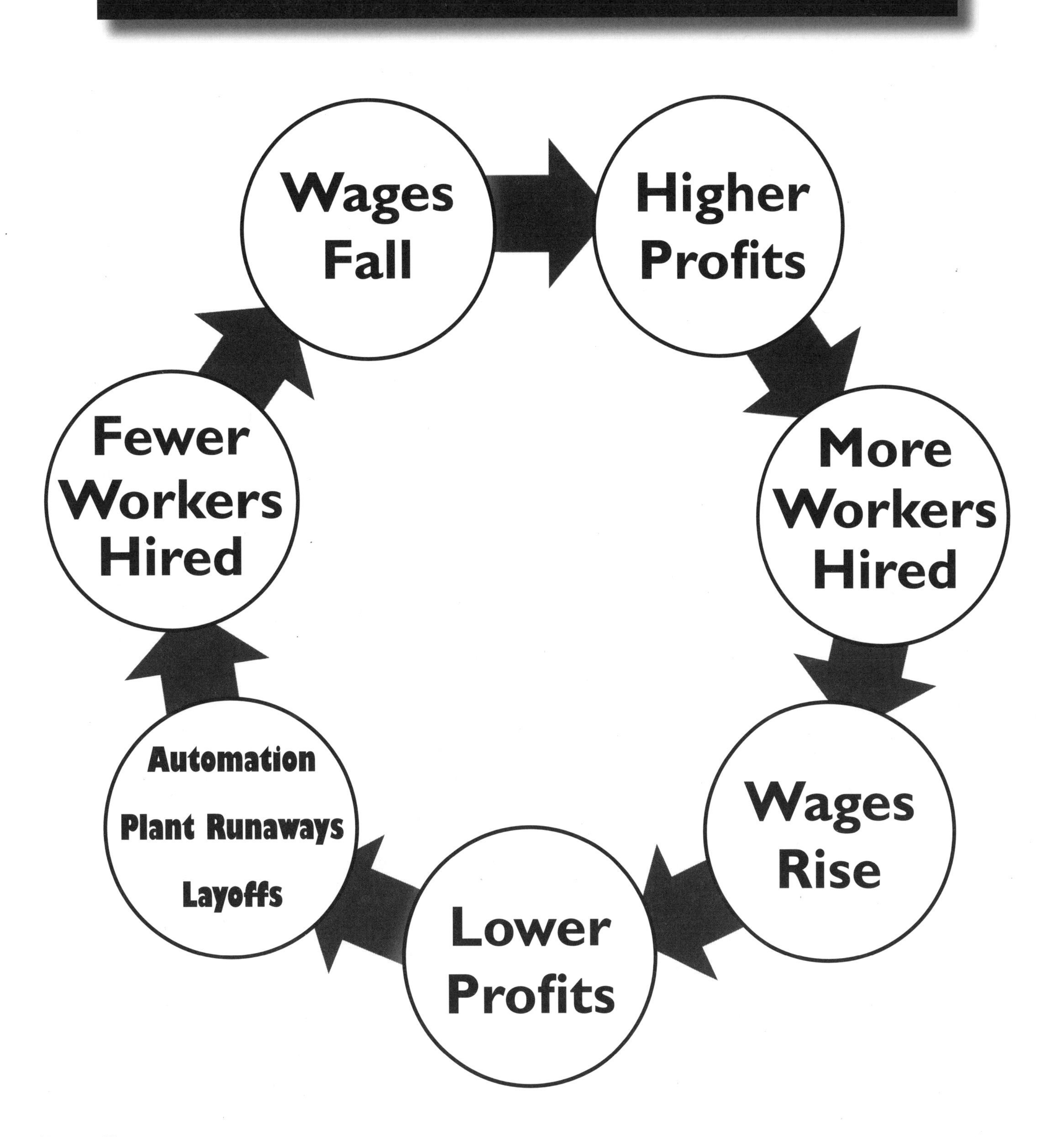

Chart 8b

Objectives:

- *Examine monetary policy and the role of the Federal Reserve Bank (Fed)*
- *Review how the Fed raises and lowers interest rates*
- *Determine who benefits and who is harmed from the Fed's policy of controlling inflation*
- *Define "interest," "inflation," and "fiscal policy"*

Concepts and Key Terms:

- *Federal Reserve Board*
- *monetary policy*
- *interest rates*
- *unemployment*

Instructional Time:

- *55 minutes*

Preparation:

For the Bellringer Activity 9.1:

- *Laminated 8.5" x 11" placards with the following titles: three with "The Bank" (give the banks local bank names); one with "The Federal Reserve Board" (a.k.a. 'The Bankers' Bank'); three with "New Business" (give the businesses local business names); one with "The Economy"*
- *Eight copies of the Fed Role Play script*
- *Play money*
- *A large piece of paper labeled "Prime Rate" at the top. Write the current prime interest rate just below the title. You can find the current prime rate on the financial pages of your newspaper.*
- *Handout: "The Fed and Interest Rates." One for each student.*

For Activity 9.2:

- *Make handouts of Chart 9a, Federal Reserve Policy. One for every two students.*

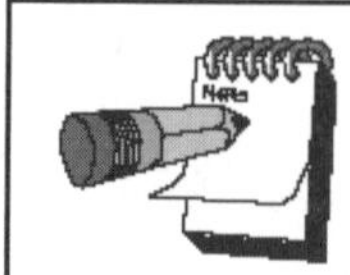

Note to Teacher

This lesson works best after teaching Lesson 8 on the Business Cycle.

Conducting the Lesson

Bellringer Activity 9.1: The "Fed" Role Play

1. Begin with a definition of *interest.*

> **DEFINITION:**
>
> ***Interest*** is the "price paid for the use of credit or loanable funds over a period of time. It is stated as a rate — that is, as a percentage of the amount borrowed. Thus an interest rate of 10% annually means that the borrower pays 10¢ interest per $1 borrowed per year, or $10 per $100 borrowed per year, and so on." (Milton H. Spencer and Orley M. Amos, Jr. *Contemporary Microeconomics*, New York: Worth Publishers, 1993.)

2. Ask for eight volunteers. Give each volunteer one of the laminated placards and a script.

3. Have the volunteers act out the Fed Role Play. Students read and discuss the handout "The Fed and Interest Rates," which provides more background information on the Federal Reserve Board. Explain that when the Federal Reserve exercises its right to increase or decrease interest rates, this is an example of **monetary policy.**

4. Ask students in whose favor (whose "desired levels of output and employment") they believe monetary policy is being made?

5. Discuss why there is a need to slow economic growth in the context of what students learned about the business cycle and recession in Lesson 8.

The Fed Role Play Script

THE FED	*(Walks over to* ***THE ECONOMY****)* "So, how are things going?"
THE ECONOMY	"Not so good. We need to ENCOURAGE economic growth. Why don't you help me out by lowering interest rates so people will borrow more money from banks and invest it in new and existing businesses?"
	*(****THE FED*** *walks over to the chart labeled "Prime Rate," crosses off the written number — the current prime interest rate — and changes the interest rate to one full point lower than the existing rate.)*
	(The three ***BANKS*** *converse loudly among themselves.)*
BANK #1	"Did you see the Fed just lowered its interest rates? Let's go get a loan."
	(The ***BANKS*** *walk to* ***THE FED****)*
BANK #2	"May we have three loans please?"
THE FED	"Sure."
	*(****THE FED*** *hands each of the* ***BANKS*** *some play money.)*
	(The three ***NEW BUSINESSES*** *approach the* ***BANKS****.)*
NEW BUSINESSES	*(In unison)* "We heard the interest rates were just lowered. May we have three loans please?"
BANKS	*(In unison)* "No problem!"
	(The three ***BANKS*** *separately hand money to each of the three* ***NEW BUSINESSES****.)*
THE FED	*(Walks over to* ***THE ECONOMY****)* "Just wanted to check in and see how you are doing these days."
THE ECONOMY	"Wow, we have too much investment, I think it is time to SLOW economic growth. Will you help me out here?"
THE FED	"Of course, right away."
	*(****THE FED*** *walks over to the chart labeled "Prime Rate," crosses off the current number and writes one number higher for the interest rate.)*
	(The ***BANKS*** *walk to* ***THE FED****)*
BANK #1	"May we borrow some money?"

THE FED	"Sure, but you do know the interest rates are a bit higher now."
	*(**THE FED** hands each of the **BANKS** some play money.)*
	*(The three **NEW BUSINESSES** approach the **BANKS**.)*
NEW BUSINESS #1	"May we have three loans please?"
BANKS	"Sure, but the interest rate is just a little higher."
NEW BUSINESS #1	"Well, I'll take a very small loan then. I'll hire fewer new employees than I had planned to."
NEW BUSINESS #2	"I don't think I can afford a loan at that interest rate. Thanks anyway. I'll have to lay off some of my employees."
NEW BUSINESS #3	"I know I can't afford a loan at that interest rate. I'm going to have to go out of business and lay off all my employees."

The Federal Reserve Bank and Interest Rates

Interest rates – the amount charged by banks to borrow money – are largely determined by the Board of Governors of the Federal Reserve System, popularly known as "The Fed." This board is a panel of bankers who are appointed by the President to 14-year terms. The Chairman of the President's Council of Economic Advisors serves as the head of the Fed. Alan Greenspan was Fed Chair from 1987 - 2005. Now, the Fed is led by Ben Bernancke.

In addition to regulating banks and controlling the money supply, the Fed raises and lowers the interest rate that it charges to its member banks on loans, also known as the "discount rate."

When the Fed raises interest rates, the cost of borrowing money to start or expand a business rises. When the cost of borrowing is higher, people tend to buy fewer homes, cars, and other items that are bought on credit. The economic slowdown, in turn, tends to lower the demand for workers, and the unemployment rate rises.

In general, when the Fed lowers interest rates, the costs of starting or expanding a business and buying homes and cars drops. This raises the demand for workers, and the unemployment rate drops.

Why would the Fed ever want to see the unemployment rate go up? This is an important political question. One thing that often happens when unemployment is low is that the inflation rate rises. With more people working, there is more demand for products. This can result in higher prices.

Certainly no one likes it when prices are going up. But inflation is not necessarily all bad for the average family. For one thing, inflation is usually caused by higher incomes, which means that families can keep pace with rising prices because they are making more money. But inflation is also a friend to anyone who has borrowed money for a house or a car. Even as incomes and prices rise, the amount of the monthly payment stays the same. Finally, homeowners see the value of their houses rise, which adds to their net worth.

But there is one group of people for whom inflation is a pure disaster: investors, especially holders of fixed-rate bonds. When inflation is high, it's tougher for these investors to make money, because their investment returns must outpace inflation. As inflation rises the difference between the rate of interest they're receiving and the inflation rate narrows. This lowers their income. Also, just as inflation helps debtors, it hurts creditors, because their costs are rising as people pay them back with dollars that are worth less and less.

This is why Wall Street often reacts to higher unemployment as if it was good news. With more people out of work, the inflation rate is less likely to go up. That's good news for investors, bad news for people trying to get a job.

Additional Resources:

The Federal Reserve Board - The Most Important Source of Poverty in the United States by Dean Baker, November 3, 2005. Center for Economic & Policy Research (http://www.cepr.net/pages/seminars.htm).

The Complete Idiot's Guide to the Federal Reserve, by Lita Epstein & Preston Martin (2003). Alpha Books. ISBN 0-02-864323-2.

Secrets of the Temple: How the Federal Reserve Runs the Country by William Greider (1989). Simon & Schuster. ISBN 0-671-67556-7.

Activity 9.2: Who Really Benefits from the "Anti-Inflation" Policy?

1. Ask students to work in pairs. Provide each pair with a handout of **Chart 9a, "Federal Reserve Policy"**

2. Ask students to examine the chart and answer the following questions:
   - a) What two factors are being examined?
   - b) Over what time period?
   - c) What trend began in the 1970s?
   - d) What can you can conclude about the "Anti-Inflation" policy from the chart?

3. Discuss students' answers and then make the following points using these answers:
   - a) Stock Prices (S&P 500 Index) & the Hourly Wage.
   - b) 1957-2003.
   - c) Stock prices began going up while hourly wages continued to fall.
   - d) The "Anti-Inflation" policy helps investors but slows wage growth.

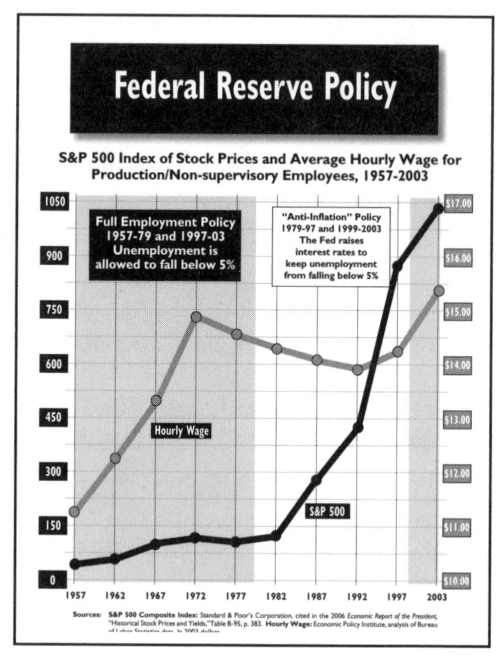

Chart 9a

> **DEFINITION:**
>
> ***Fiscal policy*** is the use of the government budget to affect an economy. When the government decides on the taxes that it collects, the transfer payments it gives out, or the goods and services that it purchases, it is engaging in fiscal policy.[6]

> **TALKING POINTS:**
>
> Before the 1970s, the Fed followed closer to what could be called a "full employment" policy that allowed unemployment to fall to relatively low levels, even if that meant that the inflation rate would go up. For example, from December 1965 to January 1970, the unemployment rate never went above 4%. During this time, hourly wages for production workers rose sharply, while stock prices were basically flat.
>
> However, starting in the 1970s, the Fed departed from its "Full Employment" policy, generally following an "Anti-Inflation" policy. In trying to predict when inflation might be going up, the Fed looks closely at the unemployment rate: lower unemployment = higher wages = inflation. Some economists argued that if the unemployment rate was allowed to fall below 5%, the inflation rate would rise.
>
> The Fed acted as if it accepted this argument. As a result, when the unemployment rate declined too much, the Fed would raise interest rates to slow the economy. Sometimes, the unemployment rate would rise, throwing people out of work. Sometimes, the unemployment rate would hold steady, meaning that some jobless people weren't hired. During the "Anti-Inflation" policy years, hourly wages for production workers fell, and the stock market entered into the longest upswing in its history (1977-2000).
>
> Between 1997 and 2000, the Fed briefly returned to the "Full Employment" policy of the 1950s and 1960s. When the unemployment rate began to fall below 5% in 1997, the Fed decided not to raise interest rates. More people went back to work. Wages started to go up again for the first time in 24 years. However, in 2001, after the dot.com bubble burst and the stock market declined steeply, the Fed again began to raise interest rates.

Federal Reserve Policy

S&P 500 Index of Stock Prices and Average Hourly Wage for Production/Non-supervisory Employees, 1957-2003

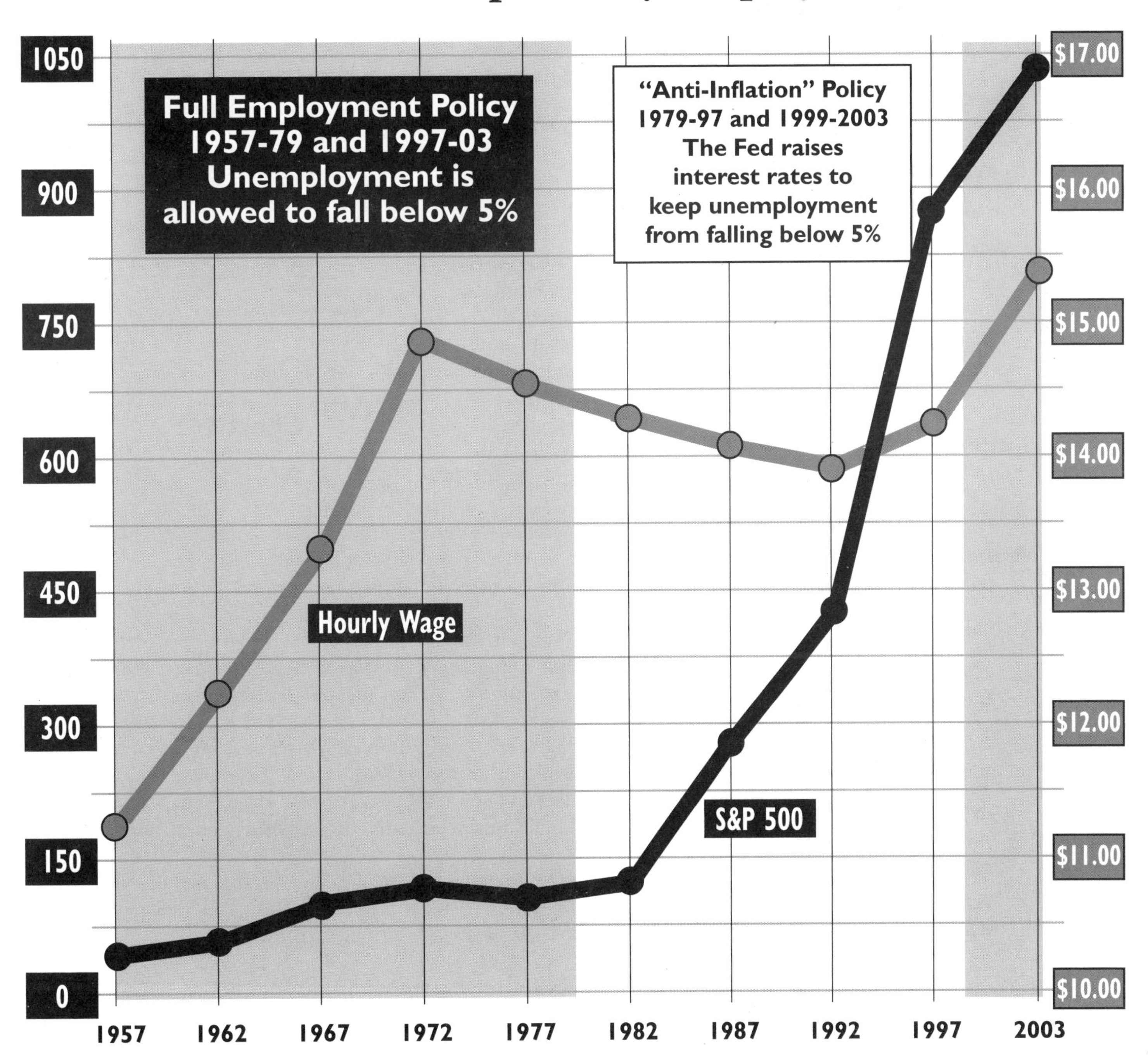

Sources: **S&P 500 Composite Index:** Standard & Poor's Corporation, cited in the 2006 *Economic Report of the President,* "Historical Stock Prices and Yields," Table B-95, p. 383. **Hourly Wage:** Economic Policy Institute, analysis of Bureau of Labor Statistics data. In 2003 dollars.

Chart 9a

Objectives:

- *Define the concepts of wealth and assets.*
- *Compare "wealth" and "income."*
- *Apply an understanding of the definition of wealth by providing examples of wealth for different income and racial groups.*
- *Dramatize the dramatic shift in wealth from 1976 to 2004.*

Concepts and Key Terms:

- *wealth*
- *wealth compared to income*
- *current concentration of wealth in the U.S.*
- *shift in concentration of wealth in the U.S. from 1976 to 2004*

Instructional Time:

- *55 minutes*

Preparation:

For the Bellringer Activity 10.1:

- *Chart 10a, What is Wealth?*

For Activity 10.2:

- *Ten chairs without armrests*
- *CD or tape player (optional)*
- *8.5" x 11" laminated placard: "Wealthiest 10% of the U.S. Population"*
- *Chart 10b, Ownership of Household Wealth in the U.S.*

Conducting the Lesson

Bellringer Activity 10.1: Examples of Wealth

1. Review **Chart 10a, What is Wealth?**

What is Wealth?

★ **What is wealth and how is it different from income?**
Wealth = What you own minus what you owe. Income is money that flows in. Wealth is money that remains after the bills are paid.

★ **You can have high income and no wealth.**
For example, if you earn $100,000 a year and spend $110,000, you have no wealth, just debt. At the end of the year, your wealth will be negative (-$10,000).

★ **You can have low income and still have some wealth.**
For example, if you earn $20,000 a year and save $100 a month, at the end of the year your wealth will be over $1,200 (plus the interest you gain on your savings account).

★ **What you own is often referred to as "your assets."**
There are four major types of assets: 1) homes; 2) liquid assets, including cash, bank deposits, money market funds, and savings in insurance and pension plans; 3) investment real estate and unincorporated businesses; and 4) corporate stock, financial securities, and personal trusts.

★ **What does debt consist of?**
Debt consists primarily of mortgage debt (usually on one's home), credit card debt, student loans, auto loans, and consumer loans.

Chart 10a

2. Ask students to pair off, brainstorm, and record their answers to the following questions regarding the different kinds of wealth:

a) What are some examples of assets that lower-income people might have? (e.g.: cash, checking account, TV set, used car.)

b) What are some examples of assets that middle-income people might have? (Examples: cash, savings or checking account, equity in a house, nice car, small funds).

c) What are some examples of assets that upper-income people might have? (Examples: luxury car, boat, equity in an expensive house and vacation home, stocks.)

d) What are some examples of assets owned by the top one percent of people in the U.S.? (Examples: several houses and apartments, real estate, large stock and bond holdings, businesses, artwork and other collectibles.)

3. Bring the group back together and discuss their answers to each question. Ask them to think about how they would describe their parents' wealth or their own wealth.

4. Review and reiterate by asking students how wealth is different than income. Ask, how it is possible to have negative wealth?

5. Ask students what other questions they have about wealth and income.

> **TALKING POINTS:**
>
> Wealth is what you own minus what you owe.
>
> Income is your paycheck or wages, or government benefit check, or dividend check, or your profit from selling an investment.
>
> Wealth is what you have in the bank and the assets you own.
>
> 18% of the population currently has no assets or negative assets; they owe more than they own. Some of these people may live in big houses and drive big cars, but they may not actually own any of it. They are in debt.

Activity 10.2: Who Owns How Much? (The 10 Chairs)

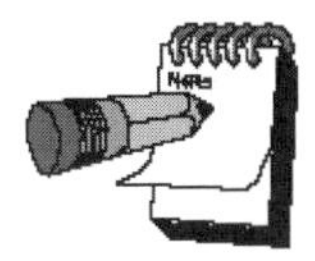

Note to Teacher

This activity strives for dialogue between you and the volunteers in their roles as well as dialogue and reflection among the students observing the activity. You may want to add music to the activity to spice it up. Announce that you are going to play musical chairs. However you may still conduct the activity in the same manner as explained below, without the music.

1. Line up ten chairs across the front of the room facing the students, *prior* to the start of the activity, and set up a CD player with some lively music.

2. Ask for ten volunteers. Identify one person who will represent the "Wealthiest 10% of the U.S. Population" and give that person the placard to wear. Ideally, choose someone who is tall and who will play up this role, a "ham."

3. Ask the volunteers to stand in line, one behind each of the chairs. Explain that each chair represents 10% of all the private wealth in the U.S. and that each of the volunteers represents 10% of the population of the U.S. Explain that "(Insert student's name) is representing the "wealthiest 10% of the U.S. population."

4. While students are standing in a line, one behind each chair, explain this is what wealth would look like if it were evenly distributed in the U.S. — one person, one chair. If wealth were evenly distributed, every household would have a net worth of $380,100. Talk with students about what that might be like. Explain that in fact, life in the United States — or anywhere else, for that matter — is not like that.

5. Explain that different statistical groupings of people in the U.S. own different percentages of wealth. Explain that typically, reliable economic data takes two to three years to be analyzed and in this lesson we are using the most recent available information, which is from 2004. Ask students to guess how much of the total wealth they think the wealthiest 10% of the population owned in 2004. Write their guess on the board so you can refer to it later.

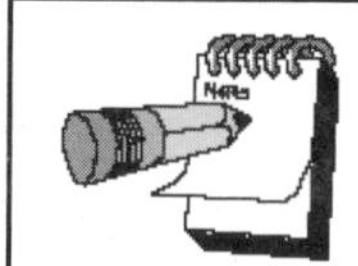

Note to Teacher

A variation on this exercise is to have each person sit in a chair while the teacher makes the point that this picture of equal wealth distribution has never existed. When students have to give up their chairs one by one so the top 10% can stretch out even more, it ups the "punch" of the activity.

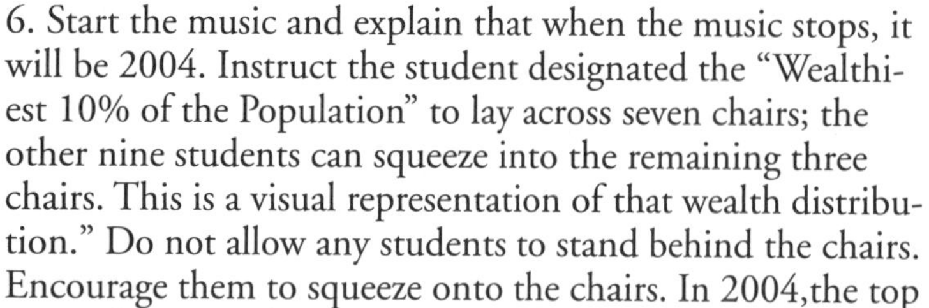

6. Start the music and explain that when the music stops, it will be 2004. Instruct the student designated the "Wealthiest 10% of the Population" to lay across seven chairs; the other nine students can squeeze into the remaining three chairs. This is a visual representation of that wealth distribution." Do not allow any students to stand behind the chairs. Encourage them to squeeze onto the chairs. In 2004,the top 10% of the population owned nearly 70% of all the private wealth and therefore this one student gets to stretch across seven chairs. Ask the students trying to squeeze into the remaining three chairs to come up with one word or short phrase to describe how they feel about this situation.

7. Explain that even within the top 10% there is greater disparity. For example, let's let the arm of the volunteer representing the top 10%, now represent the wealthiest 1% of the population (top 10% student stretches out his arm). In 2004, the share of the top 1% is nearly 33% of all wealth, or equal to almost three and a half chairs. That's more chairs than the bottom 90% have combined. Reiterate by writing the following statement on the board: "The Wealthiest 1% own more wealth than the bottom 90% combined!" Mention that this disparity has grown significantly in the last 25 years (as Chart 10b will show).

8. Ask the volunteers to note the circumstances they are in and their own feelings about these circumstances. Ask them the following questions:

a) How are you feeling at the top?

b) How about in the bottom 90%?

c) How's life at the bottom?

d) Who would you push off the chairs to make room? Why?

e) Look at that person at the top, how would you imagine he uses his chairs (wealth)?

f) Ask the person farthest from "The Top 10%" if she can even see the guy at the top.

g) Are there any students on the floor? Who do they represent? (The homeless.)

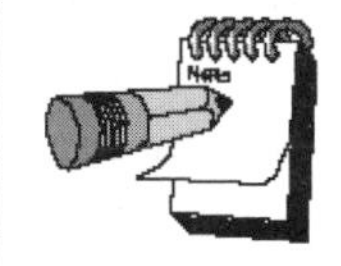

Note to Teacher

There are many analogies to be made during this exercise. Ask students if they feel uncomfortable. Make sure to leave them in position long enough so they feel some discomfort. Ask them how they are demonstrating their discomfort or anger. Do they take it out on the top 10%, or are they fighting among themselves for the three chairs? See the Multicultural and Gender Focus option below to take this a step further.

9. Suggest to the nine students that perhaps their condition is their own fault. Perhaps if they worked harder, they wouldn't be in this spot. Or ask the poorest person (someone who has fallen off the chairs or is on the edge of falling off): "Don't you think everyone else would be better off if you stopped mooching off welfare?"

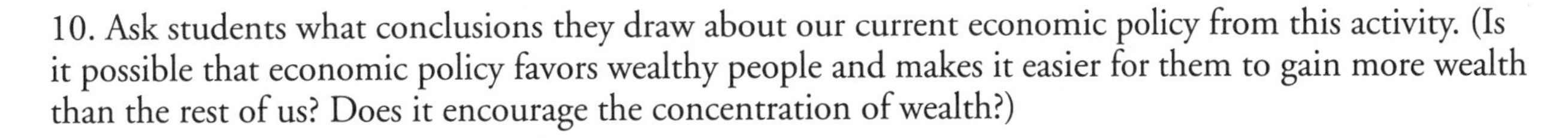

10. Ask students what conclusions they draw about our current economic policy from this activity. (Is it possible that economic policy favors wealthy people and makes it easier for them to gain more wealth than the rest of us? Does it encourage the concentration of wealth?)

11. Display **Chart 10b, Ownership of Household Wealth in the United States** to reinforce or summarize the 10 Chairs activity. Note that not only has there been a significant increase in the overall private wealth owned within the U.S. (the wealth "pie" has grown) but the share of that wealth owned by the top 1% has also grown significantly, and out of proportion to the rest of the 99% of families in the country. Note also that those on the bottom of the economic scale have seen their net worth drop dramatically in the last few decades, with many families in debt and owing more than they own!

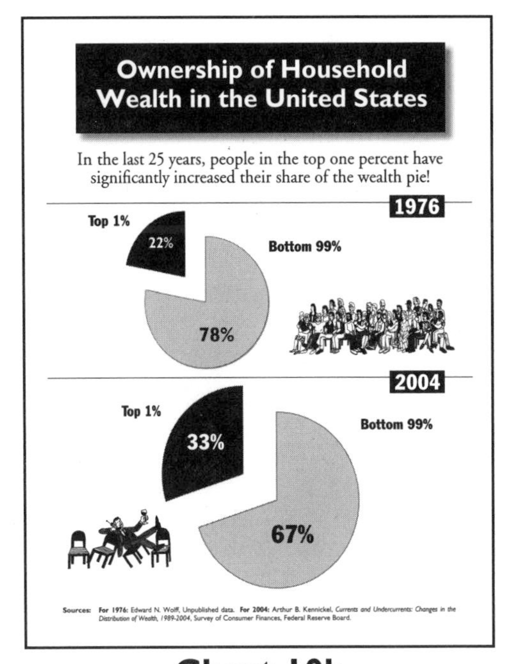

Chart 10b

Optional Activity 10.3: Looking at Wealth Through Race and Gender Lenses

During the 10 Chairs students may actually direct their anger at the person representing the top 10%. In reality people often direct their anger at those around them as they compete with each other for jobs, etc. The top 10% remains largely invisible to the rest while wedges based on race, gender, sexual orientation, age, and class are driven between people and we all battle each other for more space on the few remaining chairs.

1. Ask students to take their seats and then hold a brief discussion with the entire class. Ask them to offer some examples of this "fighting among the bottom 90%" and ask them to name some scapegoats (possible answers: undocumented immigrants, beneficiaries of Affirmative Action policies, welfare recipients, etc.).

2. Have students look at **Charts 10c** and **10d**. These show the distribution of wealth by race. Ask students what explanations they have for why there is such a gap in the amount of wealth owned by white people and the amount owned by people of color.

Note to Teacher

There's much more to say about the increasing concentration of wealth and the racial wealth divide than could be included in one 50-minute class period. You must choose which facts and points to emphasize rather than try to jam everything in.

Also, we recommended that you teach Lessons 10, 11 and 12 in consecutive class periods.

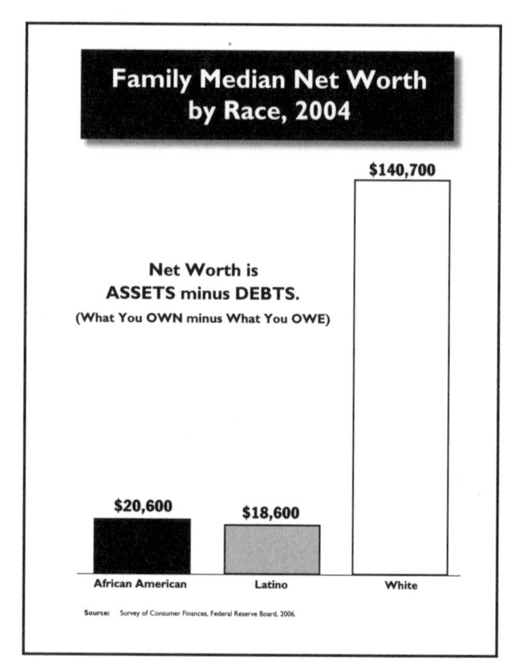

Chart 10c

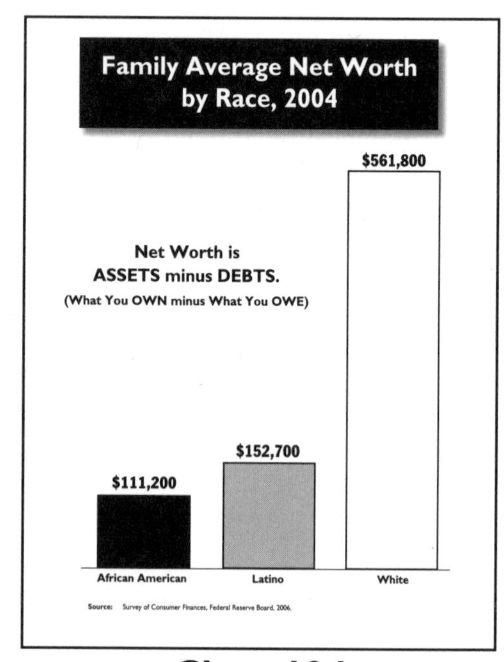

Chart 10d

What is Wealth?

★ What is wealth and how is it different from income?

Wealth = What you own minus what you owe. Income is money that flows in. Wealth is money that remains after the bills are paid.

★ You can have high income and no wealth.

For example, if you earn $100,000 a year and spend $110,000, you have no wealth, just debt. At the end of the year, your wealth will be negative (-$10,000).

★ You can have low income and still have some wealth.

For example, if you earn $20,000 a year and save $100 a month, at the end of the year your wealth will be over $1,200 (plus the interest you gain on your savings account).

★ What you own is often referred to as "your assets."

There are four major types of assets: 1) homes; 2) liquid assets, including cash, bank deposits, money market funds, and savings in insurance and pension plans; 3) investment real estate and unincorporated businesses; and 4) corporate stock, financial securities, and personal trusts.

★ What does debt consist of?

Debt consists primarily of mortgage debt (usually on one's home), credit card debt, student loans, auto loans, and consumer loans.

Chart 10a

Ownership of Household Wealth in the United States

In the last 25 years, people in the top one percent have significantly increased their share of the wealth pie!

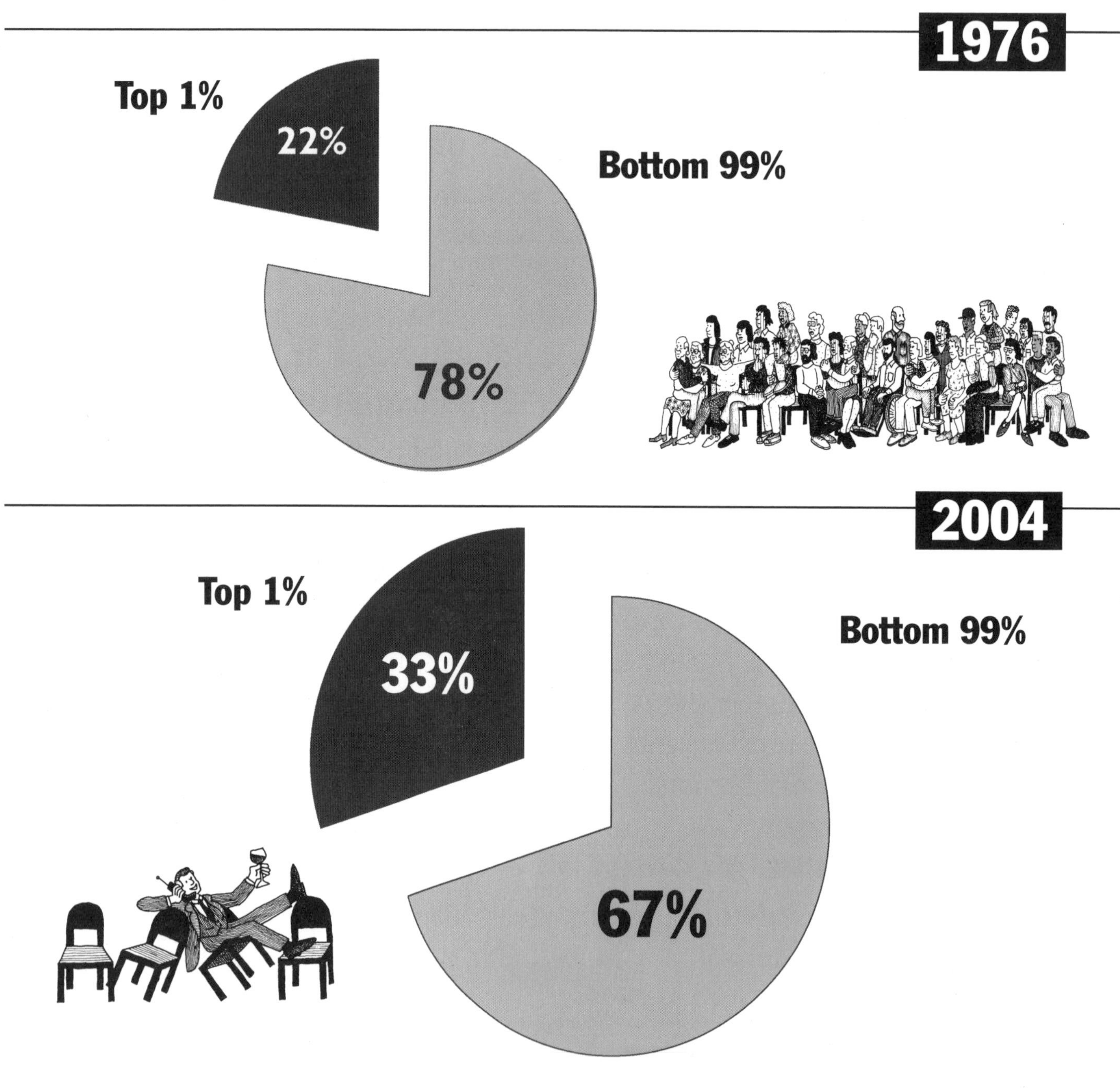

Sources: **For 1976:** Edward N. Wolff, Unpublished data. **For 2004:** Arthur B. Kennickel, *Currents and Undercurrents: Changes in the Distribution of Wealth, 1989-2004*, Survey of Consumer Finances, Federal Reserve Board.

Chart 10b

Family Median Net Worth by Race, 2004

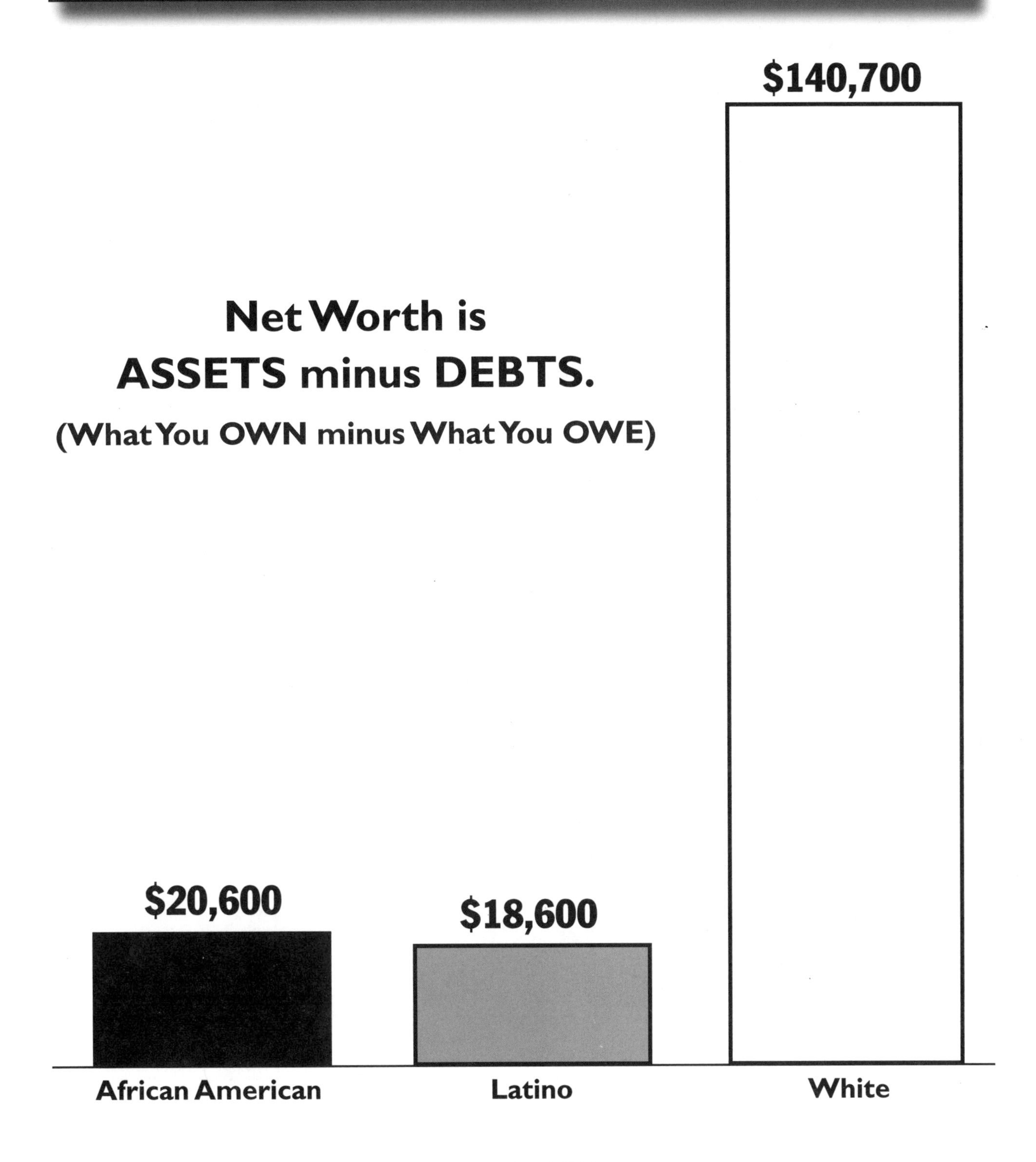

Source: Survey of Consumer Finances, Federal Reserve Board, 2006.

Chart 10c

Family Average Net Worth by Race, 2004

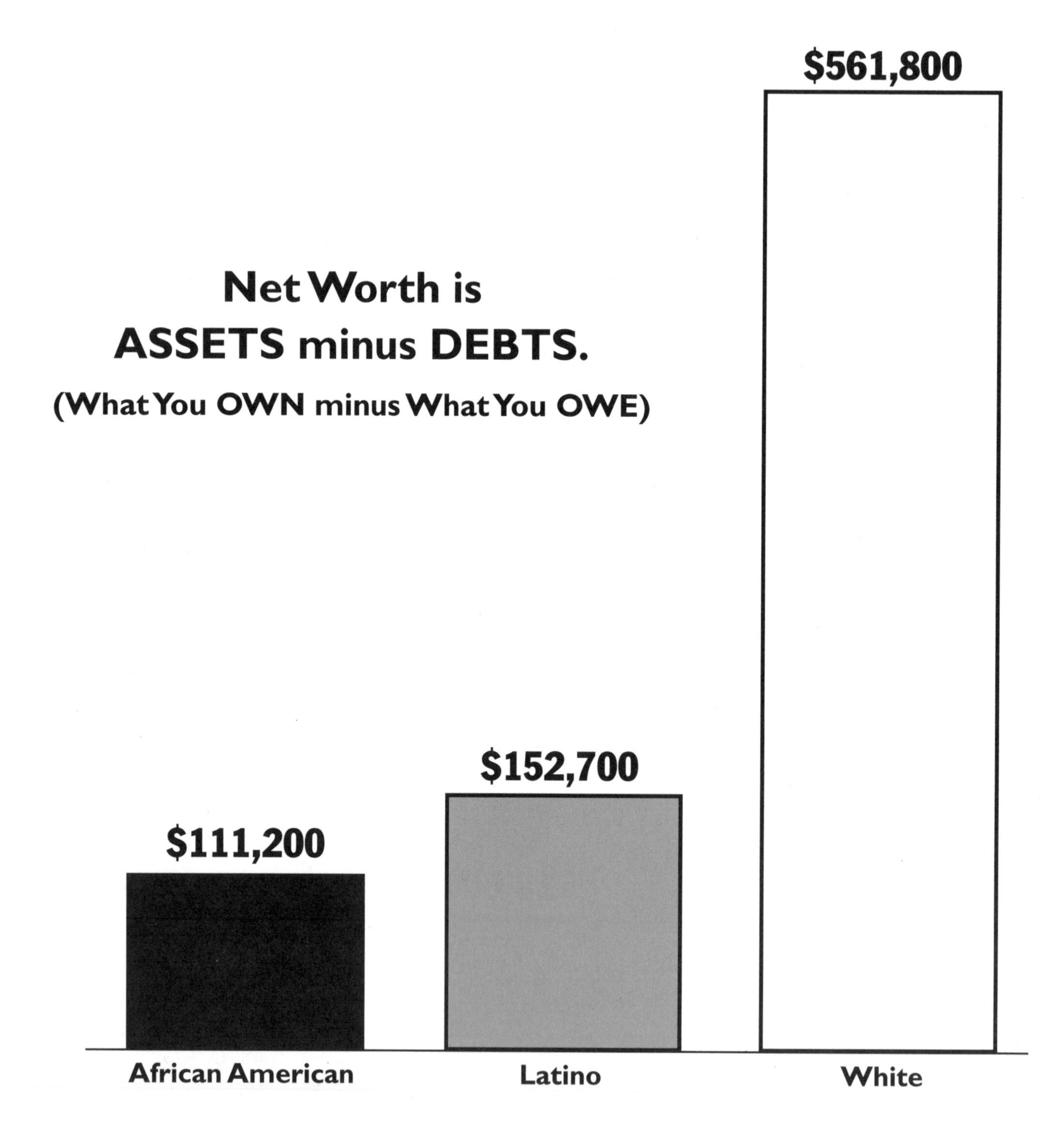

Source: Survey of Consumer Finances, Federal Reserve Board, 2006.

Chart 10d

Objectives:

- *Find out how many American households hold different types of assets.*
- *Demonstrate how investments in savings accounts and stocks function.*

Concepts and Key Terms:

- *how savings accounts function*
- *how stocks function*
- *interest*
- *dividends*
- *assets*

Instructional Time:

- *55 minutes*

Preparation:

For the Bellringer Activity 11.1:

- *Several large pieces of paper taped to the walls, equal distance apart, around the room.*
- *Ten large magic markers*
- *Chart 11a, Percentage of Families Owning Various Assets, 2004*

For Activity 11.2

- *Make up large individual stock certificates for five easily recognized companies, preferably one or two that are local, and tape to the chalkboard (e.g., Disney, General Motors, Sony, Verizon, Wal-Mart)*
- *Plenty of play money, including five $1,000 bills*
- *Three 8.5" x 11" laminated placards labeled "Storeowner," "Banker," and "Investor"*

Conducting the Lesson

Bellringer Activity 11.1: How Many Families in the U.S. Own Savings Accounts? How Many Own Stock?

1. Divide students into small groups of four or five. Hand each group a magic marker and provide the following instructions:

   a) Each group should choose one of the pieces of paper taped to the wall.

   b) Have each group estimate what percentage of families in the U.S. have checking and/or savings accounts, what percentage own their own home, and what percentage own stock.

   c) Have each group draw a bar chart on the paper taped to the wall containing estimates for the three categories.

2. When all students are done, discuss all the "guesses" and have the class vote on the one they think is most accurate. Then reveal **Chart 11a, Percentage of Families Owning Various Assets, 2004.**

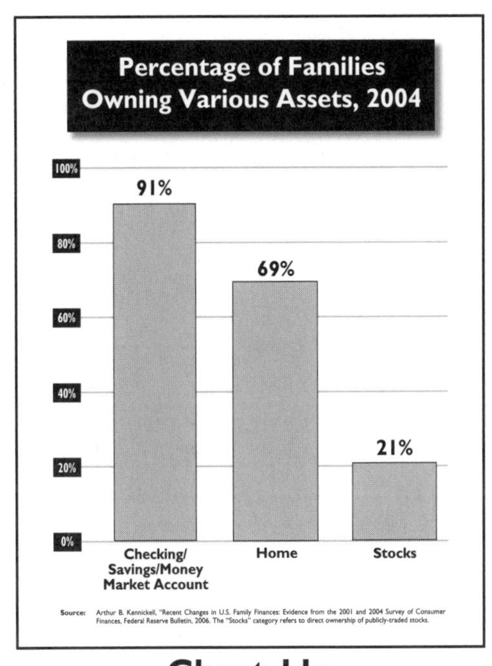

Chart 11a

Activity 11.2: How do Savings Accounts and Stocks Work?

People often have their wealth invested in savings accounts or stocks. The next two demonstrations will explain how these both work. It is helpful to write the interest rates on the board as you narrate this demonstration.

Savings Accounts

1. Recall from Lesson 9 the definition of interest (price paid for the use of credit or loanable funds over a period of time.) Inflation is stated as a rate, that is, as a percentage of the amount borrowed. Thus, an interest rate of 10% annually means that the borrower pays 10 cents interest per $1 borrowed per year, or $10 per $100 borrowed per year, and so on.

2. Ask for three volunteers: a person with money to put in a savings account, in other words, an *investor*; a *banker*; and a *store owner*.

3. Give the volunteers their identifying placards, and give the investor a $1,000 bill, and the banker and store owner some of the fake money.

4. Narrate the following scene: The Investor approaches the bank and puts her money in a savings account at the bank, with a promised 3% interest. The Banker now lends the money to the store at an interest rate of 10%. The Storeowner uses the money to buy more goods to sell in his store and to sell the goods at a profit. Stop at this point and ask the Storeowner what he wants to sell.

5. Tell students that one year has passed. The Storeowner now owes the bank $1,100 ($1,000 + 10% interest). The Banker now owes the Investor $1,030 (1,000 + 3% interest). The Banker gets to keep $70 as profit. The Investor gets to keep $30 out of the deal. A small profit, but since it was a savings account it was guaranteed by the federal government with no risk. The Storeowner was able to make a profit by selling the goods at a higher price than he bought them.

Stocks

6. Define "stock."

7. Tape the five stock certificates to the chalk board. Ask for five volunteers and hand each volunteer a fake $1,000 bill. Ask each person which company's stock she/he wants to buy. Hand each certificate to the student who buys it.

8. Tell students that one year has passed. Stock owners are now receiving dividends. Define "dividends." Hand students fake money from $1 to $50.

DEFINITIONS:

A ***stock*** is a share of ownership of a business such as Disney or Microsoft. Officially, in exchange for cash, an investor becomes a part owner of the business. The share of stock is a claim on a share of the profits of the business. Some of these profits are distributed to the stockholders in the form of ***dividends.*** In recent years, however, many investors haven't focused as much on dividends. They buy a stock in the hopes that its price will go up, so that they can sell it at a profit.

Dividends are earnings (income) that stockholders receive from the company on a regular basis (monthly, quarterly, or yearly.

9. Now students sell their stocks (students hand the stock certificates to the teacher) and get the amounts based on the change in the value of the stock. Some students made a lot of money, but some lost money for their $1,000 investment. Unveil the following information on the board and hand out the amounts based on the sale price.

Company	**Sale Price**
Disney	$1,100
General Motors	800
Sony	950
Verizon	1,001
Wal-Mart	1,200

10. Point out that there is more risk in putting your money in stocks than in putting it in a savings account. In general, the greater the financial risk you take, the higher the potential return will be.

TALKING POINTS:

In the 1990s, the value of many stocks rose dramatically and many investors gained a lot of wealth. A typical investor who put $10,000 into the stock market on January 1, 1990 and left it alone would have gained $40,122 by the end of 1999. In other words, that investor's wealth would have quadrupled. However, between March 11, 2000 and October 9, 2003, the largest stock exchange in the U.S., called the NASDAQ market, lost 78% of its value in what has come to be known as the DOT COM bust (based on the number of internet-related companies that failed during that period). That means that our sample investor who had a total investment of $50,122 in 1999, may have ended up on October 9, 2002 with only $11,026!

While a growing percentage of individuals own stocks and mutual funds – over 50% in 2004 – most of the ownership is concentrated in the hands of a few. Eighty-five percent of all stocks are owned by the wealthiest 10% of households. And the wealthiest 1% own 46% of all stocks and mutual funds.

Percentage of Families Owning Various Assets, 2004

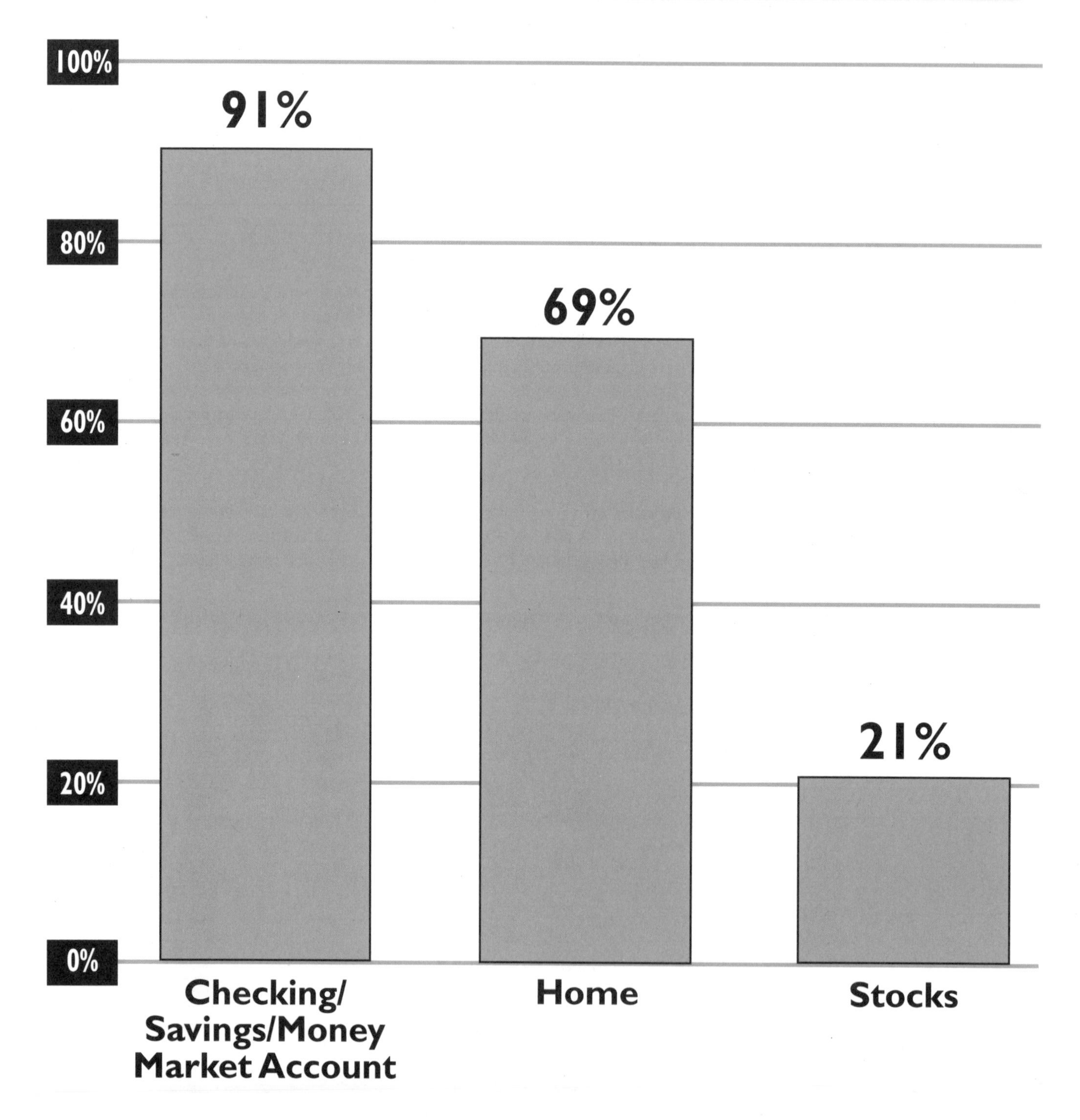

Source: Arthur B. Kennickell, "Recent Changes in U.S. Family Finances: Evidence from the 2001 and 2004 Survey of Consumer Finances, Federal Reserve Bulletin, 2006. The "Stocks" category refers to direct ownership of publicly-traded stocks.

Chart 11a

Objectives:

- *Explore how wealthy Americans acquired their fortunes.*
- *Compare levels of wealth and the lifestyles, assets, and power each level brings.*

Concepts and Key Terms:

- *concentration of wealth*
- *trickle-down theory*

Instructional Time:

- *55 minutes*

Preparation:

For Bellringer Activity 12.1:

- *Any props you can scrounge up to make this more like a baseball game are encouraged. Examples: wear an umpire's uniform while teaching the lesson; arrange the chairs bleacher style on one side of the room and put the bases on the other side, etc.*
- *Set up first, second, third, and home base in your classroom*
- *A megaphone (if you take students outside to the baseball field for this exercise)*
- *Five 8.5" x 11" laminated placards, labeled "Born on Home Plate," "Born on Third Base," etc., accompanied by notes found on page 80, for the student to read.*

For Activity 12.2:

- *Charts: 12a, Small and Medium Amounts of Wealth Can Give You Security, 12b, Large Amounts of Wealth Add Luxury, and 12c, Huge Wealth Can Give You Unfair Power Over Other People.*

Conducting the Lesson

Bellringer Activity 12.1: Who Owns How Much and How Did They Get It?

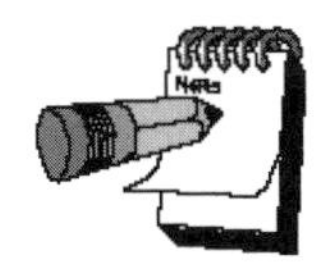

Notes to Teacher

Starting where Lesson 10 left off showing the distribution of wealth in the U.S., we now look closer at who these extremely wealthy people are and how they got to be so wealthy. This lesson goes to the very core of examining whether or not the U.S. is a true meritocracy, where the most able rise to their rightful positions.

You can go into more detail explaining the *Forbes Magazine* annual release of the 400 wealthiest individuals in the U.S. UFE examined the 2005 Forbes 400 list <www.forbes.com/400richest> and grouped those listed into five categories borrowed from the game of baseball. Keeping with the baseball rule that "ties go to the runner," we gave list members the benefit of the doubt. For example, if we couldn't be sure whether a member belonged on second or third base, we assigned him/her to second base.

1. Begin by telling the students they are going to play baseball today. Explain that in order to examine the 400 wealthiest individuals in America, we will use a baseball analogy.

2. Ask for five volunteers and provide each volunteer with one of the placards.

3. Ask each volunteer to stand in the correct place (1st base, 2nd, etc. The volunteer holding the "In the Batter's Box" placard may stand halfway out the door).

4. Begin at home plate and ask the volunteers to read their notes. Encourage them to "ham it up." Stop after each individual card is read and clarify what the card means. Do this by questioning the "fans" in the "bleachers" to make sure they understand what the volunteer read. For example, after "Born on Home Plate" speaks, explain that 42% of the wealthiest

people in the U.S. inherited substantial sums or property and then later built that stake into a greater fortune.

5. When all the volunteers have read their cards, ask them to have a seat (on the bases is fine) and spend some time conducting a mini-presentation using the talking points on page 81. Solicit feedback from students on the various points. If time does not permit covering all of the points, pick and choose the ones that will likely generate the most discussion. If you conducted Lesson 1 discussing the American Dream, you may want to touch on that subject again and see if students' opinions have changed regarding the American Dream.

Born on Home Plate: 42%

"My name is Christy Walton (#7 on the Forbes list). My net worth is $15.6 billion. I became a billionaire when my husband John Walton, Wal-Mart heir, died in a plane crash in June 2005.

Born on Third Base: 6%

"My name is Philip Anschutz (ranked #31 on the Forbes list). My net worth is $7.8 billion. In *Forbes Magazine* I am described as 'self-made' but I guess I have to admit that inheriting oil and gas fields sure helped me increase my wealth." My team and I inherited wealth in excess of $50 million from a large and prosperous company. What do you think of the new name for our team, 'The Silver Spooners?'"

Born on Second Base: 7%

"My name is Herbert V. Kohler (ranked #52 on the Forbes list with a net worth of $4.5 billion). My grandfather founded a company in 1873 to make hitching posts and cemetery ornaments for midwestern farmers, and I built it into the second largest plumbing supplies company in the U.S. Unlike those 'Silver Spooners,' my team and I inherited more than $1 million but less than $50 million."

Born on First Base: 14%

"Hi, I'm Bill Gates (#1 on Forbes list with a net worth of $53 billion). I consider myself self-made. I made my own fortune and so did the other guys on my team who inherited less than $1 million. I mean sure, Mommy and Daddy were comfortable professionals. And so what if they did pay my way to Harvard until I dropped out. OK, most of my team members did get some money from their parents to start their own businesses."

Born in the Batter's Box: 31%

"I'm Wayne Huizenga (#153 on the Forbes list with a net worth of $2.1 billion). I did not inherit great wealth. When my parents divorced, I lived with my mother, driving a truck and pumping gas after school and on weekends to help with expenses. I made it to the Forbes list on my own by buying a garbage truck and starting a waste-hauling company. With the money I made I was able to buy the 19-store Blockbuster video-rental chain and build it into a huge company. I hope more people can continue to do the same thing but I know how tough it is for our team to win when some players start out so far ahead."

TALKING POINTS:

Between 1996 and 2005, the total combined net worth of the Forbes 400 increased from $476 billion to $1.13 trillion — a gain of 137%. For the same time period, median weekly earnings for full-time non-supervisory workers grew at annual rates between 1.8% and 5%. (Remind students inflation also ranged between 1.4% and 3.5% during this time period and therefore these workers' "real" earnings barely grew at all.)

Wealth is now more concentrated in the U.S. than at any time since the 1920s. After the "Great Depression" of the 1930s, *"demand-side"* economic theory suggested that to grow the economy the government needed to stimulate demand for goods and services. It did so by creating job programs, including the WPA (Works Progress Administration), which helped bring an end to the depression and were the basis for economic policies for many years. Nonetheless, in the 1980s, as well as today, government policy changed, and working people have seen a significant decline in their economic well-being. For most people, declining net worth (growing personal indebtedness — exceeding 115% of household income in 2004, according to the Federal Reserve Board) means less *true* home ownership; no stake in pension funds, etc.

Trickle-down theory, also known as *"supply-side economics,"* especially popular among wealthy asset owners, implies that government should do everything in its power to lift the tax "burden" from private wealth. Doing so, according to these theories, will result in increased economic prosperity for everyone. Wealth accumulated at the top will be invested/spent and will eventually "trickle down" to even the lowest wage owners.

The over-emphasis on helping increase private wealth through tax cuts has produced unprecedented deficits (more than $1.3 trillion projected in the coming decade), rising interest rates, and has overburdened and impoverished the other partners in wealth creation: workers, communities, small businesses, small savers, and the natural environment. After the massive tax cuts initiated in 2000 and 2003, which overwhelmingly benefited the wealthiest 1%, many communities, cities, and states have found themselves struggling to provide basic services such as education, emergency medical care, law enforcement, etc. And, despite these massive tax cuts based on supply-side theory, job growth and workers' earnings have remained stagnant.

Too much wealth in too few hands fuels speculation from the top, de-stabilizing the jobs and security of many people. Besides, there are only so many racehorses, works of art, or face lifts any one person can have. More money in more people's hands would be a better fuel for the economy. As economist Randy Albelda put it, "Mink coats don't trickle down."

The shift in the ownership of income and wealth — and the changing nature of work — will likely hit the next generation particularly hard. Many young people who grew up in middle-class families may never have a standard of living approaching their parents — and therefore will increasingly be dependent on their parents' savings (equity) to help them build any security. Lower income youth face the prospect of a lifetime of economic insecurity.

We are in danger of becoming an "inheriting society" rather than an "achieving" or "opportunity society," as those who get an early ticket on the asset train pull away, with government help, from those who rely on their work for a living. An opportunity society should be measured not by the great wealth of people who reach the Forbes 400 but by the opportunity for all people to attain economically secure lives.

Activity 12.2: How Rich is Rich?

1. Solicit students' ideas about what differing amounts of wealth can give you, before revealing the information in **Chart 12a, Small and Medium Amounts of Wealth Can Give You Security, Chart 12b, Large Amounts of Wealth Add Luxury,** and **Chart 12c, Huge Wealth Can Give You Power Over Other People.**

2. We've been using negative examples of what someone can do with huge wealth. Of course there are positive things wealthy people can do with their money. Ask students to name positive examples. Possibilities include starting a non-profit foundation or giving money away to social change organizations. (See www.responsible wealth.org for examples.)

3. Ask students to provide some examples of the impact on democracy by the tremendous concentration of wealth in the hands of a relatively few people. (Lesson 18 focuses more on this topic.)

4. As you present **Chart 12c, Huge Wealth Can Give You Unfair Power Over Other People,** allow students to make the connection between money and power. For each of the dollar figures, provide the first part of the "You might." (Example: You might own lots of apartment buildings.) Then, ask students to come up with suggestions of how someone in this position and with this amount of money might hold lots of power and abuse it. Have them complete the following sentence: "You have the power to..." and then share these or your own answers with the students.

Small and Medium Amounts of Wealth Can Give You Security

If you have this much wealth:	You might:
$500	Have a savings cushion to prevent debt when your expenses are greater than your income.
$1,500	Own a used car.
$5,000	Have a savings cushion to cover 3 months of living expenses in case of sickness or unemployment.
$15,000	Own a new car with no debt payments.
$30,000	Make a down payment on a house or condo; build up equity.
$50,000	Be able to send your children to college.
$200,000	Own your home (a big house in a rural area, a medium-sized house in the suburbs, or a condominium in a large city).
$300,000	Have enough investment income to live on at retirement age 65, when combined with Social Security. In other words, old age security.

Chart 12a

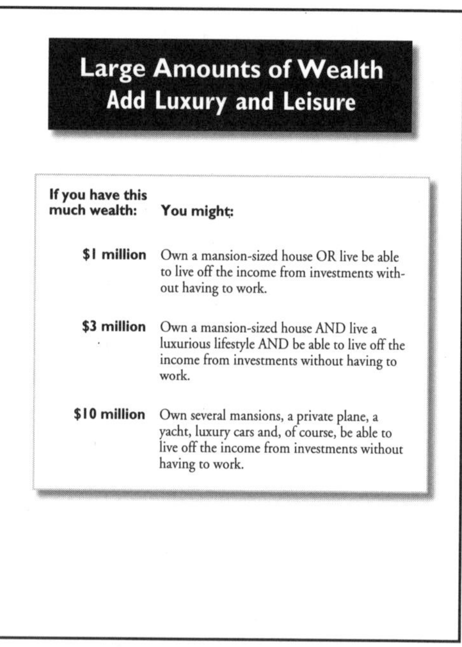
Large Amounts of Wealth Add Luxury and Leisure

If you have this much wealth:	You might:
$1 million	Own a mansion-sized house OR live be able to live off the income from investments without having to work.
$3 million	Own a mansion-sized house AND live a luxurious lifestyle AND be able to live off the income from investments without having to work.
$10 million	Own several mansions, a private plane, a yacht, luxury cars and, of course, be able to live off the income from investments without having to work.

Chart 12b

Huge Amounts of Wealth Can Give You Unfair Power Over Other People

If you have this much wealth:	You might:
$10 million	Own lots of apartment buildings; you have the power to raise rents or sell the apartments as condos and kick low-income tenants out.
$50 million	You have the power to make big contributions to so many candidates that politicians will create tax breaks and corporate welfare (subsidies, etc..) just for your company.
$300 million	Own a sports team; you have the power to threaten to move to a different city if your home city won't build you a stadium.
$600 million	Own a big company; you have the power to close down your American factories and open sweatshops in Third World countries.
$1 billion	Own most of the stock in a huge company; you have the power to buy up competitors to your company and shut them down so your company can get their customers.
$10 billion	Make millions buying and selling foreign currency; you have the power to sell so much of one country's money at once that the currency will dramatically drop in value.

Chart 12c

TALKING POINTS:

Individuals with incredibly huge amounts of wealth can make decisions that can be very harmful to many people. Concentrated wealth and power can lead to the following abuses:

- The judicial system is more favorable to those with money. Defendants who could afford their own attorneys are incarcerated less often than those who were represented by public defenders.

- People with a lot of money can use campaign contributions to influence politicians to make laws in their interest.

- Many people feel that money has such an influence over politics that they become disillusioned, cynical, apathetic, and don't bother to take part in elections. Voter participation in the US has dropped to record low numbers. Only a little more than 58% of registered voters turned out for the contentious 2004 presidential election. By contrast, in the 1964 Presidential election, nearly 70% of the voting-age population went to the polls. When people drop out of electoral politics, we no longer have a legitimate representative democracy and decisions are made without the people's consent.

- Extraordinary fortunes produce tremendous economic and social power, which can be exercised through large contributions to political campaigns, well-financed personal candidacies (examples include Ross Perot, Steve Forbes, Michael Bloomberg, and Jon Corzine), or the formation of family dynasties (e.g., the Rockefellers, Kennedys, and Bushes.) And this pushes spending on all electoral campaigns ever higher. For example, according to the Federal Election Commission, Congressional candidates spent $711.6 million in 2004, an increase of 15% over 2002. Senate candidates spent $278 million, up 22% over 2002.

- For the average family, by contrast, wealth provides an economic safety net rather than a source of social power and political advantage. Savings serve as a fallback source for times of economic stress.

Suggested Homework:

Reflecting on the three charts and the entire lesson, have students write a paragraph answering the following question: What do you think is positive about great wealth? What is harmful? Explain your answers. Lesson 13 will include a values clarification exercise and students may be called on to read their paragraphs in conjunction with this exercise.

Small and Medium Amounts of Wealth Can Give You Security

If you have this much wealth:	You might:
$500	Have a savings cushion to prevent debt when your expenses are greater than your income.
$1,500	Own a used car.
$5,000	Have a savings cushion to cover 3 months of living expenses in case of sickness or unemployment.
$15,000	Own a new car with no debt payments.
$30,000	Make a down payment on a house or condo; build up equity.
$50,000	Be able to send your children to college.
$200,000	Own your home (a big house in a rural area, a medium-sized house in the suburbs, or a condominium in a large city).
$300,000	Have enough investment income to live on at retirement age 65, when combined with Social Security. In other words, old age security.

Chart 12a

Large Amounts of Wealth Add Luxury and Leisure

If you have this much wealth:	You might:
$1 million	Own a mansion-sized house OR be able to live off the income from investments without having to work.
$3 million	Own a mansion-sized house AND live a luxurious lifestyle AND be able to live off the income from investments without having to work.
$10 million	Own several mansions, a private plane, a yacht, luxury cars and, of course, be able to live off the income from investments without having to work.

Chart 12b

Huge Amounts of Wealth Can Give You Unfair Power Over Other People

If you have this much wealth:	You might:
$10 million	Own lots of apartment buildings; you have the power to raise rents or sell the apartments as condos and kick low-income tenants out.
$50 million	You have the power to make big contributions to so many candidates that politicians will create tax breaks and corporate welfare (subsidies, etc..) just for your company.
$300 million	Own a sports team; you have the power to threaten to move to a different city if your home city won't build you a stadium.
$600 million	Own a big company; you have the power to close down your American factories and open sweatshops in Third World countries.
$1 billion	Own most of the stock in a huge company; you have the power to buy up competitors to your company and shut them down so your company can get their customers.
$10 billion	Make millions buying and selling foreign currency; you have the power to sell so much of one country's money at once that the currency will dramatically drop in value.

Chart 12c

Objectives:

- *Define stocks and bonds*
- *Explore ownership of stocks and mutual funds in the U.S., including ownership by race.*
- *Explore how wealth begets wealth.*
- *Examine the percentages of family savings in the U.S. and compute a family savings "cushion."*

Concepts and Key Terms:

- *compound interest*
- *mutual fund*
- *stock ownership*
- *gross inequalities*
- *the color of wealth*

Instructional Time:

- *55 minutes*

Preparation:

For the Bellringer Activity 13.1:

- *Record clips of the evening stock report from radio or TV network news for several consecutive nights*
- *Several pieces of flipchart paper taped to the walls, equal distance apart, around the room*
- *Ten large magic markers*
- *Chart 13a, Ownership of Stocks and Mutual Funds in 2004*

For Activity 13.2:

- *Charts 13b, Family Savings: Living on the Edge*
- *One student copy of the "What's Your Savings Cushion" form for each family scenario you create (You can use the family scenarios found with this lesson and/or create your own)*

Conducting the Lesson

Bellringer Activity 13.1: Who Owns Stock in the Stock Market?

1. Ask students to listen closely to the recording you're about to play. Begin by playing a recording of the stock market report from the radio. (This is easily recorded from most public radio stations.) Students may be more familiar with the TV network news report of the Dow Jones Average. Ask for a show of hands of students who have heard of the Dow Jones or the NASDAQ.

2. Even if students are not familiar with any of this, they have likely heard that some people made a fortune in the stock market. (The "dot.com" boom of the late 1990s is a recent example.) Call on a student and ask what has been happening lately in the stock market and she/he may know the market had great ups and downs in the last ten years.

3. Ask students how they know when the stock market is doing well. Do they hear about it in the news? Have their families experienced financial gain from stocks? On rare occasions there will be students who own some stock and actually follow the market.

4. When it is established that most people know the market has done well because they were told it was doing well, rather than experiencing it, divide students into small groups of four or five, hand each group a magic marker and provide the following instructions:

a) Each group should choose one of the pieces of paper taped to the wall.

b) Have each group estimate what percentage of stocks and bonds are owned by the Top 1%, the Next 9%, and the Bottom 90% of American households. Then have each group draw these percentages in the form of a pie chart on the poster. Provide the groups about three minutes to complete this task. (You may need to start students off with a hypothetical answer. For example: "Do you think the bottom 90% of the population owns 80% of the stocks?" Draw in a wedge covering 80% of the circle and label it with "Bottom 90%.")

5. When all students are done, discuss all the guesses and have the class vote on the one they think is most accurate. Then reveal **Chart 13a, Ownership of Stocks and Mutual Funds in 2004.**

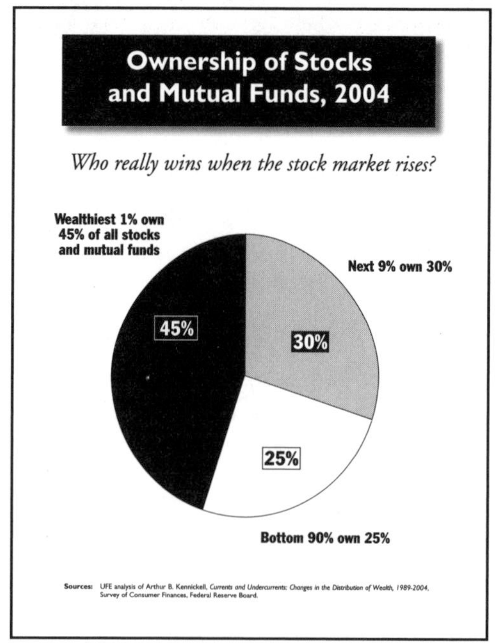

Chart 13a

6. A mutual fund is a form of collective investment that pools money from many investors and invests the money in stocks, bonds, short-term money market instruments, and/or other securities. In a mutual fund, the fund manager trades the fund's underlying securities, realizing capital gains or loss, and collects the dividend or interest income. The investment proceeds are then passed along to the individual investors.

7. How close were students in their estimates? Ask them to take a seat and use the following talking points to stimulate discussion. We hear a lot about how a booming stock market benefits everyone, but as this chart shows, most families in the U.S. have little or nothing invested in the stock market and therefore do not benefit directly when stock prices rise.

TALKING POINTS:

In 2004, 17% of all income went to the top-earning 1% of households, who owned 37% of stock market holdings. In comparison, the lower 90% of income earners owned only 21% of the stock market. Of these folks, the bottom 60% of the population (in terms of income) owned only 2.3 % of the stocks in the market. The trend since 2001 shows that these folks are cashing in what little they have. The less money you make, the less likely you are to own stocks and enjoy the earnings they provide.

On the other hand, the amount of stocks owned by the wealthy is going up. Wealth begets wealth. The impact of compounding interest multiplies wealth for asset holders. Investing in financial markets is a major way the super rich make their fortunes.

During market down-turns, like the bursting of the "dot com bubble," economic analysts can say: "Don't worry, the middle class isn't really hurting because they don't own much stock." Yet these same commentators turn around and say everyone benefits when the stock market goes up.

Source: www.epinet.org/content.cfm/webfeatures_econindicators_jobspict_20050304.

8. Remind students how interest works and then explain compound interest, interest computed on a principal sum (in this case the amount you loan or invest) and also on all the interest earned by that principal sum as of a given date.

9. In Lesson 10 we discussed the risks involved in playing the stock market. Knowing more about the market now, who do you think is more likely to take these risks and therefore more likely to profit from the stock market? (The super rich, because they have comparatively very little to lose.) Why do you think the stock market report is given so frequently by the media? What other indicators would you suggest for determining the health of the economy (e.g., the labor market, wages, etc.).

Activity 13.2: When the Savings Run Out

1. As the wealthiest people in the U.S. continue to profit whenever the stock market rises, 45% (almost half) of all families in the U.S. only have financial reserves for about three months. That's 50 million families! Listen to this description of the economic situation many families in the U.S. are in:

> "What would happen to your family if the primary breadwinner lost her/his job? The key to true economic security for most families are their assets, particularly cash. Money stored up in a savings account can tide a family over in an emergency such as an illness or a layoff. Most financial planners suggest having six months' worth of income saved for just such times. However, this is an impossible goal for many families. Consider the nearly 200,000 families affected by the layoffs in the auto industry during 2005 and 2006. Or the tens of thousands of families left stranded by Katrina's rising flood waters and inadequate disaster relief efforts. Lacking decent incomes, cash savings, or substantial assets, many people are forced to work extra hours or take a second or even a third job just to survive."

2. Introduce **Chart 13b, Percentage of Families Whose Savings Would Run Out in 3 Months or Less.** In Lesson 3 we discussed how many Americans can't afford to put money away into savings these days. This chart shows how different it might be for a Black, White, or Latino family facing economic hardship in 1995.

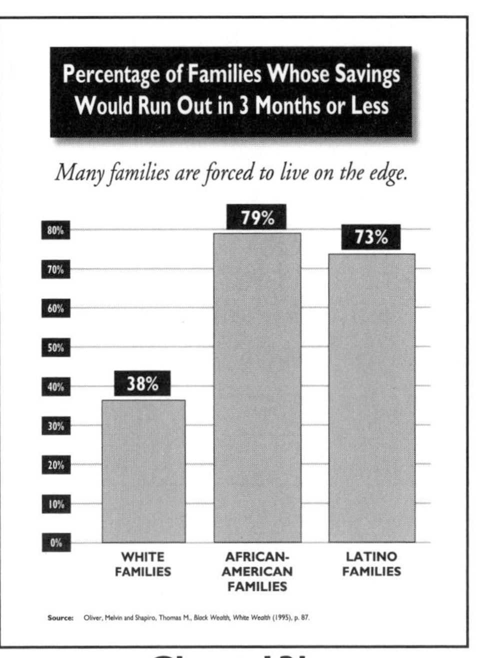

Chart 13b

> **TALKING POINT:**
>
> In 2001, if we lined up all the White households by amount of cash they had in savings and checking accounts, from those with the most to those with the least, half had more than $4,200 and half had less. In 2003, the middle-ranked White households had a bit more ready cash for an emergency: $5,000. Among African-American households, the middle-ranked households in both 2001 and 2003 had only $100 available for an emergency! Consider the implications of this information for struggling households given that a calculated minimum family budget just for essentials is about $12,000 per month. (Based on the 'Basic Family Budget' calculations for a two-parent family with two children, using data from www.epi.org).

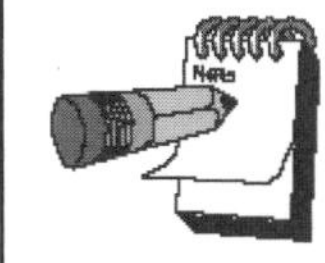

Note to Teacher

This activity can be done by students at home with parental involvement or it can be done in class using the "family scenarios" provided below.

3. Pass around a hat or basket with the "family scenarios" in it (see next page). Each student selects a scenario, reads it aloud, and chooses as many students as the card instructs to be a part of her/his "family."

4. After choosing "family scenarios," students will use the "What's Your Savings Cushion" form to figure their family's savings cushion.

5) When you are done, offer that students may want to discuss this activity with their parents if their parents feel comfortable discussing financial matters as a family.

Family Scenarios

1. You are a single mother with two children in elementary school. You work full-time as a sales clerk at The Gap. You make $14,250 a year and have cash savings of $450. (3-person family)

2. You are a father with three children, ages 2, 4 and 6. You work full-time as a fire fighter, making $42,000 a year. Your partner stays home and keeps the children. You have cash savings of $3,000. (5-person family)

3. You are a single female attorney working for large law firm. Your salary is $85,000 a year and you have cash savings of $18,000. (1-person family)

4. You are a mother of three and a welfare recipient, receiving $9,000 a year. You have cash savings of $100. (4-person family)

5. You are a father with five children. Two children are in college and three are still in private school. You are a doctor, making $160,000 a year. Your wife is a public school teacher making $39,000 a year. You have cash savings of $12,000. (7-person family)

6. You are a recent college graduate. You just accepted a job as a sales person for a new telecommunications company. Your salary is $34,000 per year. However, you have only worked for two months so you have cash savings of $0.00. (1-person family)

7. You are a machinist for Ford. You work 40 hours per week on the night shift. On occasion you receive overtime so your annual salary is approximately $36,000. You did have several thousand dollars, but because you are a newlywed, you just spent most of it on your honeymoon. You have cash savings of $1,100. (2-person family)

8. You are a CEO of a large company that had a record year of profit making. Your salary is $1 million dollars. You have four children, ages 10, 12, 14, and 16. Your partner works part-time as an artist. You have cash savings of $5 million. (6-person family)

What's Your Savings Cushion?

If your family's breadwinner lost a job today, how long could the family survive at the poverty line before running out of money? To find out, complete this form.

a. Estimate your cash savings and enter the figure on line a. a. ______________________

b. Look at the Family Size/Poverty Line table below to determine the monthly poverty-level minimum for your family. Enter that amount on line b. b. ______________________

c. Divide line a by line b. The result is the number of months your family could live at the poverty level before your savings run out. c. ______________________

Single parent raising:							
Number of children:	0	1	2	3	4	5	6
Monthly income at Poverty line	$1,090	$1,122	$1,311	$1,656	$1,913	$2,134	$2,340

Source: U.S. Census Bureau. Poverty thresholds for single parent families with children under 18 for 2005 (http://www.census.gov/hhes/www/poverty/threshld/thresh05.html).

TALKING POINTS FOR A FOCUS ON RACE:

It is important not to leave the impression that more African-Americans are poor because white people work harder or some other possible "blame the victim" explanations.

There is, after all, a larger number of white families than African-American families whose savings would run out in three months or less. African-Americans make up just 12% of the U.S. population.

While it is true that a greater percentage of families of color live close to the edge than white families, this can be explained by policies that favored some groups (principally white men) and disadvantaged others. Add to this: years of discrimination in workplaces and schools; discrimination in the administration of government programs, such as the G.I. Bill of Rights, denied to African-American WW II veterans; lack of equal educational opportunities afforded to white people; and lack of inherited wealth, among other reasons.

For a full discussion of the racial wealth divide, see *The Color of Wealth* (listed at the end of this lesson), a book produced in 2006 by United for a Fair Economy.

Bonus Reading

The Color of Wealth - The Story Behind the U.S. Racial Wealth Divide by Meizhu Lui, Bárbara Robles, Betsy Leondar-Wright, Rose Brewer, and Rebecca Adamson (The New Press, 2006). *The Color of Wealth* is the first book to lay out the obstacles placed in the path of asset building by government actions and inactions for four different racialized groups, and to detail the boosts given to white people by public policy. The book's message is a hopeful one; the very success of programs to move white men into the middle class shows that it can be done for everyone. Inspiring case studies and realistic policy ideas point the way towards a real opportunity society.

Students often make anecdotal arguments when discussing the advancement of young people of color. They cite examples of sports celebrity achievement, such as Michael Jordan, Tiger Woods, Michael Vick, etc. Stanley Eitzen's book *Fair and Foul: Beyond the Myths and Paradoxes of Sport* goes to the heart of these arguments and presents hard facts on what percentage of high school students actually receive college scholarships or ever make it to professional teams. For a short version of this topic, see Eitzen's essay "Upward Mobility Through Sport?" at http://www.zmag.org/zmag/articles/mar99eitzen.htm.

Activity 13.3: Gross Inequalities... Time for a Change

1. Ask students to form a standing circle, as large as the classroom will permit. Announce: "We have just seen how the wealthiest people in our society are continuing to increase their wealth. We then examined how many Americans are no longer able to save money for emergencies and many would be at the poverty line within a few months. Taking this into consideration listen to a few more facts about growing inequality, and participate in a 'Values Clarification' activity to decide how you feel about this issue."

2. Announce: "When you listen to some of the following 'Gross Inequalities' statements ("gross" is a pun on Gross Domestic Product), if you believe it is time citizens do something to change this growing inequality, move inside the circle to form a smaller circle. Once in the smaller circle, look around to see who shares this view with you. Then move back to the larger circle before the next statement is read.

Note to Teacher

If you assigned the homework at the end of Lesson 12, this is a good time to include students' paragraphs.

"If we pay them starvation wages— why do they need a lunch break?"

GROSS INEQUALITIES

Is it time for us to do something to change the inequalities described in these statements?

Statement 1

Estimates of the costs of providing basic education and health care for all people, reproductive health care for all women, and adequate food and safe water for all the people in the world is $50 billion — less than the net worth of the richest man in the world.

Statement 2

The three richest people in the world have assets that exceed the combined GDP of the 57 poorest countries. (GDP is explained in Lesson 3. GDP data for countries is from the International Monetary Fund, 2005.)

Statement 3

The wealth of the 225 richest people is equal to the annual incomes of nearly half of the world's population (over 2.9 billion people).

Statement 4

This year, as *Forbes Magazine* reported in October 2006, for the first time, everyone on the Forbes list has at least $1 billion. The net worth of the 400 richest people in the U.S. climbed $120 billion, to $1.25 trillion. Half that increase — $60 billion — would have been enough to bring all poor Americans up to the official poverty line.

Statement 5

An opportunity society should not be measured by the great wealth of people who reach the Forbes 400 list but by the opportunity for all people to attain economically secure lives.

Statement 6

There is something wrong with a society that ignores, denies, hides or tries to justify the fact that one-fifth of its children live in poverty and many go hungry at night, while some individuals within the society have such enormous and extravagant wealth that it seems as if they could never spend it all.

3. If this activity motivates students to address this problem and they start asking what they can do, you may want to go to Lesson 19, 20 and 21.

Race and Statistics

"Racial and ethnic classifications are increasingly mediated by the Census Bureau. While originally conceived simply to provide consistent categories for use by federal agencies, the census' definitions of race and ethnicity have had the unintended consequence of shaping the very discourse of race and the distribution of vast resources in the U.S. These categories have become the de facto standard for state and local agencies, the private and nonprofit sectors, and the research community. In addition, these categories inordinately influence group identities and forms of political mobilization.

"Yet racial categories are inherently unstable and shifting. We can never have categories that will be conceptually valid, measurable, and reliable over time. Yet we cannot simply abandon the use of racial and ethnic categories. Without them, we cannot monitor and track racial inequity and discrimination — for example, racial profiling. However "unscientific" and imprecise these categories may be, some form of racial classification is needed to discern trends and discriminatory patterns."

— Michale Omi, "Counting in the Dark" in *ColorLines* (Spring 2001).

Ownership of Stocks and Mutual Funds, 2004

Who really wins when the stock market rises?

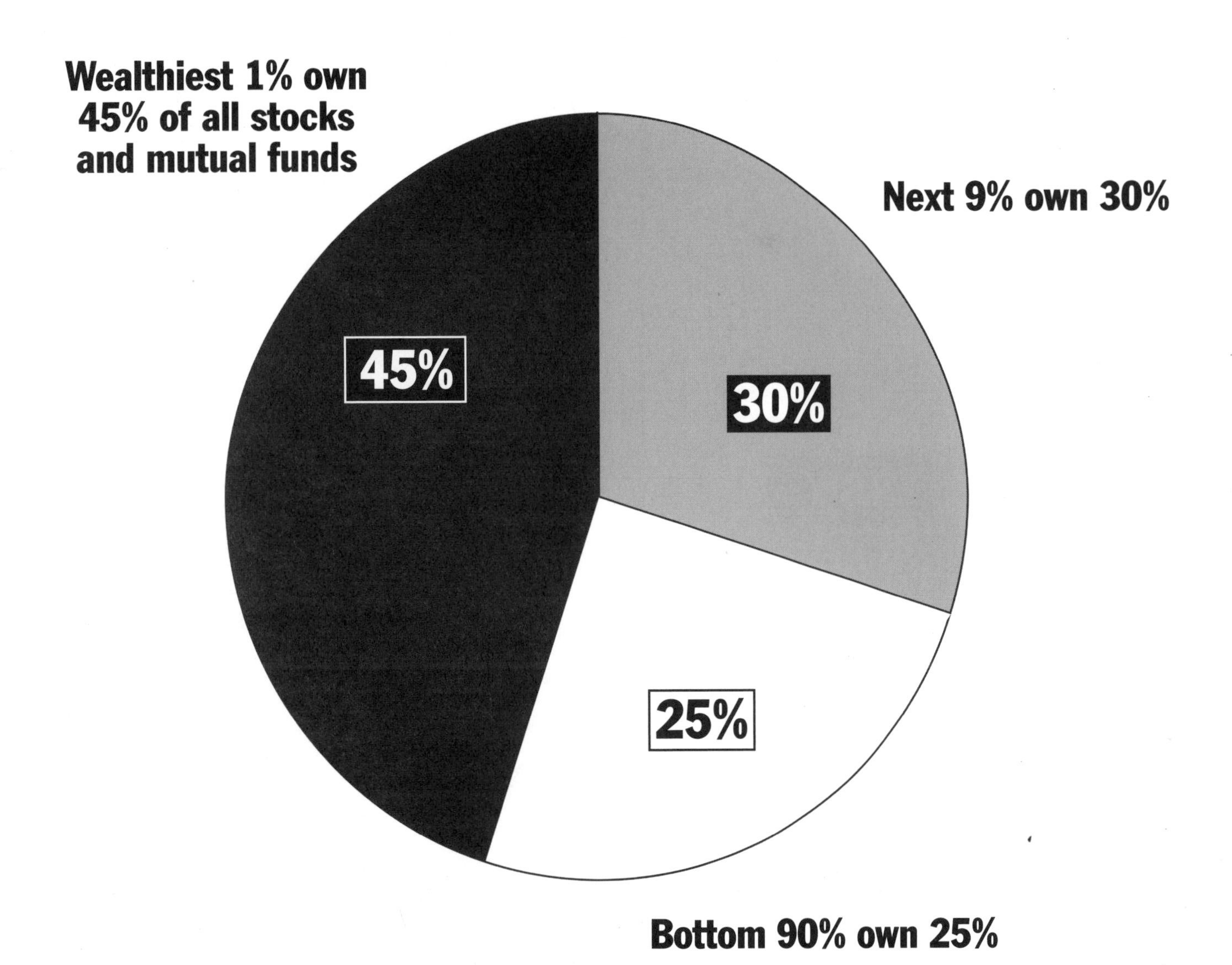

Sources: UFE analysis of Arthur B. Kennickell, *Currents and Undercurrents: Changes in the Distribution of Wealth, 1989-2004*, Survey of Consumer Finances, Federal Reserve Board.

Chart 13a

Percentage of Families Whose Savings Would Run Out in 3 Months or Less

Many families are forced to live on the edge.

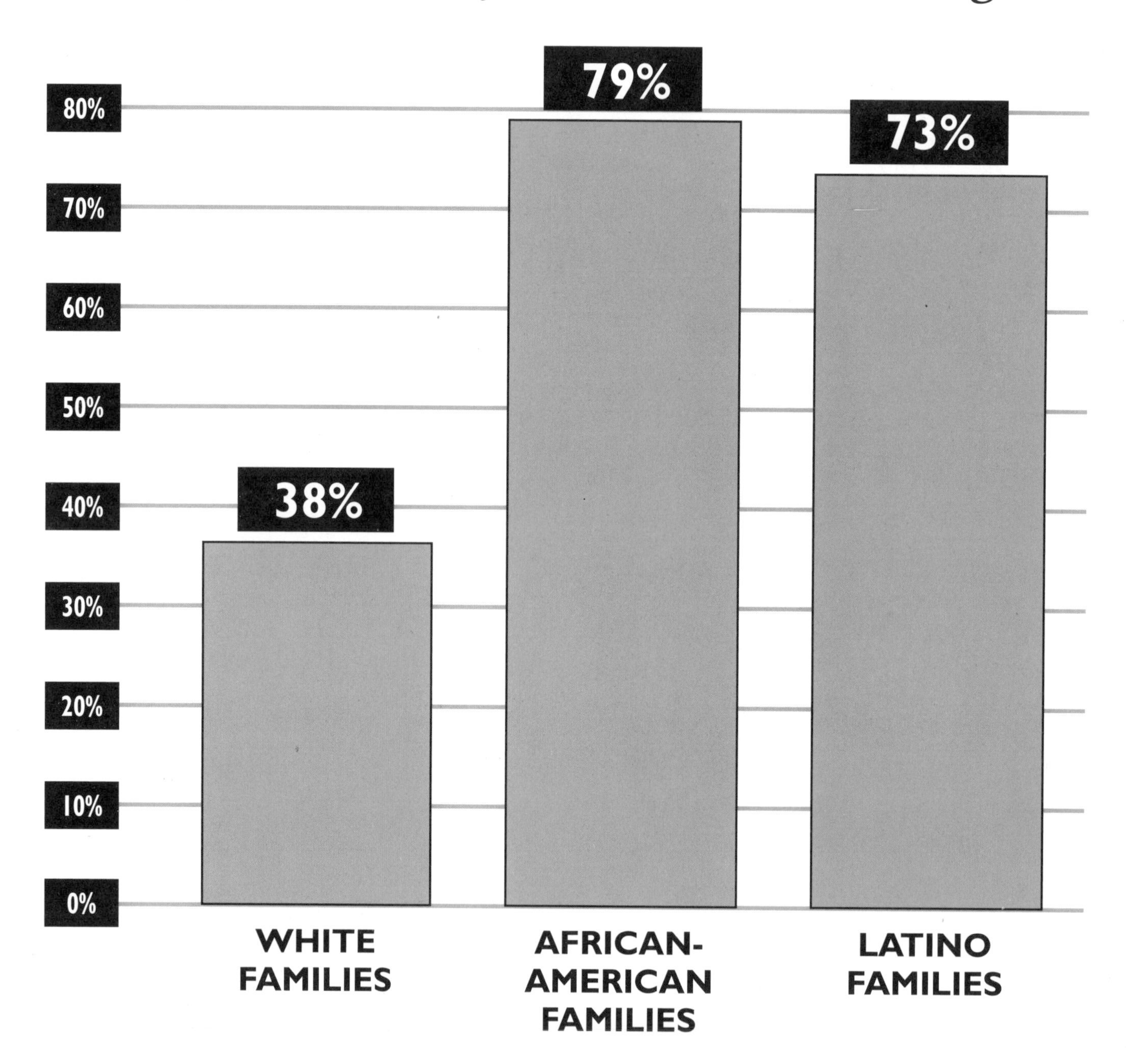

Source: Oliver, Melvin and Shapiro, **Thomas** M., *Black Wealth, White Wealth* (1995), p. 87.

Chart 13b

Lesson 14: Power Shift Led to Rule Changes

Objectives:

- *Experience class discrimination and discuss reactions to this discrimination.*
- *Address the shift in power leading to rule changes that have fostered growing economic inequality in the U.S.*
- *Explore the connections between rule changes, including those that affected the ability of working people to organize into unions, and the concentration of power and wealth in the U.S.*

Concepts and Key Terms:

- *labor unions*
- *class discrimination*
- *power shifts leading to inequality*
- *rule changes leading to inequality*

Instructional Time:

- *55 minutes*

Preparation:

For the Bellringer Activity 14.1:

- *Arrange the desks in one large semi-circle facing the front of the room (optional, yet provides optimum conditions for the simulation).*
- *Cut up small pieces of colored paper. Decide on the number of colors based on the number of students in your class. For a class with 30 students use six blue, 16 green, and eight pink. (Choose any three colors.)*
- *Fill a paper bag with the pieces of colored paper.*
- *Tape*
- *Write the following set of rules on the board, a poster, or an overhead (do not reveal the rules until students have selected a color from the bag):*

  a) Members of the same color group may speak freely among themselves.

  b) "Blues" may speak to members of any other group.

  c) "Greens" may speak freely to "pinks," yet may only speak to "blues" when spoken to first.

  d) "Pinks" may speak only to members of their own color group, unless spoken to first.

  e) "Blues" may raise their hands at any time to ask or answer a question; "greens" and "pinks" may raise their hands only to ask, but not to answer, a question.

  f) The teacher is a member of the "blues."

  g) Rules cannot be changed or disobeyed.

  h) If rules are disobeyed, "blues" will determine the punishment.

- *Charts 14a, The Power Shift Since the 1970s, 14b, Rule Changes Since the 1970s, 14c, The Wheel of Misfortune and 14d, Union Membership, 1930-2004*

Conducting the Lesson

Bellringer Activity 14.1: Class Discrimination Simulation

In this simulation students will experience preferential treatment based solely on the color of a group to which they are randomly assigned. Before and during the simulation, make sure students understand that they are taking on randomly selected roles in a hypothetical situation. The length of time they assume these roles is up to you, but a suggested time is 15 to 30 minutes.

1. Explain the following to students: "You will be taking part in a simulation that will demonstrate a concept. At some point it may become obvious what concept the simulation is demonstrating. When the simulation ends there will be an opportunity to discuss your reactions to it."

2. Pass around the bag and the tape and have each student draw a colored slip of paper and tape it to her/his shirt. When all students have drawn a color, ask them to sit together by color (with blues in the middle of the two colors).

3. Show students the Rules listed in the Preparation section and explain each rule. Announce: "For the next 15 minutes, class will be conducted under a set of rules based on group color."

4. Tell students you will now begin the day's lesson as usual.

5. Results you might experience include:
   a) Greens and Pinks organizing a walkout of the classroom.
   b) Greens and Pinks uniting and tearing the Blues' colored slips from their shirts, in essence, stripping them of their power.
   c) Greens and Pinks begin goofing off, not paying attention or intentionally trying to fall asleep. (In this case, eventually call the simulation to an end. Make the connection to real life — those people who are not heard and who are being oppressed often give up hope, goof off in class, drop out of school, etc.)

NOTES ON THIS ACTIVITY:

The simulation can take several different angles eventually leading to different outcomes. In turn, you will have the opportunity to foster dialogue on several topics. The purpose for using the simulation during this lesson is to promote unity among the Greens and Pinks so they will organize and rise up against the oppressive Blues. (It doesn't take much time before the Blues begin abusing their authority.) The subject matter to be discussed in Activity 14.2 is the role unions play in a free market economy and the changes in the presence of unions since the 1970s. After the simulation, students should see the parallel between the subject matter discussed in the lesson and what occurred during the simulation.

As soon as someone from the Greens or Pinks breaks a rule, ask the Blues to come up with a "reasonable" punishment, suggesting a punishment such as standing on one leg at the chalkboard with her/his nose in a circle, etc. Greens and Pinks may not accept their punishment. As the teacher, and as a Blue, you can encourage them to "play by the rules" and "play the game."

When a Blue breaks a rule quickly (and quite obviously) overlook it, and that will draw complaints from the Greens and Pinks. Answer coyly, "What can I say? She's a fellow Blue; I think I will overlook it."

As a Blue, you can also become corrupt, by overlooking greens and Pinks when their hands are raised and instead calling on a fellow Blue. This may encourage Greens and Pinks to get in more trouble with the Blues as they rebel against the unfair treatment.

You have to closely monitor this activity so that students do not get angry or too rowdy. It does not always end the way you want, and you will have to find different ways to draw it to a close.

Mini-Lecture: Power Shift Has Led to Rule Changes

Present this *mini-lecture* under the simulation rules:

> A significant shift in power has occurred in the last 25 years, to corporations and the very wealthy on the one hand, and away from workers, low-income people, and the middle class, on the other hand. This power shift is in large part due to a decline of unions, the increasing impact of big money in political campaigns, and the weakening of many civic institutions. The power shift has enabled corporations and their directors and wealthy individuals and families to alter rules and social policies which has resulted in the growing concentration of wealth and power. We think of this process as a circle or spiral of mutual influences. More power for the fat cats yields rule and policy changes which yields a concentration of wealth which yields more power and enables more changes, and so on.

There are several charts and many talking points to help students understand the notion of the recent shift in power and the rule changes that have accompanied and strengthened the increasing power imbalance.

This lesson addresses the rule changes regarding union membership. Lesson 15 addresses the rule changes regarding global treaties. Lesson 16 addresses rule changes regarding taxes; Lesson 17 addresses the effects of these rule changes specifically on minorities; and Lesson 18 addresses the rule changes' impact on the political process. Other rule changes are discussed throughout the book.

The more the "Talking Points" are changed into thought provoking questions, the more lively the simulation will become as the greens and pinks become eager to participate.

Option: Provide a reward (such as bonus points for the day's class participation grade) and explain that the group who answers the most questions will receive the reward. This will immediately bother the Greens and the Pinks as they realize the system is set up against them.

a. Read the factors that are "On the Rise" and "In Decline", listed in **Chart 14a, The Power Shift Since the 1970s.**

b. Make sure students understand the terms in the chart. Ask, "What evidence do you see of this over-class creating divisions in America? What are some of these divisions? As economic insecurity climbs up the economic ladder, reaching into formerly comfortable middle class homes, resentment and anger grows. Has middle class America finally become resentful of this economic insecurity? How do you know this? Provide examples."

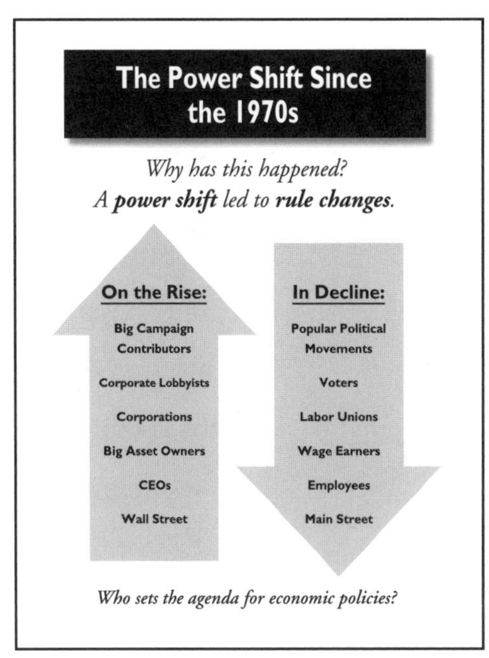

Chart 14a

TALKING POINTS:

This alarming growth in inequality was not the result of sun spots or some other great mystery. It is the outcome of specific policy choices made by human beings.

An "owning" class, predominatly white and male, has succeeded in changing the rules to shift the tax burden off corporations and the wealthy and onto the middle and working classes. Those who hold assets have been rewarded at the expense of wage earners. ("Assets" is defined and explained in Lesson 10.)

For example, a multimillion-dollar lobbying effort to repeal the federal estate tax has been aggressively led by 18 super-wealthy families, worth a total of $185.5 billion. These families and their businesses, which include the families behind Wal-Mart, Gallo wine, Campbell's soup, and Mars Inc., maker of M&Ms, have financed and coordinated a 10-year effort to repeal the estate tax. Repeal would collectively net them a windfall of $71.6 billion. (See the report, Spending Millions to Save Billions; *The Campaign of the Super Wealthy to Kill the Estate Tax* by Public Citizen and United for a Fair Economy <www.faireconomy.org/reports/2006/EstateTaxFinal.pdf> for more details.)

c. Instead of the sentiments of middle class resentment being directed toward the concentration of wealth and unbridled corporate power, people are looking down the economic ladder, scapegoating those less privileged than themselves. Ask students to provide some examples of scapegoating. (Possible answers: blaming job losses on immigrants or women, blaming the budget deficit on welfare recipients, etc.)

d. Display **Chart 14b, Rule Changes Since the 1970s,** and **Chart 14c, The Wheel of Misfortune,** and discuss.

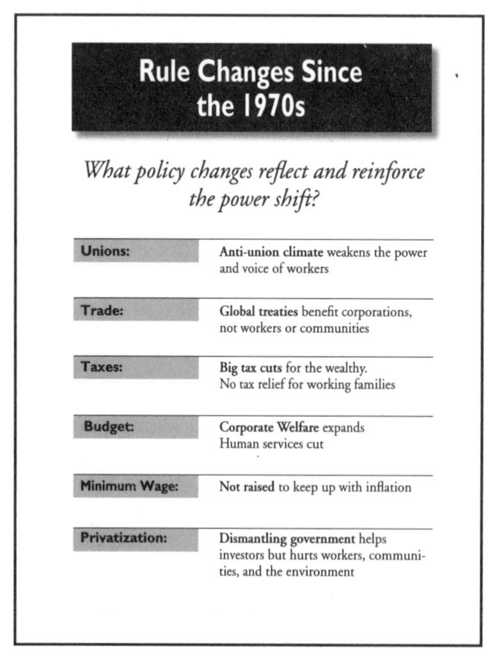

Chart 14b

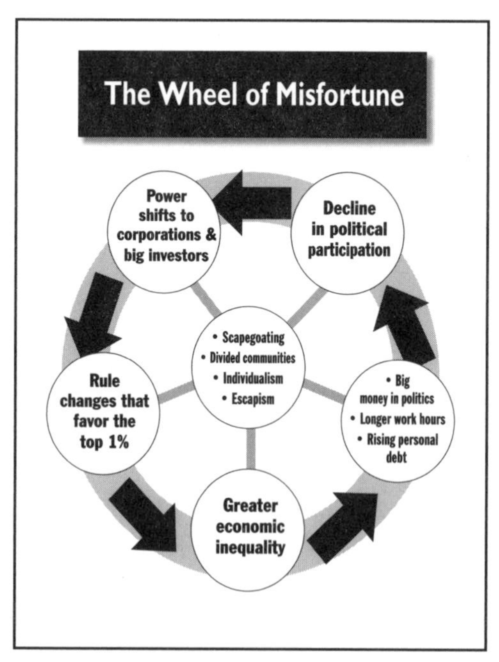

Chart 14c

TALKING POINTS:

At other times in our country's history — between World War II and the 1970s, for example — there was a so-called "social contract" between big business and workers: In exchange for thirty to forty years of loyal, diligent labor, many corporations promised to provide job security and benefits, including health insurance and pensions. In general, as the economy grew after World War II, many workers saw their standard of living rise. The "social contract" also benefited corporations because they got a loyal and productive workforce plus plenty of consumers who could afford to buy their products.

This social contract was enforced by the strength of organized labor, and by relatively high levels of political participation. There was more of a balance of power — both at the bargaining table and in the halls of Congress — between corporations and their (mostly white and male) employees that resulted in increased benefits for many workers and a stronger, more cohesive society.

With the increasing imbalance of power, we have entered what one could call a "cycle of inequality" or a "wheel of misfortune." As working families are squeezed by stagnant incomes and society becomes more economically insecure for them (even as some sectors "prosper"), we find that we have to work harder and longer to stay in place. That leaves us less time to look after our families and our communities — our civic and political life begins to wither.

Corporation executives, super wealthy families, and conservative ideologues often find ways to fill that civic vacuum, capitalizing on working families' frustrations and insecurity to tout economic policies that sound good at first but which will actually widen the growing divide in wealth and income.

They tell us that an "unfettered free market" will solve the problems of job loss, stagnant wages, high college tuition and health care costs, crumbling schools, and disinvestment in urban areas. They denigrate "big" government and public investment, further alienating people from the political and collective action that could bring real economic security and prosperity with a modicum of fairness.

As in the past, our challenge is to find places on this wheel of misfortune to enter the political struggle, stop the motion, and begin reversing the direction. This time, we must work to ensure that the gains achieved are shared across racial and gender lines as well.

e. Display **Chart 14d, Percentage of the Workforce Represented by a Labor Union 1930-2004**, and discuss.

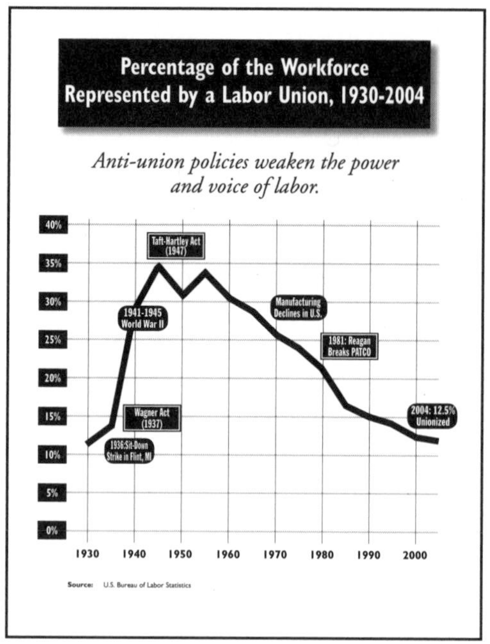

Chart 14d

TALKING POINTS:

What would it be like to work ten hours a day for seven days a week? Who has seen the bumper sticker that reads: "The Labor Movement: The folks who brought you the weekend?"

In 1936, a brand new union, the United Auto Workers, literally sat down on the job at the General Motors plant in Flint Michigan, to press for recognition and for a 30-hour work week, time-and-a-half for overtime, and other benefits. A month into the strike, GM recognized the UAW, and 18 months later the union had its first contract and won a measure of financial security. Contracts with Chrysler and Ford followed.

However, the big corporations began chipping away at the gains made by organized labor. After World War II, legislators acting in the interest of the corporations passed laws, such as the Taft-Hartley Act (1947), which made it difficult for workers to use the tools of the 1930s — such as industry-wide strikes and striking while a contract is in effect.

In 1981, President Reagan fired the striking air traffic controllers, breaking the PATCO union. This sent a strong signal to management that the federal government was less interested in standing up for the rights of striking workers. The number and effectiveness of strikes dropped throughout the 1980s and 1990s. For the first time in decades, employers began to replace workers who were out on strike with "scabs" (people who continue to work or who are hired when workers go on strike).

The decline of organized labor as a countervailing institution to the corporate power elite in America has paralleled the drop in wages and the increases in inequality.

Because labor unions are weaker, they no longer play as significant a role in pushing for wage and salary fairness.

6. At this point you should probably bring the simulation to a close if it has not already brought itself to a close. Ask for a volunteer to explain what the simulation was demonstrating. Verify that students were experiencing class discrimination. The Blues were "upper-level income earners," the Greens were "middle-level income earners," and the Pinks were "lower-level income earners."

7. Ask a member of each group how they felt about what was happening. Conduct a discussion around the outcome of the simulation and tie it to the subject matter discussed in the mini-lecture. Several points you may want to coax from the students or explain yourself if they apply to what occurred during the simulation:

Simulation	Real Life
Students randomly chose a color from the bag and ended up lucky or unlucky.	People are born into families with different amounts of money and therefore fall into different classes and are given different opportunities.
The Greens and Pinks did not have equal treatment in the justice system. The teacher and other Blues were often unfair to them because of who they were and because they were outsiders.	Poor people often cannot afford good legal advice and therefore are disproportionately represented in the country's jails and prisons. People with money are able to "buy" their way out of punishment for their crimes.
Because Greens and Pinks did not have equal treatment in the justice system and were sometimes either targeted for misbehavior or overlooked when they were trying to participate and get ahead, they began to drop out of the system, fall asleep, talk and get in more trouble, etc.	When people with little money see no hope (in achievement or in going to college, etc.) because they see the system as unfair and holding them back, they get discouraged and often give up or stop trying to succeed. Have you seen examples of this in your classes at school?
There were fewer Blues yet they were still able to control the greens and pinks at the beginning of the simulation. Greens and Pinks working together were able to stand up to the Blues and demand a more fair situation.	When people unite, (e.g. labor in unions), they are able to demand more fair wages, salary and working conditions. There is power and strength in numbers!

Activity 14.2

If students feel comfortable discussing the issue of class discrimination, ask them to provide examples of real life situations they have experienced. Another way to approach this issue is to ask if they have experienced age discrimination. Often teens are treated differently (and with less respect) than adults when they enter stores or restaurants. Explain how the same discrimination often occurs to lower-income earners when they enter stores, restaurants, and banks or go on job interviews.

The Power Shift Since the 1970s

Why has this happened?

A ***power shift*** *led to* ***rule changes.***

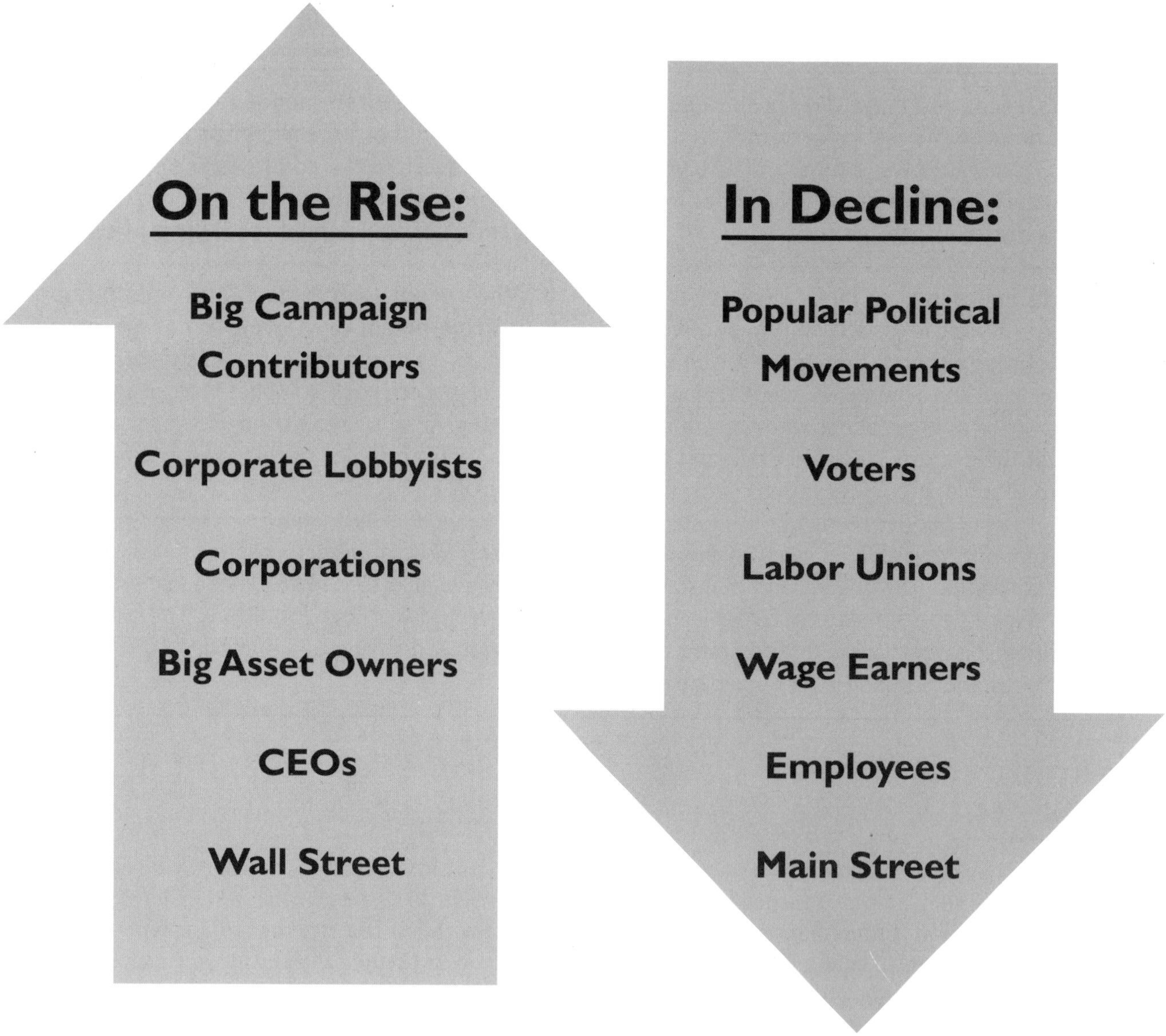

On the Rise:

- Big Campaign Contributors
- Corporate Lobbyists
- Corporations
- Big Asset Owners
- CEOs
- Wall Street

In Decline:

- Popular Political Movements
- Voters
- Labor Unions
- Wage Earners
- Employees
- Main Street

Who sets the agenda for economic policies?

Chart 14a

Rule Changes Since the 1970s

What policy changes reflect and reinforce the power shift?

Unions:	**Anti-union climate** weakens the power and voice of workers
Trade:	**Global treaties** benefit corporations, not workers or communities
Taxes:	**Big tax cuts** for the wealthy. No tax relief for working families
Budget:	**Corporate Welfare** expands Human services cut
Minimum Wage:	**Not raised** to keep up with inflation
Privatization:	**Dismantling government** helps investors but hurts workers, communities, and the environment

Chart 14b

The Wheel of Misfortune

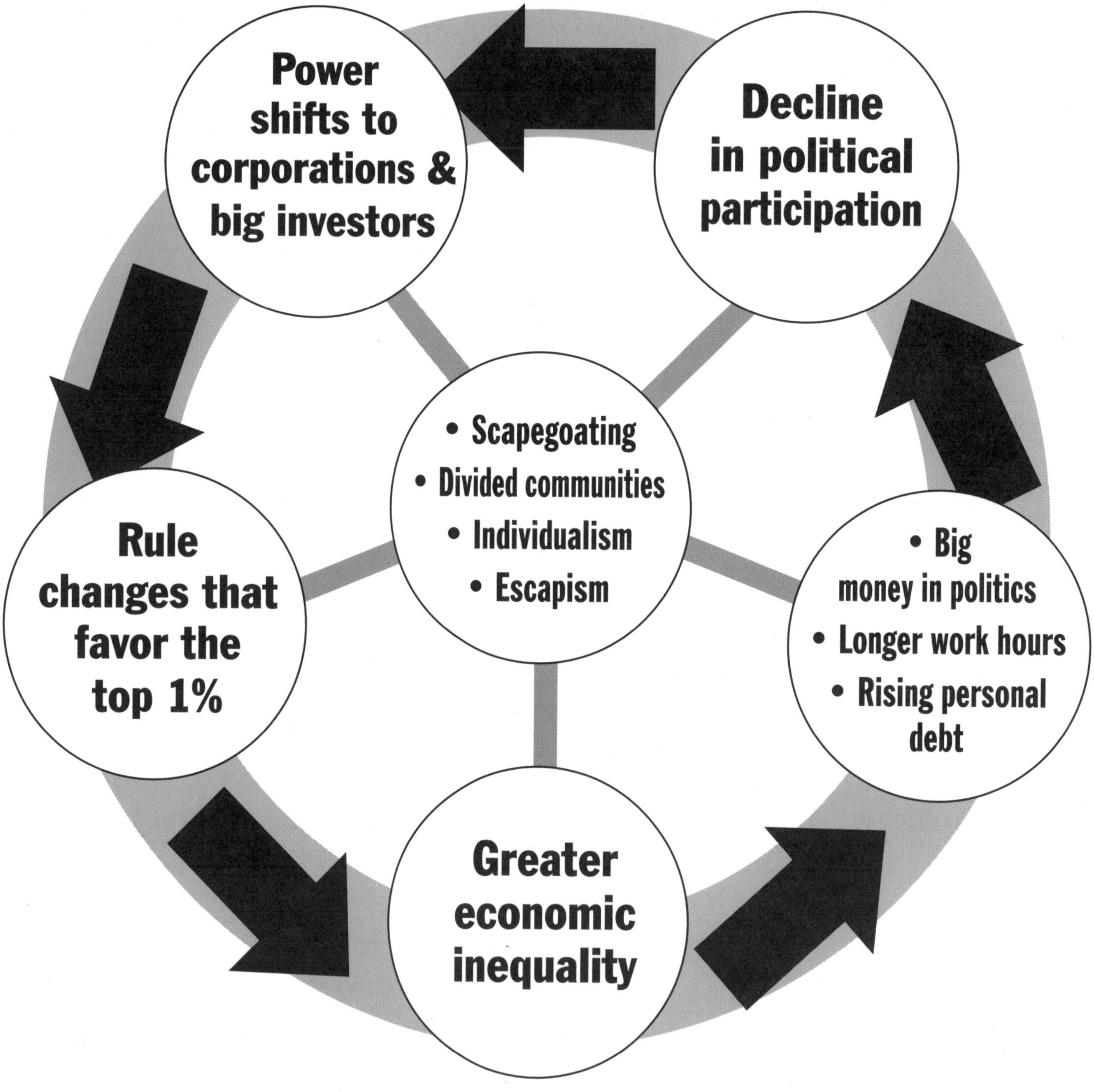

Power shifts to corporations & big investors

Rule changes that favor the top 1%

Greater economic inequality

- Big money in politics
- Longer work hours
- Rising personal debt

Decline in political participation

- Scapegoating
- Divided communities
- Individualism
- Escapism

Chart 14c

Percentage of the Workforce Represented by a Labor Union, 1930-2004

Anti-union policies weaken the power and voice of labor.

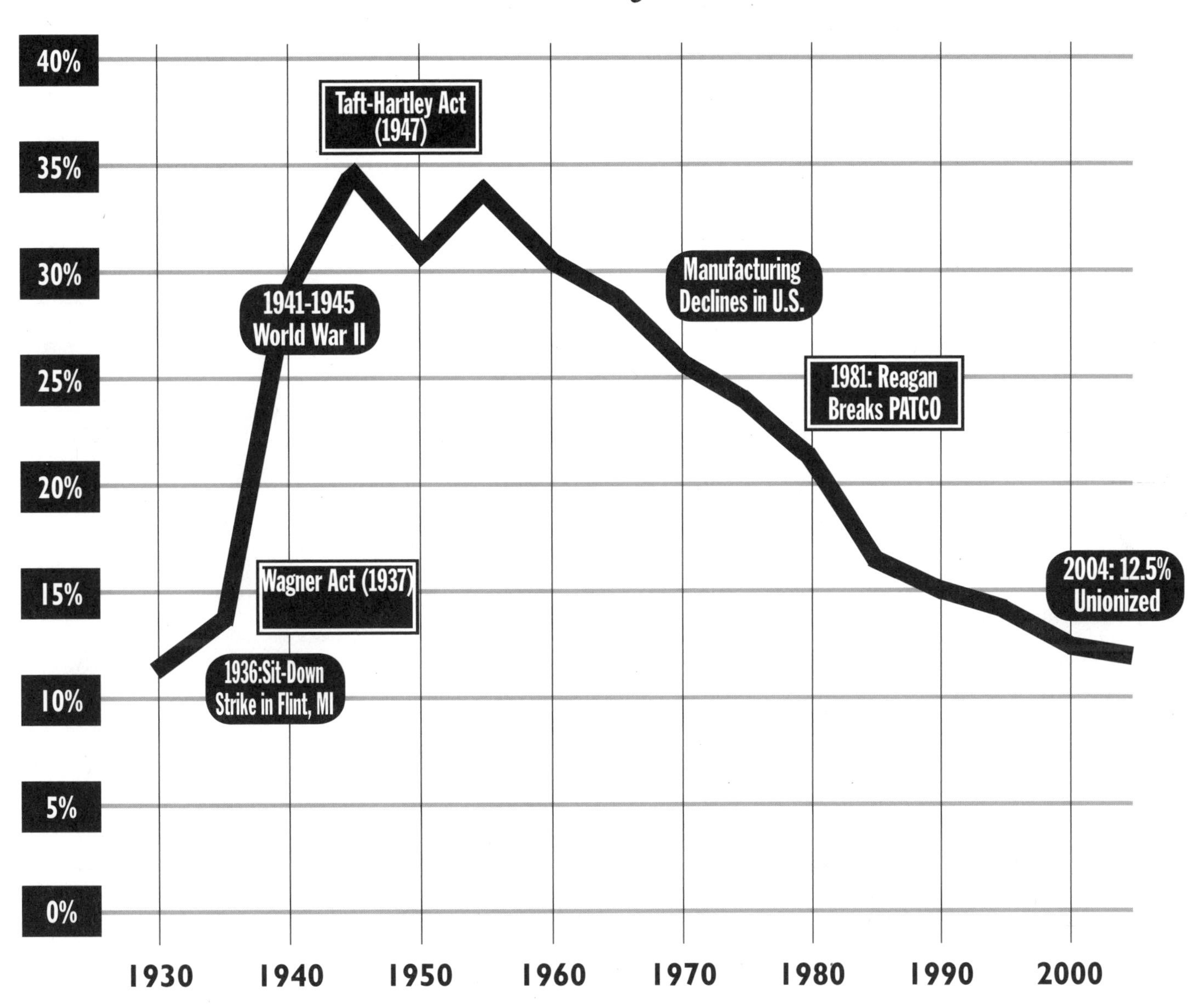

Source: U.S. Bureau of Labor Statistics

Chart 14d

Lesson 15: The Race to the Bottom

Objectives:

- *Examine the implications of regional and global trade agreements on inequality in the U.S.*
- *Review how trade agreements benefit corporations at the expense of workers, communities, the environment.*
- *Explore how global trade agreements pose a threat to our democracy.*

Concepts and Key Terms:

- *global trade*
- *North American Free Trade Agreement (NAFTA)*
- *General Agreement on Trade and Tariffs (GATT)*
- *multinational corporations*
- *race to the bottom*

Instructional Time:

- *55 minutes*

Preparation:

For the Bellringer Activity 15.1:

- *Several candy bars (at least six)*
- *Auction Scoring Guide (see instructions, p. 110)*
- *Copies of the handout "Transnational Capital Auction: A Game of Survival" (one for each student)*
- *Copies of the "Transnational Capital Auction Credit Sheet" (one for each country group)*
- *Copies of the "Bids to Capital" slips, enough so that each group has one per round*
- *Copies of the handout "Transnational Capital Auction Follow-up" (one for each student)*

Conducting the Lesson

Chart 15a, Global Trade Treaties, and the talking points on page 109 may by helpful to use during the class demonstration or to prepare for the global trade issue before teaching it.

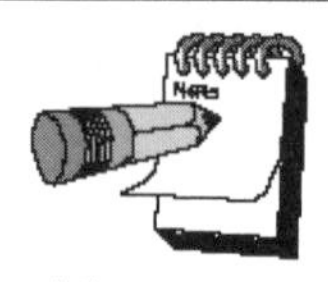

Note to Teacher

Lesson 14 discussed the shift in power and subsequent rule changes that have occurred since the 1970s. This lesson focuses on the rule changes regarding trade, with an emphasis on how so-called "free trade" treaties help corporations at the expense of workers

Global Trade Treaties

Trade treaties like CAFTA and NAFTA reduce "barriers" to trade. The worldwide result:

- **Jobs** shift to low-wage countries
- Weakened **worker rights**
- Lower **wages** and higher **poverty**
- **Environmental** damage
- Cuts in **social safety nets**
- **Economies** collapse in developing nations
- Rise in **emigration**

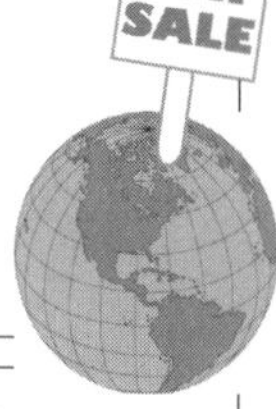

Proposed investment treaties such as the FTAA (Free Trade Area of the Americas):

- Would allow multinational corporations to **overturn local laws** as "barriers to free trade."
- Will threaten laws that protect community lending, health and safety, pay equity, pro-human rights government, public control of water, education, etc.

Chart 15a

TALKING POINTS:

Why is inequality rising in the U.S. and around the world? One big reason is global trade and investment policies that carefully spell out the rights of corporations and investors while ignoring workers, communities, and the environment.

Because there is no democratic accountability, large multi-national corporations dominate the agenda of the International Monetary Fund (IMF), the World Bank, and the WTO. The WTO committee that's developing automobile standards for the planet, for example, had 26 industry representatives and only two consumer representatives trying to influence government regulators.

The IMF, World Bank, and other international financial institutions (IFIs), impose Structural Adjustment Policies (SAPs) on borrowers to ensure debt repayment and economic restructuring that favors foreign investment. The SAPs require poor countries to reduce spending and/or privatize services such as health, education, and development in order to get the funds to repay their loans. In effect, the IFIs demand that poor nations lower the standard of living of their people.

The GATT (General Agreement on Trade and Tariffs), is a set of trade rules established in 1947. Regulating trade in goods, GATT spells out, for example, how a company such as Time Warner could sue Malaysia if the government allows local bootleggers to peddle Michael Jackson CDs. Yet the treaty says virtually nothing about human rights, conditions for workers, the right to organize labor unions, minimum wage standards, factory safety, or protections for the environment.

Treaties like GATT and NAFTA (North American Free Trade Agreement) have created governing bodies that float above the democratic institutions of nation states, while setting the rules for how the global economy will work. The World Trade Organization (WTO), established in 1995, expanded the GATT to include setting and enforcing the rules that govern trade in services and intellectual property, as well as goods. Officials of the WTO, who are elected by no one, meet behind closed doors and decide on rules and policies that allow corporations to have rights above and beyond our city and state laws. Under the WTO, corporations even have the right to sue nations for "loss of future profits" due to regulations that protect workers' rights and the environment.

NAFTA, the agreement that went into effect in 1994 to regulate trade among the U.S., Canada, and Mexico, has not fulfilled its promise of job creation other than low-wage, no-benefit, no-security employment. In addiion to this NAFTA-related shift in employment patterns, greater and greater numbers of people have experienced economic dislocation from their homeland and are forced to search for jobs elsewhere that will bring them some measure of economic security and a better life for their families. For example, U.S. exports of corn into Mexico increased by over 1000% in the first three years of NAFTA, resulting in the collapse of thousands of small Mexican farms and the emigration of tens of thousands of displaced farm workers into the U.S. in search of employment.

The Central America Free Trade Agreement (CAFTA) expanded NAFTA to five Central American nations (Guatemala, El Salvador, Honduras, Costa Rica and Nicaragua) and the Dominican Republic. It was signed in May 2004 and passed through the U.S. House of Representatives by one vote in the middle of the night by the U.S. Congress in July 2005. NAFTA and CAFTA are pieces in the free-trade jigsaw puzzle which caused the "race to the bottom" in labor and environmental standards, promoted privatization and deregulation of key public services, and contributed to the economic and political instability and subsequent mass emigration.

Due to strong resistance by several of the CAFTA countries' parliaments, the Bush administration was forced to delay the planned Jan. 1, 2006 implementation, and has instead sought to negotiate bilateral trade agreements with several nations in Latin America.

Resistance has also taken the form of alternative trade agreements such as ALBA (Alternativa Bolivariana para las Américas). ALBA advocates a socially-oriented trade block rather than one strictly based on the logic of deregulated profit maximization. ALBA appeals to the egalitarian principles of justice and equality, the well-being of the most dispossessed sectors of society, and a reinvigorated sense of solidarity toward the underdeveloped countries of the western hemisphere, so that with the required assistance, they can enter into trade negotiations on more favorable terms than has been the case under the dictates of developed countries.

Bellringer Activity #15.1: The Race to the Bottom

This activity is based on "The Transnational Capital Auction" by Bill Bigelow. It appears in *Rethinking Globalization: Teaching for Justice in an Unjust World,* avaliable from Rethinking Schools, 1001 E. Keefe, Milwaukee, WI 53212; 800-669-4192; rsbusiness@aol.com; www.rethinkingschools.org.

This simulation game was written by Bill Bigelow to help students grasp some aspects of *capital* (cash or goods used to generate income either by investing in a business or income property) as a force in today's world, and to help students see *capital* as a kind of living entity that has certain needs and inclinations. The game is a metaphor for the "auction" that *capital* holds to determine who in the world will make the most attractive bid for its "services." Students engage in this dynamic from the standpoint of "Third World" elites, and simulate a phenomenon that has been called the "race to the bottom," whereby these elites compete against one another to attract capital. The game's "punch line" is an examination of the social and ecological consequences of the auction.

1. Before the activity, create the Auction Scoring Guide on the board or on an overhead transparency. It should look something like this:

		Groups						
		1	2	3	4	5	6	7
Rounds	1							
	2							
	3							
	4							
	5							
	Total							

2. If you have at least 21 students in your class, divide them into seven groups. Ask the groups to form around the classroom, as far away from one another as possible.

3. Distribute copies of "Transnational Capital Auction: A Game of Survival," "Transnational Capital Auction Credit Sheet," and the "Bids to Capital" slips. Read aloud with students "Transnational Capital Auction: A Game of Survival." It should be obvious, but emphasize the distinction between "Friendly to Capital" credits and game points. Answer any questions students might have. Review the "Transnational Capital Auction Credit Sheet." Point out that a group earns more credits the friendlier it is to capital. Show them the candy bars and announce that the three groups with the most game points will win all the candy bars.

4. Begin the first round. Tell students to make their bids on each of the categories and to total up their "Friendly to Capital" credits on the "Bids to Capital" slips. Note that this is really the hardest round because students don't have any way of knowing what the other groups are bidding. The teacher plays "Capital" in the game, and wanders around the classroom as the small groups decide on their bids, urging them to lower the minimum wage, taxation on corporate profits, and the like: "Come on, show that you really want me to invest in your country."

5. After each group has submitted its bid, write them up on the board or overhead. Award the first game points based on the results — again, 100 game points for the third highest number of "Friendly to Capital" credits, 50 for the second highest, and 25 for the first. After this first round has been played and the points are posted, the teacher as "Capital" scoffs at the losers and urges them to get with the program and start making some bids that will attract Capital. (From this point on — for better or worse — the competition to "win" or for candy bars, takes over, and students continue to "race to the bottom" of conditions for their respective countries. Sometimes they even realize what they're doing as they decide their bids. "This is just like *The Price is Right* oppression style," one student was overheard to say.)

6. After each round of bids, continue to post the Friendly to Capital credit scores and award game points for that round. Keep a running total of each country team's game points. As "Capital," the teacher continues to urge students lower and lower: "Team five, do you think I'm going to come to your country if your tax rate is 30%? Come on, next round let's get that way down."

7. For the fifth and final round, ask each student to write down the group's last bid, separate from the "Bid to Capital" slips — not just the number of credits, but the actual minimum wage, the child labor laws, etc. For their homework writing assignment, each student needs to know the specific social and environmental conditions created by the auction.

8. Award the candy bars to the "winners." Distribute the homework assignment: "Transnational Capital Auction Follow-up."

9. The next day, have a discussion about their answers to the homework assignment. Additional questions to raise are:

> What do you think the consequences might be of living in a nation without environmental laws?
>
> What might "Capital" do? What do you imagine might be the social effects of such low wages? (You might want to list these on the board or overhead.)
>
> How do you think families would be able to survive?
>
> How might a family supplement its income? (You can point out that even if a country did have child labor laws, the lower the wages for adults, the greater the pressure on a family to send its children to work. If students don't point it out, the teacher should note the relationship between the "race to the bottom" and increased immigration. Of course, there are other factors leading to immigration, such as the dramatic rise in cash crop agriculture which throws peasants off the land, but it is vital that students see the interconnectedness of global issues.)
>
> Why did you keep driving down conditions in your country?
>
> Why didn't you get together and refuse to bid each other down?

Note to Teacher

Encourage students to ground their answers in their own experiences with the "Transnational Capital Auction." It is very important that, if possible, students be left with the sense that the downward leveling they experienced in the auction is not inexorable. There are things that people can do, are doing. Students need to see "big pictures" in order to understand seemingly disconnected events in countries around the world. But it's vital that they not be defeated by this awareness (see the last Talking Point on page 109).

Who benefits and who doesn't benefit from the "Race to the Bottom?"

How could people in various countries get together to stop attacks on their social and environmental conditions?

What could we do in this country to respond to the "Race to the Bottom"?

10. Ask students to make one list of possible benefits of investment and another of the harmful effects.

Optional Activity:

Have students play the game again, the second time representing labor and environmental activists rather than the country's elite.

Transnational Capital Auction: A Game of Survival

You are leaders of a poor country. Each of your countries was either colonized by European countries or dominated by them economically and militarily. You need to attract foreign investment ("Capital") from transnational corporations for many different reasons. Of course not all your people are poor. Many, including a number of you, are quite wealthy. But your wealth depends largely on making deals with corporations that come to your country. You get various kickbacks, bribes, jobs for members of your families, etc. Some of this is legal and some not. But in order to stay in power you also need to provide jobs for your people, and the owners of capital (companies such as Nike, Disney, Coca-Cola, Levi-Strauss, etc.) are the ones who provide thousands of jobs in their factories. The more jobs you can bring into your country, the more legitimacy you have in the eyes of the people. And your government collects taxes from these companies, which help keep your government working, and also help you pay back loans to the International Monetary Fund (IMF), and other foreign-owned banks. The bottom line is this: you badly need these companies to invest capital in your country.

But there's a problem. You must compete with other poor countries who also need capital. Corporations are not stupid, and so they let you know that if you want their investment, you must compete with other countries by keeping workers' wages low, having few laws to regulate conditions of work (overtime, breaks, health and safety, child labor, etc.), not enforcing laws that are on the books, having weak environmental laws, making sure that workers can't organize unions, having low taxes on corporate profits, etc. Basically, companies hold an *auction* for their investments. The countries who offer the companies the most "freedom" are the ones who get the investment capital.

The Game:

The goal is to win the game by ending up with the most game points after all five auction rounds. Each country team's goal is to win by attracting capital.

The team who bids the third highest number of "Friendly to Capital" credits in a round is awarded 100 game points; the team with the second highest number of Capital credits is awarded 50 game points; and the team with the highest number of Capital credits is awarded 25 game points. The other teams get no points for the round.

The auction is *silent* — you don't know until the end of each round who has bid what.

Again, Capital will go where the people are friendliest to it. However, the friendlier you are to Capital, the angrier it may make your own people. For example, Capital wants workers to work for very little and not worry about environmental laws. But that could start demonstrations or even rebellions, which would not be good for Capital or for you as leaders of your country. That's why the team bidding the highest number of Capital credits does not get the highest number of game points.

Last rule: your team may be the highest (Capital credit) bidder twice and not be penalized. But for each time you are the highest bidder more than twice, you lose ten game points — ten the first time, twenty the second time, etc. This is the "rebellion penalty."

Good luck!

Minimum Wage	"Friendly to Capital" credits
$5.00	0
4.75	10
4.50	15
4.25	20
4.00	25
3.75	30
3.50	33
3.25	37
3.00	40
2.75	43
2.50	46
2.25	49
2.00	52
1.75	55
1.50	58
1.25	61
1.00	64
.85	67
.75	70
.65	73
.55	76
.45	79
.35	82
.30	85
.25	88
.20	91
.15	94
.10	97
.05	100

Tax Rate of Corporate Profits	"Friendly to Capital" credits
75%	0
70%	5
65%	10
60%	15
55%	20
50%	25
45%	30
40%	35
35%	40
30%	50
25%	60
20%	70
25%	75
10%	80
5%	90
no taxes	100

Child Labor Laws	"Friendly to Capital" credits
Child labor below 16 is illegal, enforced	0
Child labor below 16 is illegal, weakly enforced	15
Child labor below 16 is illegal, not enforced	30
Child labor below 14 is illegal, enforced	50
Child labor below 14 is illegal, weakly enforced	70
Child labor below 14 is illegal, not enforced	85
No child labor laws	100

Worker Organizing	"Friendly to Capital" credits
Unions are fully legal, allowed to organize	0
Unions are fully legal but some restrictions on strikes	15
Only gov't-approved unions with some restrictions on strikes	30
Only government-organized unions	50
Unions are banned and have no right to strike	70
Unions banned, no right to strike, military patrol in factories	85
Unions banned, no strikes, military patrol in factories, suspected labor organizers jailed, military breaks up strikes	100

Environmental Laws	"Friendly to Capital" credits
Strict environmental laws, enforced	0
Strict environmental laws, weakly enforced	15
Strict environmental laws, rarely enforced	30
Some environmental laws, enforced	50
Some environmental laws, weakly enforced	70
Some environmental laws, rarely enforced	85
Almost no environmental law	100

Bids to Capital

Country # _____ Round # _____

Minimum wage credits _____

Child labor credits _____

Worker organizing credits _____

Taxation rate credits _____

Environmental laws credits _____

Bids to Capital

Country # _____ Round # _____

Minimum wage credits _____

Child labor credits _____

Worker organizing credits _____

Taxation rate credits _____

Environmental laws credits _____

Bids to Capital

Country # _____ Round # _____

Minimum wage credits _____

Child labor credits _____

Worker organizing credits _____

Taxation rate credits _____

Environmental laws credits _____

Bids to Capital

Country # _____ Round # _____

Minimum wage credits _____

Child labor credits _____

Worker organizing credits _____

Taxation rate credits _____

Environmental laws credits _____

Bids to Capital

Country # _____ Round # _____

Minimum wage credits _____

Child labor credits _____

Worker organizing credits _____

Taxation rate credits _____

Environmental laws credits _____

Bids to Capital

Country # _____ Round # _____

Minimum wage credits _____

Child labor credits _____

Worker organizing credits _____

Taxation rate credits _____

Environmental laws credits _____

Transnational Capital Auction Follow-up

Complete these on a separate sheet of paper. Be as thoughtful as you can be.

1. Look over your auction bids for the final (fifth) round of the Transnational Capital Auction — on minimum wage, child labor, worker organizing, taxation rates, and environmental laws. If Capital were to accept your bid and come to your country, what would be the real human and environmental consequences there? (Answer in detail.)

2. Based on your experience with the Capital Auction, agree and/or disagree with the following statement, and back up your answer with evidence: Poor countries need investment, so it's a good thing when transnational companies invest capital there.

3. The Global process that we simulated in class is sometimes called "downward leveling" or the "race to the bottom." What, if anything, could people in poor countries do to stop this race to the bottom?

4. True story: An international investment director works for a company that formerly manufactured all its products in the U.S., paying wages (with benefits) that averaged around $16/hour. Now, every month, he travels to places like Indonesia, El Salvador, and Nicaragua looking for sites to produce his company's products. He says that he would prefer to keep all their production in the U.S. Based on this situation and what you know, why do you think this person's company feels forced to send production to countries that have a lot of "Friendly to Capital" points?

5. What impact do you think the "race to the bottom" has on workers in this country? In what ways might it affect your lives? In answering this question, reflect on the three quotes below.

> "It is not that foreigners are stealing our jobs, it is that we are all facing one another's competition."
>
> — William Baumol, Princeton University economist

> "Downward leveling is like a cancer that is destroying its host organism – the earth and its people."
>
> — Jeremy Brecher and Tim Costello, *Global Village or Global Pillage*

> "Globalization has depressed the wage growth of low-wage workers [in the United States]. It's been a reason for the increasing wage gap between high-wage and low-wage workers."
>
> — Laura Tyson, former chair of the U.S. Council of Economic Affairs

Activity #15.2: How Trade Agreements Threaten Democracy

1. Have students count off into groups of four or five. Ask each group to come up with ways that global trade agreements are a threat to national sovereignty and democracy. Encourage them to be creative and to come up with at least one complete hypothetical situation. Have one student in each group serve as scribe and record the group's ideas. You may want to provide them with real examples to get them thinking.

Examples

A democratically elected government, such as the mayor and other elected officials in a city, may choose to create a living wage ordinance or law, stating that any business receiving city subsidies or doing contractual work for the city must pay workers a living wage, or must hire local workers.

In the late 1980s, Denmark's democratic government chose to deny sales of any non-recyclable bottles in the country. In the mid-1990s, a foreign bottling company challenged this decision and took it before the World Trade Organization. The WTO threatened sanctions against Denmark if they did not open their markets to non-recycling bottling companies. Denmark conceded, even though it went against the decision of their democratically-elected government.

2. Calling each group to the front of the class one group at a time, ask them to explain some of the ideas their group generated.

Additional Resources

Books

Alternatives to Economic Globalization: A Better World is Possible by John Cavanaugh and Jerry Mander (Berrett-Koehler Publishers, 2004).

Confessions of an Economic Hit Man by John Perkins (Plume Publishers, 2005).

Dispatches from Latin America: Experiments Against Neoliberalism by Vijay Prashad (South End Press, 2006).

Field Guide to the Global Economy (Revised Edition) by Sarah Anderson and John Cavanaugh with Thea Lee (The New Press, 2005).

Globalization: Opposing Viewpoints by Louise I. Gerdes (Greenhaven Press, 2005).

Making Globalization Work by Joseph Stiglitz. (Penguin Press, 2006).

People Before Profit: The New Globalization in an Age of Terror, Big Money, and Economic Crisis by Chales Derber (Picador, 2003).

Real World Globalization, 8th Edition by Dollars & Sense (2004).

Whose Trade Organization? - A Comprehensive Guide to the WTO by Lori Wallach and Patrick Woodall with Public Citizen (The New Press, 2004).

World on Fire: How Exporting Free Market Democracy Breeds Ethnic Hatred and Global Instability by Amy Chua (Anchor Press, 2004).

Videotapes

Banking on Life and Debt, 30 minutes. The World Bank, the IMF, structural adjustment, and three case studies (Brazil, Phillipines, Ghana). Narrated by Martin Sheen. Produced by Maryknoll World Productions, PO Box 308, Maryknoll, NY, 10545-0308, 800-227-8523.

Beyond McWorld: Challenging Corporate Rule, 35 minutes. Shows college students talking about and organizing around the issues of free trade, corporatism and globalization. Phone: 416-516-2472, email: just@interlog.com. Accompanying workbook *Challenging Corporate Rule: A Workbook for Activists,* by Tony Clarke and Sarah Dopp.

Deadly Embrace, 30 minutes. The World Bank, structural adjustment, and Nicaragua. $25 from Elizabeth Canner, 617-666-5122 or email lizcanner@hotmail.com.

Global Village or Global Pillage, 28 minutes. How people around the world are fighting the "race to the bottom." Narrated by Ed Asner. Available from www.nationalfilmnetwork.com.

The Hidden Face of Globalization, 34 minutes. Sweatshops in Bangladesh and their connection to Wal-Mart and Disney. Available from Crowing Rooster Arts and the National Labor Committee.

Now with Bill Moyers (60 minutes) from his television series. Available from www.shoppbs.org.

- *A Question of Fairness* (11/21/03) - NAFTA, outsourcing, and off-shoring.
- *Rich World, Poor Women: The True Face of the Global Economy* (9/5/03) - The impact on poor women in the developing world by the policies of the World Bank, the IMF, and the WTO.
- *Trading Democracy* (2/1/02) - NAFTA, gasoline additives, and contaminated drinking water.

Uprooted: Refugees of the Global Economy, 28 minutes. Three stories (of the Phillipines, Bolivia, Haiti) that illustrate the relationship between neoliberal trade policies and immigration. Produced by the National Network for Immigrant and Refugee Rights (NNIRR) www.nnirr.org.

Global Trade Treaties

Trade treaties like CAFTA and NAFTA reduce "barriers" to trade. The worldwide result:

- **Jobs** shift to low-wage countries
- Weakened **worker rights**
- Lower **wages** and higher **poverty**
- **Environmental** damage
- Cuts in social **safety nets**
- **Economies** collapse in developing nations
- Rise in **emigration**

Proposed investment treaties such as the FTAA (Free Trade Area of the Americas):

- Would allow multinational corporations to **overturn local laws** as "barriers to free trade."
- Will threaten laws that protect community lending, health and safety, pay equity, pro-human rights government, public control of water, education, etc.

Chart 15a

Lesson 16: America: Who Really Pays the Taxes?

Objectives:

- *Examine the connection between public services and taxes.*
- *Practice putting together a family budget.*
- *Define progressive, regressive, flat, sales, and income taxation strategies and explore the impact of each on middle- and low-income families.*
- *Define trickle-down economics.*
- *Compare U.S. income tax rates from 1950 to the present and identify who carries the tax burden.*
- *Define gross and net income.*

Concepts and Key Terms:

- *taxes*
- *progressive tax*
- *regressive tax*
- *flat tax*
- *sales tax*
- *personal budgeting*
- *trickle-down economics*
- *corporate welfare*
- *gross income*
- *net income*
- *revenue*

Instructional Time:

- *55 minutes*

Preparation:

For the Bellringer Activity 16.1:

- *Call a few apartment buildings to determine the cost of a nice one-bedroom apartment in your local area.*
- *Review the Monthly Income, Taxes, and Expenses Sheet and fill in the expense items to fit your community (ex. state tax, rail commuter fee, etc.).*
- *Monthly Income, Taxes, and Expenses overhead transparency sheet or blank transparency with expenses written in, and an erasable marker*

For Activity 16.2:

- *Chart: 2006 Federal Income Tax Brackets. Keep this covered until you have completed the budgeting activity.*
- *Create three empty income tax graphs on the board (see activity description)*
- *Charts 16a, 2006 Federal Income Tax Brackets, 16b, Federal Tax Rates, 16c, Effect of 1977-2003 Tax Law Changes on Yearly Tax Bill, and 16d, Progressive and Regressive Taxes.*

For Activity 16.3:

- *thick pad of sticky notes*
- *magic markers (1 for every 2 students)*
- *Charts: 16e, Who is Really on Welfare and 16f, Examples of Corporate Welfare.*

Conducting the Lesson

Bellringer Activity 16.1: Why Should I Care About Taxes

1. Ask for a show of hands by students who have already paid taxes at some point. Tell students that to really care about the subject of taxes, you usually have to first start paying taxes. Since many students may not pay income taxes yet, or may only pay a small amount of taxes, explain that we are going to take a look into the future when they take their first job and have to begin paying a significant amount of taxes.

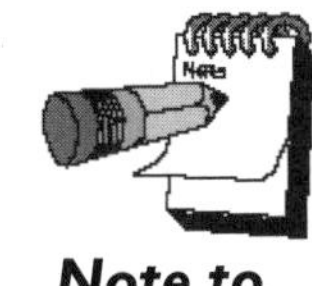

Note to Teacher

Lesson 14 discussed the power shift and subsequent rule changes that have occurred since the 1970s. This lesson focuses on the rule changes regarding taxes.

2. Conduct the following budgeting activity, preferably on an overhead, so you can reveal the expenses and costs of living one by one. You can use the blank form on the next page. As you reveal each expense, ask students to guess the approximate cost.

a. Let's say each of you just graduated from college with a basic liberal arts degree or business degree (no advanced degree and not necessarily a high-tech computer degree). What do you think the average college graduate will make in the year 2010? (Figures may run a bit high; coax students down to $40,000 – $45,000. In 2005, according to *Business Week*, the median real earnings of wage-earners with a BA between the ages of 25 and 34 was about $40,000.) Record this number at the top of your chart.

b. Show students the federal (and, if applicable, the state) taxes taken out of their monthly paychecks. Then calculate their monthly amount to live on after taxes. Begin going through expenses one by one. Students are usually amazed at what is left over after expenses are paid. They will immediately begin telling you how they will get a roommate and use other cost cutting measures. Draw their attention to the lack of money for savings, buying new furniture, making car repairs, or taking a vacation.

c. An example of the completed chart is shown on the next page. A blank chart for you to fill in with the class can be found on the page after that.

TALKING POINTS:

According to a study commissioned by the American Institute of Certified Public Accountants, the finances of young people living in the U.S. are worse off now than for people their age 20 years ago. People aged 25 to 34 years old had a median net worth of $3,746 in 2004, down from $6,788 in 1985. Moreover, their average debt is $4,733, up from $3,118 in 1985.

The percentage of this age group maintaining an interest-bearing savings account fell from 61% in 1985 to 47% in 2004.

Sample Monthly Income, Taxes, and Expenses Sheet

Income and Taxes [1]

Annual Salary for a recent college graduate (known as Adjusted Gross Income)	$40,000
Subtract: Standard Deduction	– $5,150
Result: Taxable Income	$34,850
Calculate Federal Income Tax: (on taxable income only)	
Take 10% on each dollar up to $7,550	$755
Add 15% on each dollar between $7,550 and $30,650	$3,465
Add 25% on each dollar between $30,650 and $74,200	$1,050
Result: Total Federal Income Tax	$5,270
Add: Payroll Tax[2] (7.65% on all wage income)	$2,666
Add: State Income Tax (2.3%[3] of Taxable Income)	802
TOTAL State, and Federal Taxes	$7,738
After Tax Income (subtract Total State and Federal Taxes from Annual Salary)	$32,272
Monthly After Tax Income (divide After Tax Income by 12)	$2,690

Monthly Expenses

Monthly Income after Taxes	$2,690
1 bedroom apartment	– 850
Utilities (phone, electricity, internet provider, water)	– 175
Small Used Car, financed for 4 years (total: $11,000)	– 230
Car Insurance, for driver under 26 years old	– 150
Gas for commute to work	– 200
Food ($20 a day)	– 600
Clothes	– 175
Remaining Total	$310

1. Calculations are based on a single person living alone.

2. Payroll tax includes 6.2% for social security and 1.45% for Medicare.

3. This figure represents the average State Income Tax. From *Who Pays?: A Distributional Analysis of the Tax Systems of All 50 States, 2nd Edition* (The Institute on Taxation and Economic Policy, 2003).

Monthly Income, Taxes, and Expenses Sheet

Income and Taxes

Annual Salary for a recent college graduate (known as Adjusted Gross Income) .... ______________

Subtract: Standard Deduction .... ______________

Result: Taxable Income .... ______________

Calculate Federal Income Tax: (on taxable income only)

Take 10% on each dollar up to $7,550 .... ______________

Add 15% on each dollar between $7,550 and $30,650 .... ______________

Add 25% on each dollar between $30,650 and $74,200 .... ______________

Result: Total Federal Income Tax .... ______________

Add: Payroll Tax (7.65% on all wage income) .... ______________

Add: State Income Tax (2.3% of Taxable Income) .... ______________

TOTAL State, and Federal Taxes .... ______________

After Tax Income (subtract Total State and Federal Taxes from Annual Salary) .... ______________

Monthly After Tax Income (divide After Tax Income by 12) .... ______________

Monthly Expenses

Monthly Income after Taxes .... ______________

1 bedroom apartment .... ______________

Utilities (phone, electricity, internet provider, water) .... ______________

Car payment .... ______________

Car Insurance, for driver under 26 years old .... ______________

Gas for commute to work .... ______________

Food ($20 a day) .... ______________

Clothes .... ______________

Other .... ______________

Other .... ______________

Remaining Monthly Total .... ______________

Activity 16.2: Progressive, Regressive, Flat, and Sales Taxes

1. Begin this activity by showing students **Chart16a, 2006 Federal Income Tax Brackets.**

2. Ask the students if they think it is fair that a CEO making $100 million a year pays the same tax rate as a family making $283,150. (They will more than likely say yes, explaining it is an equal percentage. This point will be revisited below under sales tax.)

3. Create three of the following graph frames on the board. Ask for a volunteer to come to the front of the class and draw bars on one graph frame to show the current tax brackets for a single individual, using the data in the Taxable Income Chart.

2006 Federal Income Tax Brackets

	Married	Single	Rate
On each dollar between	$0 - $15,100	$0 - $7,550	10%
On each dollar between	$15,100 - $61,300	$25,750 - $30,650	15%
On each dollar between	$61,300 - $123,700	$30,650 - $74,200	25%
On each dollar between	$123,700 - $188,450	$74,200 - $154,800	28%
On each dollar between	$188,450 - $336,550	$154,800 - $336,550	33%
On each dollar above	$336,550	$336,550	35%

For example, a married taxpayer with $300,000 in taxable income would pay:

On each dollar between	$0 - $15,100	10%	$1,510
On each dollar between	$15,100 - $61,300	15%	6,930
On each dollar between	$61,300 - $123,700	25%	$15,600
On each dollar between	$123,700 - $188,450	28%	18,130
On each dollar between	$188,450 - $336,550	33%	36,812
TOTAL TAX		26.3%*	$78,982

* This is the *Effective Tax Rate* – the total tax obligation divided by the total taxable income.

Chart 16a

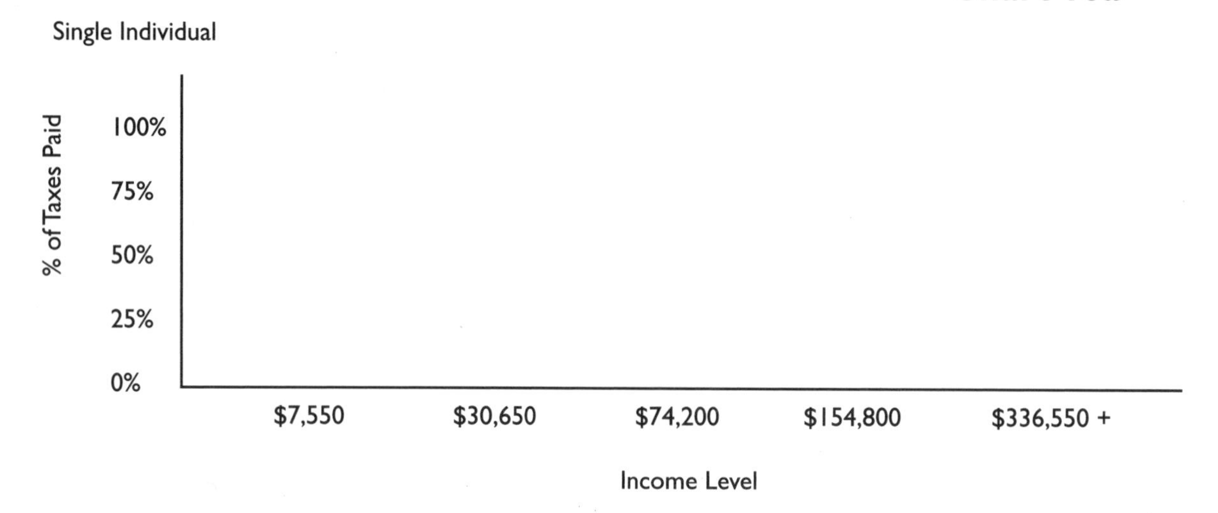

4. The bars should rise in progression from left to right, from 10% to 35%. Explain that this is referred to as a "progressive tax" – the more you earn, the higher your tax rate.

5. Ask for a volunteer to use the second graph frame to draw a bar graph of what a "flat tax" would look like.

6. The bars should all be the same height. The flat tax rate is not important, although recent proposals have called for a 17% flat tax rate. Ask students how fair they think a flat tax is to all people.

7. Ask for a volunteer to draw a line graphing a "regressive tax" on the third graph frame. The bars should fall in progression from left to right. The actual tax rates are not important.

TALKING POINTS:

A flat tax system benefits upper income earners much more than it benefits lower- to middle-income earners. For example, if a family of four has a taxable income of $40,000 and pays 17%[12] in taxes, they are left with $33,200 to live on. If an individual (such as Yahoo CEO Terry Semel) makes $230 million (his actual 2004 compensation) and pays 17% in taxes, he and his family are left with $191 million to live on.

In addition, a flat tax of 17% will not bring in enough revenue to cover current government spending. Therefore, social programs would likely be cut forcing more people into poverty and threatening the nation's infrastructure (transportation, water, energy, etc.).

8. Explain that in the past the tax rates were much more progressive than they are today. Show students **Chart 16b, Federal Tax Rates.**

9. Ask students to look at the chart and interpret what happened for the top 1% of households from 1960 to 1990 (their tax rate decreased dramatically). Ask students what was occurring for the Median household for the same period (their tax rate increased). Ask students what they think the rationale was for the tax cuts in the early 1980s? (In 1981 and 1982 it was part of "supply side" or "trickle-down" economic theory that claimed tax cuts would encourage economic growth and therefore tax revenue would rise and cover the losses from tax cuts. Tax cuts would supposedly stimulate investment, creating an income and wealth explosion.) Ask students what they think the impact was of this "trickle-down" economic policy. Was this a good thing? Why? Why not? (Most economists agree that instead of wealth trickling down as a result of these policies, it gushed up to the top.)

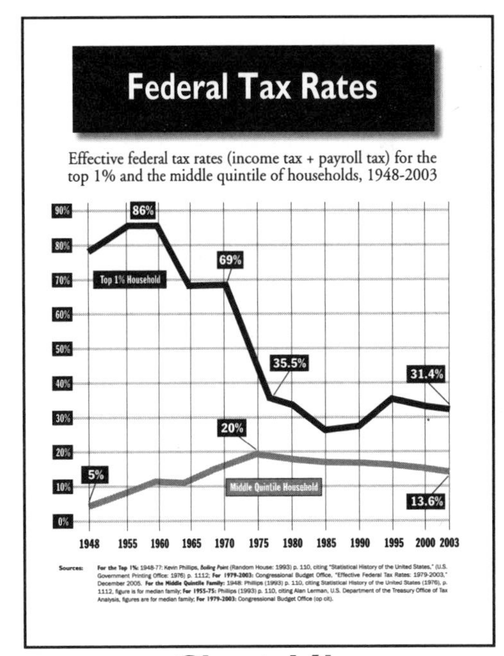

Chart 16b

TALKING POINTS:

Real estate speculation during the 1980s was fueled by provisions in the tax code that encouraged the rapid turnover (or "flipping") of investment properties. As a result, a large number of people now suffer from high rents, unattainable homeownership, or hefty mortgages that require two incomes to support. Homelessness, as well as housing insecurity in general, has also soared.

U.S.-based multinational corporations, using provisions of the tax code that they wrote and lobbied for, have taken their companies (and jobs) overseas thereby decreasing or even avoiding paying taxes.

In the 1950s, the effective top tax rate (taxable income divided by the total amount of taxes) topped 80%, although that rate was charged only on income above $400,000. ($400,000 in 1960 would be worth worth more than $2.7 million today.) This high rate affected only the top 1% of earners in the U.S. The effective rate on the median family during the 1950s was between five and ten percent.

During the 1950s, government tax and spending policies worked to build a strong middle class in this country and strengthen the opportunity for many Americans to have access to affordable education (the G.I. Bill of Rights, student loan and grant programs), homeownership (FHA and VA mortgages), and decent jobs (massive public works projects).

In the first six years of the Bush Administration half a dozen major tax cuts, coupled with higher spending on the military, ballooned the national debt (an increase of $3 billion through Fiscal Year 2007). Moreover, according to Citizens for Tax Justice, the wealthiest 1% have received an average tax break of $84,482 per family member.

10. Ask students to take a look at the impact of recent tax cuts. Display **Chart 16c, Average Annual Gain as a Result of Tax Cuts: 2001-2006.**

TALKING POINT:

From 2001 to 2006, the typical middle-income family in the U.S. received a tax cut totaling $1,855 per family member. But the family's share of the added national debt burden is $8,936 per person.

This means that the net impact of the fiscal policies of the Bush Administration is an added burden of $7,081 per person. Eventually this debt will have to be repaid.

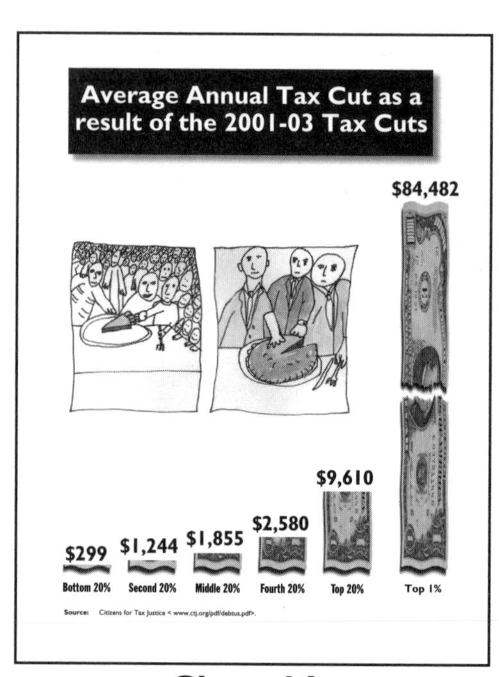

Chart 16c

12. Last, another recent federal tax reform proposal, S.25: The Fair Tax Act of 2005, sponsored by Senator Saxby Chambliss (R-GA), calls for abolishing income taxes and instituting a 23% sales tax. Display **Chart 16d, Progressive and Regressive Taxes,** and use the talking points below to lead a discussion.

TALKING POINTS:

A progressive tax is one where the tax rate rises as income rises. The reason for this is that high-income people have a greater ability to pay taxes than do lower-income people. The typical family depends on its earnings to pay for life's necessities like food, clothing, and shelter. Wealthier people have much more discretionary income left over after they pay for these basics and can therefore afford to pay taxes at a higher rate on income above a certain amount.

Over the last 20 years, the mix of progressive and regressive taxes in the average family's tax bill has shifted toward more regressive taxes.

Both *progressive* and *regressive* are relative terms. With a declining top tax rate, the federal income tax has become less progressive over time.

Progressive and Regressive Taxes

A Progressive Tax: The Income Tax

A progressive tax charges a higher effective tax rate as income rises.

	Factory Worker	CEO
Yearly Taxable Income	$30,000	$12,400,000
Income tax owed	$4,123	$4,179,861
Effective Sales Tax Rate (tax as a percentage of income)	13.7%	33.7%

The CEO pays a ***higher*** *percentage of his income than does the factory worker.*

A Regressive Tax: The Sales Tax

A regressive tax charges a lower effective tax rate as income rises.

	Factory Worker	CEO
Yearly Income	$30,000	$12,400,000
Buys a car for...	$20,000	$20,000
5% Sales Tax Owed	$1,000	1,000
Effective Sales Tax Rate (tax as a percentage of income)	3.3%	.000081%

The CEO pays a ***much lower*** *percentage of his income than does the factory worker.*

Chart 16d

Activity 14.3: Who is Really on Welfare?

1. Ask students to get in pairs. Provide each pair with one sticky note and one magic marker and ask students to write their definition or idea of "welfare" on the post-it and place it on the board at the front of the classroom when they are done. Explain that this can also be done as a word association game — what do they typically think of when they hear the word "welfare." (Ideas will vary greatly. You will likely find certain themes present in homogenous socio-economic groups. The objective of the activity is to discuss students' stereotypes of welfare recipients and then challenge the stereotypes with factual data.)

2. Discuss students' ideas, grouping them into categories, such as unwed mothers, unemployed single men, the elderly, etc.

3. Ask students to compare corporate subsidies to welfare assistance to families, known as Transitional Assistance to Needy Families. Show **Chart 16e: Who is Really on Welfare?**

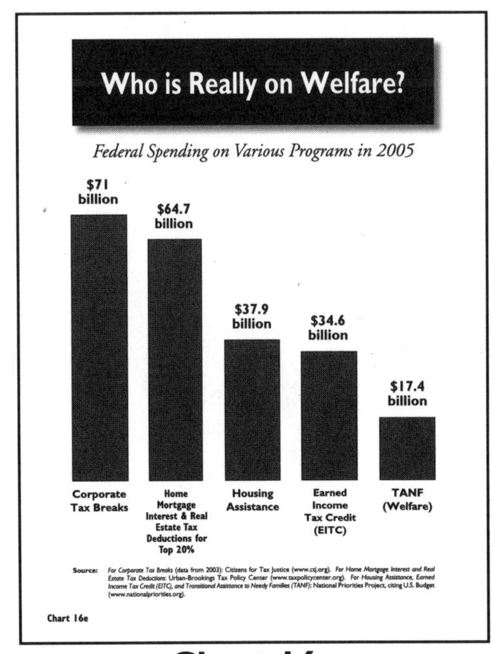

Chart 16e

4. Provide students with some examples of corporate welfare. Direct their attention to **Chart 16f, Examples of Corporate Welfare.** Explain that corporate subsidies exist in several forms:

a. Direct payments to corporations
b. Special tax loopholes and tax breaks
c. Publicly subsidized research and development with private windfalls
d. Sale of services, goods or resources at below-market rates
e. Purchase of goods and services at above-market value

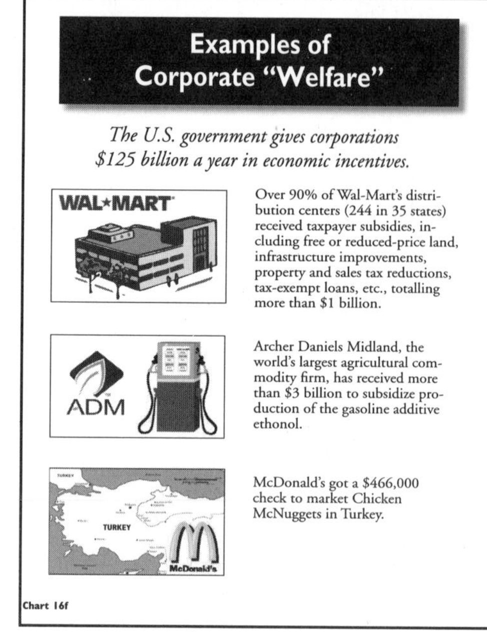

Chart 16f

6. Ask students why they likely hear more about the "lazy" welfare recipient than the corporate welfare recipient? (P*ossible answers:* Most of the media is corporately owned and benefits from corporate welfare. It would be counterproductive to their own profits to report on this subject. Discussing taxes and/or corporate welfare does not provide for flashy headline news stories. The tax code has become so obscure with its loopholes and special breaks, that details pertaining to tax cuts are often watered down by the media. It's as though they believe the details are too much for the average person to comprehend. These subjects are perceived as difficult to fit into "sound bites" that the news media today is so accustomed to using.)

Suggested Homework:

All this talk about taxes may make students resentful that they ever have to pay them. Assign a brainstorming activity for homework. Ask students to keep track — for the next 24 hours — of all the things they use that were paid for with tax dollars. For example: taxes pay for public school teachers' salaries. Was there a fire drill at school today? Taxes pay for firefighters' salaries. Taxes pay for the roads they use and the school buses students ride on the way home from school. Have them make a list including as many items as possible.

Additional Resources:

Take the Rich Off Welfare by Mark Zepezauer and Arthur Naiman (revised and expanded: 2004). Available from South End Press (www.southendpress.org/2004/items/TROW).

The Great American Jobs Scam – Corporate Tax Dodging and the Myth of Job Creation by Greg LeRoy (2005). Available from Brerret-Koehler Press (www.bkconnection.com/ProdDetails.asp?ID=1576753158).

2006 Federal Income Tax Brackets

	Married	Single	Rate
On each dollar between	$0 - $15,100	$0 - $7,550	10%
On each dollar between	$15,100 - $61,300	$25,750 - $30,650	15%
On each dollar between	$61,300 - $123,700	$30,650 - $74,200	25%
On each dollar between	$123,700 - $188,450	$74,200 - $154,800	28%
On each dollar between	$188,450 - $336,550	$154,800 - $336,550	33%
On each dollar above	$336,550	$336,550	35%

For example, a married taxpayer with $300,000 in taxable income would pay:

On each dollar between	$0 - $15,100	10%	$1,510
On each dollar between	$15,100 - $61,300	15%	6,930
On each dollar between	$61,300 - $123,700	25%	$15,600
On each dollar between	$123,700 - $188,450	28%	18,130
On each dollar between	$188,450 - $336,550	33%	36,812
TOTAL TAX		26.3%*	$78,982

*This is the *Effective Tax Rate* – the total tax obligation divided by the total taxable income.

Chart 16a

Federal Tax Rates

Effective federal tax rates (income tax + payroll tax) for the top 1% and the middle quintile of households, 1948-2003

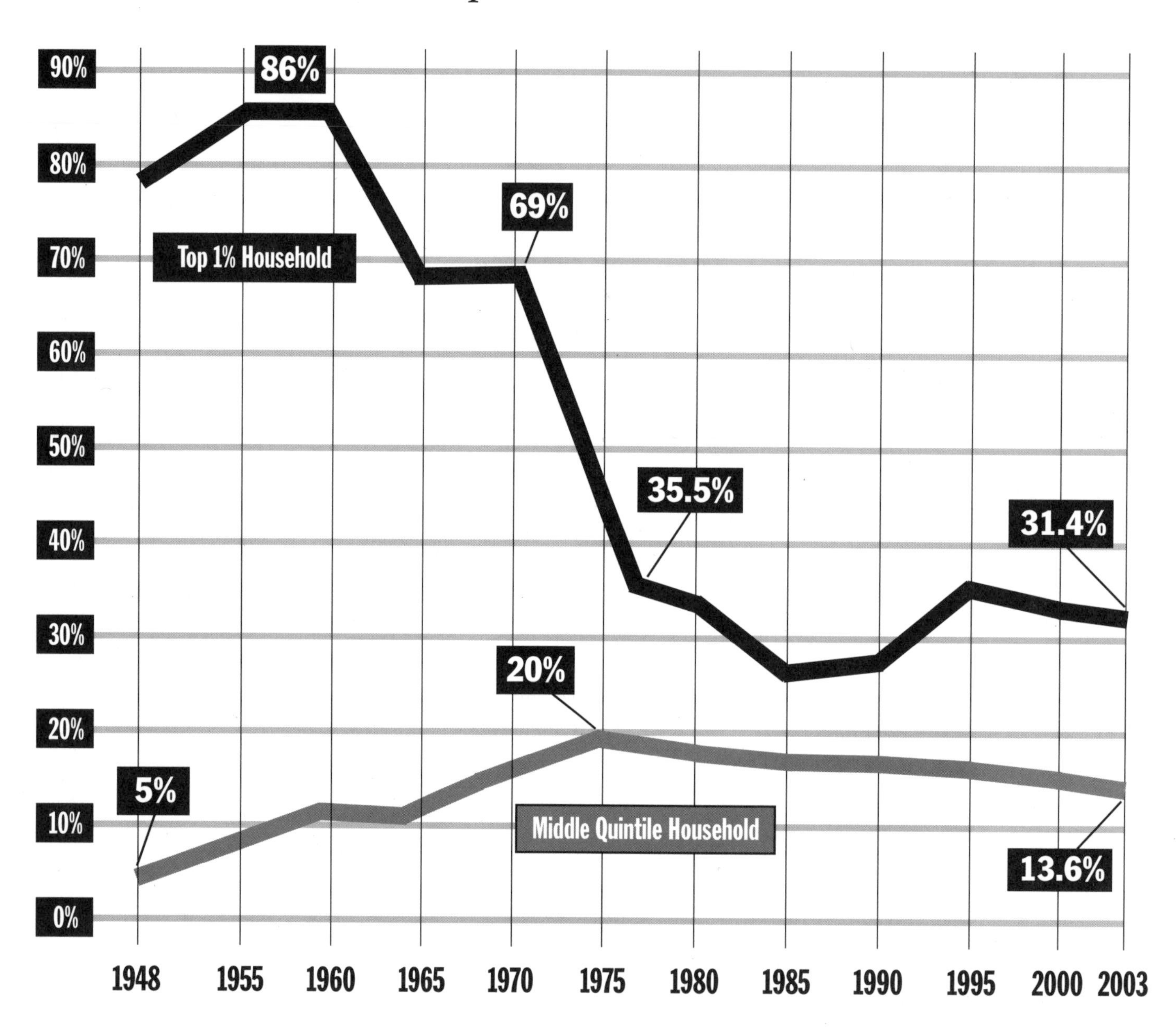

Sources: **For the Top 1%:** 1948-77: Kevin Phillips, *Boiling Point* (Random House: 1993) p. 110, citing "Statistical History of the United States," (U.S. Government Printing Office: 1976) p. 1112; **For 1979-2003:** Congressional Budget Office, "Effective Federal Tax Rates: 1979-2003," December 2005. **For the Middle Quintile Family:** 1948: Phillips (1993) p. 110, citing Statistical History of the United States (1976), p. 1112, figure is for median family; **For 1955-75:** Phillips (1993) p. 110, citing Alan Lerman, U.S. Department of the Treasury Office of Tax Analysis, figures are for median family; **For 1979-2003:** Congressional Budget Office (op cit).

Chart 16b

Average Annual Gain as a Result of Tax Cuts: 2001-2006

$84,482

$9,610

$2,580

$1,855

$1,244

$299

Bottom 20% | Second 20% | Middle 20% | Fourth 20% | Top 20% | Top 1%

Source: Citizens for Tax Justice <www.ctj.org/pdf/debtus.pdf>.

Chart 16c

Progressive and Regressive Taxes

A Progressive Tax: The Federal Income Tax

A progressive tax charges a higher effective tax rate as income rises.

	Factory Worker	CEO
Yearly Taxable Income	$30,000	$12,400,000
Income tax owed	$4,123	$4,179,861
Effective Sales Tax Rate (tax as a percentage of income)	13.7%	33.7%

*The CEO pays a **higher** percentage of his income than does the factory worker.*

A Regressive Tax: The Sales Tax

A regressive tax charges a lower effective tax rate as income rises.

	Factory Worker	CEO
Yearly Income	$30,000	$12,400,000
Buys a car for...	$20,000	$20,000
5% Sales Tax Owed	$1,000	1,000
Effective Sales Tax Rate (tax as a percentage of income)	3.3%	.000081%

*The CEO pays a **much lower** percentage of his income than does the factory worker.*

Chart 16d

Who is Really on Welfare?

Federal Spending on Various Programs in 2005

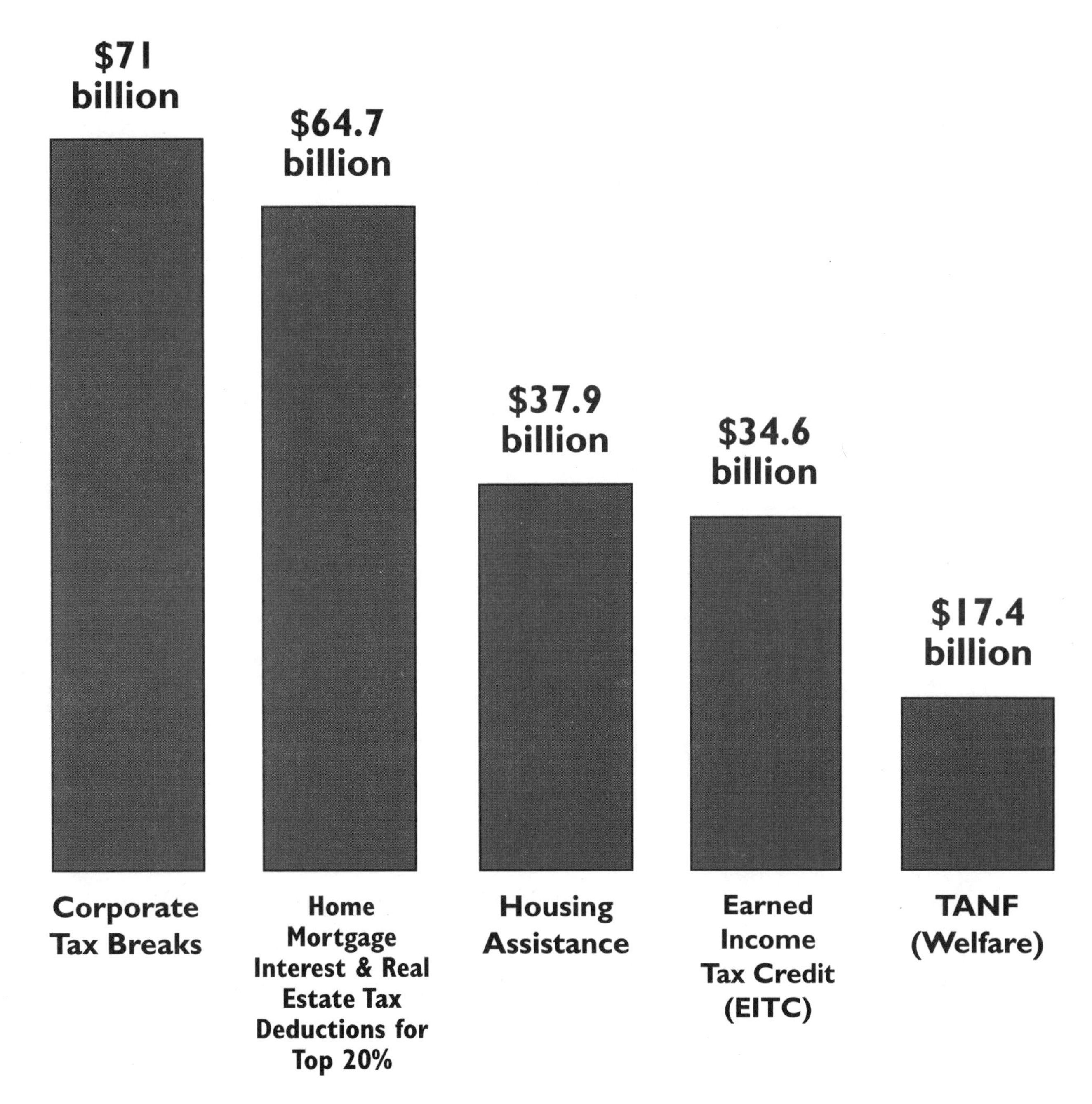

Source: *For Corporate Tax Breaks* (data from 2003): Citizens for Tax Justice (www.ctj.org). *For Home Mortgage Interest and Real Estate Tax Deductions*: Urban-Brookings Tax Policy Center (www.taxpolicycenter.org). *For Housing Assistance, Earned Income Tax Credit (EITC), and Transitional Assistance to Needy Families (TANF)*: National Priorities Project, citing U.S. Budget (www.nationalpriorities.org).

Chart 16e

Examples of Corporate "Welfare"

The U.S. government gives corporations $125 billion a year in economic incentives.

Over 90% of Wal-Mart's distribution centers (244 in 35 states) received taxpayer subsidies, including free or reduced-price land, infrastructure improvements, property and sales tax reductions, tax-exempt loans, etc., totalling more than $1 billion.

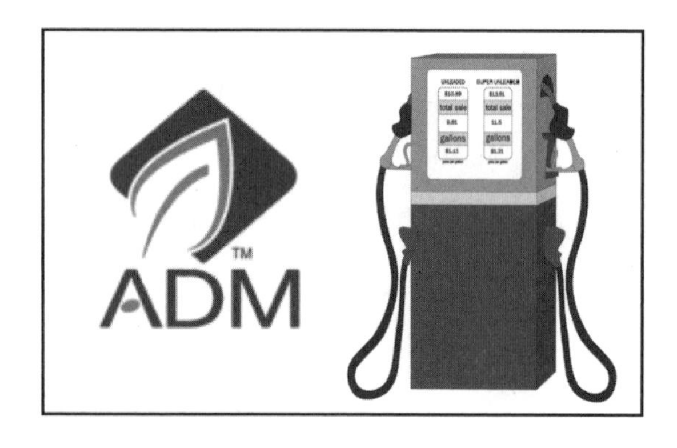

Archer Daniels Midland, the world's largest agricultural commodity firm, has received more than $3 billion to subsidize production of the gasoline additive ethonol.

McDonald's got a $466,000 check to market Chicken McNuggets in Turkey.

Chart 16f

Lesson 17 – Closing America's Racial Wealth Gap

Objectives:

- *Examine how wealth and assets are distributed along racial lines.*
- *Brainstorm explanations of the causes of the racial wealth divide.*
- *Listen to an explanation of the causes of the racial wealth divide.*
- *Review the history of asset building in the 20th century and the ways in which the government has assisted some households in asset building.*
- *Explore the historical and present-day barriers to asset accumulation for households of color.*
- *Identify several policy interventions to build assets for households of color and reduce the racial wealth divide.*
- *Evaluate the strengths and weaknesses of various policy interventions designed to reduce the racial wealth disparities.*

Concepts and Key Terms:

- *white flight*
- *wealth and assets*
- *net worth*
- *financial net worth*
- *liquidity or liquid wealth*
- *post World War II housing programs*
- *barriers to asset-building for households of color*
- *homeownership*
- *asset building accounts*
- *Individual Development Accounts*
- *race-based policies*

Instructional Time:

- *55 minutes*

Preparation:

For the Bellringer Activity 17.1:

- *One copy per student of the handout "New Orleans: A Tale of Two Cities"*
- *Charts 17a, Unemployment Rates by Race, 2005; 17b, Percentage of Families Whose Savings Would Run Out in 3 Months or Less; 17c, Family Median Net Worth in 2004*
- *Select three possible explanations for the racial wealth gap. Write these explanations on the board or on a flip chart and cover so the words are hidden. (See explanations in the activity description.)*

For Activity 17.2:

- *Sticky notes*
- *Several large magic markers*
- *Chart 17d, Timeline: Government Boosts and Blocks to Wealth Creation*

For Activity 17.3:

- *One copy of the two-page handout "Possible Solutions for Closing the Racial Wealth Gap" for each student.*

Conducting the

Lesson

Lessons 14 and 16 focused on the rule changes that are the result of a shift in power from working people to the elite. This lesson looks more closely at who is winning and more specifically at who is losing due to these changes. Although this shift in power has a negative impact on all middle and lower income Americans, it is especially hard on people of color.

Although the lesson examines the "racial wealth gap," it is limited in several ways. We look primarily at the experience of Blacks, Whites and Latinos, and for Latinos data is limited. This is because the sources of information, the U.S. Census Bureau and other primary sources, do not have good historical data about assets and wealth for Latinos, Asians, and Native Americans. Data for all groups is complicated because people with widely divergent national and cultural origins are lumped together.

Bellringer Activity 17.1

1. Begin by reading to students the excerpt from *New Orleans: A Tale of Two Worlds.* Provide each student a copy of the handout so they can read along with you. You may opt to have a read-a-round or popcorn reading (where one student calls on another when she/he finishes reading a paragraph).

2. After reading this essay ask students to close their eyes and get a mental picture of both communities that were just described. Tell them to think about the following questions but not to respond out loud.

"Picture the gated community, with green, expansive lawns, large homes, and people playing golf or sunning by their pools. What color do you imagine those people are? Now picture the other neighborhood, with people trying to salvage wrecked houses, streets filled with debris, and the smell of mold and disinfectant in the air. What color do you imagine these people are?"

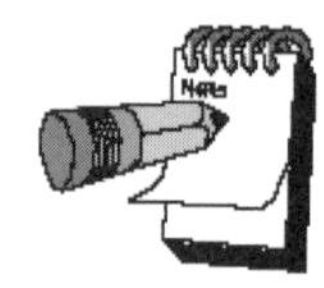

Note to Teacher

This activity suggests conducting a visualization of a divided society. It discusses the sensitive subjects of "white privilege and white flight." Students may need an introduction on sensitivity to issues such as these, or you may choose only to use the newsletter, and not to conduct the visualization.

3. Explain that it is often difficult to discuss the "color" of our communities. We want to focus on multiculturalism, celebrate diversity, and stress unity. Yet the reality of racism, and its manifestations of *white privilege and white flight,* still exist. *White flight* is the phenomenon of white people moving out of the inner city to high-priced neighborhoods to avoid living near people of color. It continues to happen today when people of color move to the suburbs and whites move even further out to newly created, often gated, communities or back to gentrified and exclusive city neighborhoods.

4. Open the class up to a discussion of how they feel about what they just read and heard. Display **Chart 17a, Unemployment Rates by Race, 2005; Chart 17b, Percentage of Families Whose Savings Would Run Out in Three Months or Less; and Chart 17c, Family Median Net Worth, 2004.** Then use the talking points that focus on the impacts that growing inequality has on people of color.

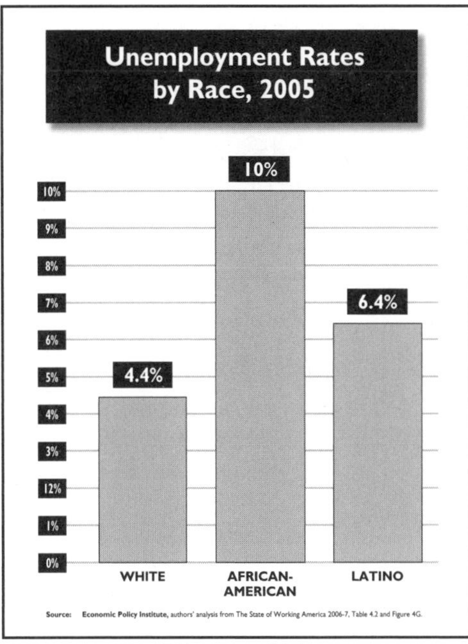

Chart 17a

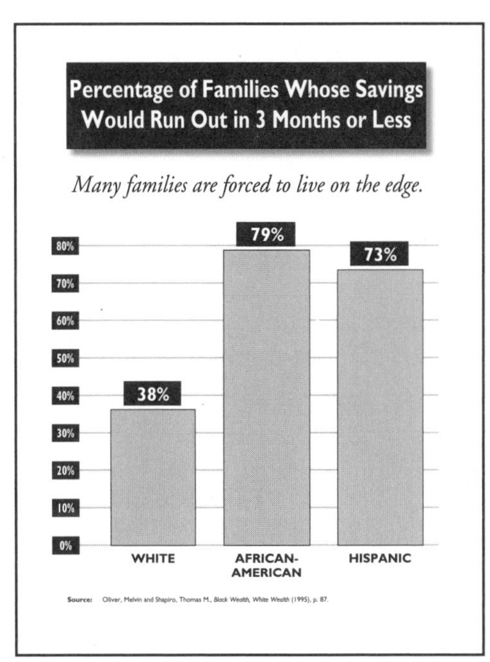

Chart 17b

TALKING POINTS

Chart 17b, Percentage of Families Whose Savings Would Run Out in Three Months or Less

Why is accumulated wealth important? Because it is what people have to fall back on in the event of a downturn in the economy, a personal setback (loss of a job, loss of income), or a disaster such as Hurricane Katrina.

If you were to go to a financial planner she/he would encourage you to save over six months of financial reserves to prepare for the event of a job loss, health emergency, divorce or other unforeseen circumstance.

Financial reserves means money you could easily get or what some people call "liquid wealth." This would include money in a bank or credit union savings or checking account — or in a money market fund that allows you to withdrawal money on short notice. But the reality is, for many people, they don't even have this minimal six-month cushion.

The chart examines what percentage of the population has three months or less of financial reserves. Almost half (45% of the population) has three months or less. This explains why many people feel some uncertainty in their financial situation and why a large percentage of the population is unable to jump on the "economic expansion wagon," by putting money in the stock market.

TALKING POINTS

There are enormous wealth disparities between white families and families of color. Net worth (assets minus liabilities or "what you own minus what you owe") includes homeownership, savings, investments, and all other tangible assets.

Median Net Worth, or the experience of families in the middle (see Chart 17c), is understood by lining up all the families by net worth, from the one with the most assets at one end of the line to the ones with the least, at the other end of the line. The family in the middle is the median, and for White families, the median is $140,700 in net worth.

The Black family in the middle has $20,600 in net worth. The Latino family in the middle has $18,600.

In 2004, White families had more than six times as much wealth as Black families and eight times more wealth as Hispanic households.

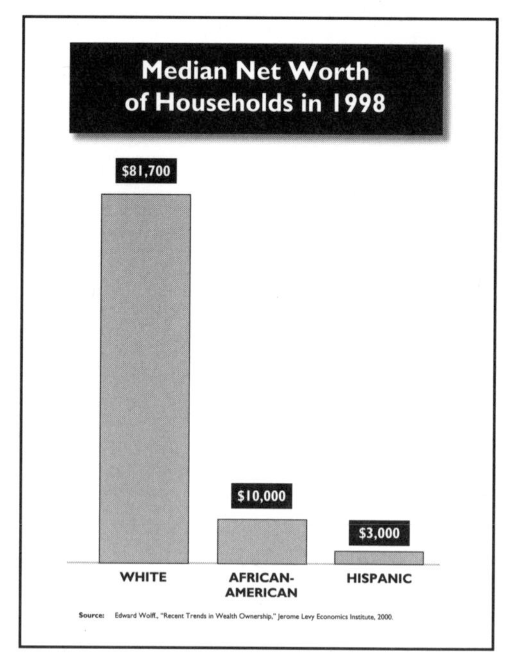

Chart 17c

5. We just reviewed some very disturbing facts. The class will now examine the reasons behind the racial wealth gap that we see reflected in the charts above. One way to begin is by examining the life experiences of the group in order to develop the story of asset building in the last century.

Write the sample explanations—accurate and mythical—on a chart in advance of the lesson and keep them hidden until ready to be used. This is not a comprehensive list, but rather a catalyst to discussion. Leave plenty of room for additional explanations from participants.

ACCURATE EXPLANATIONS FOR THE RACIAL WEALTH GAP	UNPROVEN EXPLANATIONS FOR THE RACIAL WEALTH GAP
• Long term discrimination in asset building, for example, acquiring loans.	• Cultural attitudes about saving and consumption.
• Differences in wages paid to people of color versus white people during years of discrimination and different job opportunities leading to less savings.	• Racial differences in educational ability and therefore educational achievement.
• Overall growing divide in the economy between asset owners and wage earners in the last two decades. People of color own fewer assets.	

6. One option for discussing the reasons behind the racial wealth gap is to reveal the list of sample explanations and then pose the following questions to students: From your experience, what do you think of these explanations? What is missing? What would you agree with? What would you challenge?

7. Another option for discussing the reasons behind the racial wealth gap is to ask students to brainstorm explanations for the racial wealth gap and then write their explanations on the board. Discuss each explanation as it is made.

8. Reveal the mythical explanations without labeling them "mythical." Use caution in choosing this option. Depending upon how you as the facilitator approach the comments made, it can provide an opportunity for students to self-examine their racial stereotypes.

9. Reveal the accurate and then the mythical explanations, discussing each as it is revealed.

Katrina: A Tale of Two Worlds

As New Orleans' poor were still being plucked from rooftops by Coast Guard helicopters and as the military insisted that those who had remained leave their flooded homes, New Orleans resident Ashton O'Dwyer quietly returned to his Uptown neighborhood home via private helicopter. A week after the storm, as other citizens of New Orleans waited in lines for bottles of water, Mr. O'Dwyer's city water service was restored. Two oil company engineers stopped by O'Dwyer's home and delivered herring in mustard sauce and 15 gallons of generator fuel.

The indelible images of the abandoned and forgotten — the poor, the disabled, the elderly, the young children, most of them African American — are seared into our minds. But the cross-town story of Mr. O'Dwyer and his neighbors in the Audubon Hills gated community located on some of the sparse high ground in New Orleans had not been told until the Wall Street Journal revealed it on September 8, 2005.

O'Dwyer and his neighbors commandeered a city park and turned it into a private heliport and a staging ground for the small army of security guards hired to secure their exclusive neighborhood. "New Orleans is ready to be rebuilt. Let's start right here," O'Dwyer told Journal reporter Christopher Cooper.

The flooded areas of New Orleans were three-quarters black, while in dry areas, African Americans were a minority. Over the years, many well-off white people left the city for gated suburban communities. The remaining whites tend to live on higher ground.

Almost a third of residents of the flooded neighborhoods did not own the cars on which the evacuation plan relied. If the promise to the freed slaves of 40 acres and a mule had been kept, then six generations later, their descendents would own more assets, and the mule would now be a Buick.

Now, even the rivers of disaster aid, no-bid contracts, and suspension of worker wage standards are flowing to those already on high ground. For those at the top of our badly fractured society, it's time to break out another jar of herring in mustard sauce — the helicopter is waiting.

Activity 17.2: The Wealth Building Timeline

Many people, particularly people of color, have encountered institutional barriers to getting on the "asset building train." We want to draw on our experiences to identify these barriers.

1. Break students into groups of three and ask them to discuss (and record their answers to) the following questions:

> Considering as much as you know about your family's history, going back two to three generations, what were significant events or milestones in terms of homeownership or other ways of building assets? (Do your parents own a home or a business? Did your grandparents?)
>
> Were there key barriers or key moments in homeownership or asset building? (Did they get any assistance buying their car or home, or investing in stocks from family members or the government?)

Students may or may not be able to answer questions such as these, and this may need to be a homework assignment in which they interview relatives and return with more information. Another variation is to create several more scenarios and have students, in groups of three, draw a scenario and brainstorm answers to the questions above, drawing on their knowledge of U.S. history.

2. Provide students with some examples, ideally sharing from your own family history, such as "My parents purchased a home with a down payment that was a loan from family members." "My family owned a farm in the country, but migrated to the city to work and we eventually sold the farm." "My parents were the first generation in the family to own a home." "In the 19th Century, as Irish Catholics, my great-grandparents were barred by British law from owning property. When they came to the U.S. they had nothing." "My parents had to work to buy their own car when they graduated from high school. My parents gave me a car while I was still in school."

Ask students to consider whether their grandparents owned or rented their home. Did they own a business? Did they own a farm?

TALKING POINTS

For most people, asset building is the experience of saving money and buying a home. (Assets also include savings, ownership of stocks and bonds, recreation items, second homes, etc.)

Homeownership is typically the first step (and sometimes only step) towards personal asset accumulation.

One of the biggest factors in wealth accumulation is how much wealth one's family of origin had, going back generations. Wealth accumulation is generational. When someone's family got on the "Asset Building Train" will greatly influence subsequent generations in terms of opportunity to get on the train.

3. Let students know that they have approximately five minutes for this activity. They should first share these stories with each other, and if willing, then share them with the class. To do this they should summarize the story in a short phrase and write it on a sticky note. When the whole class comes together, we will ask to hear from a few people.

Remind students that they needn't be embarrassed if they don't know much about their family's history and experience with asset building. Many people don't know.

4. When time is up, ask students to come forward and put their sticky notes on the board, then share briefly.

5. Students then listen to a mini-lecture while reviewing **Chart 17d, An Historic Timeline of Government Boosts and Barriers to Building Wealth.**

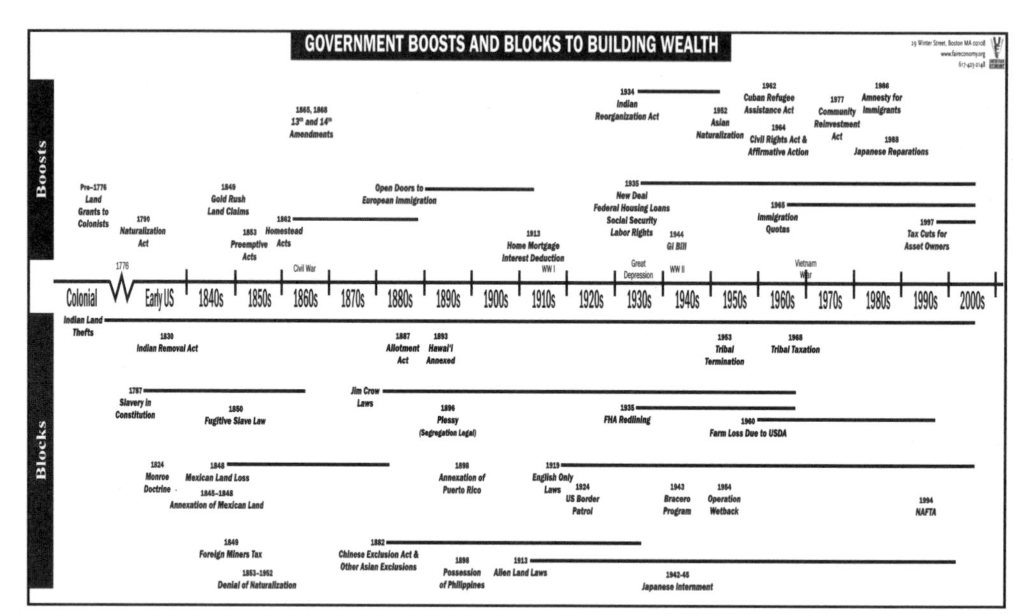

Chart 17d

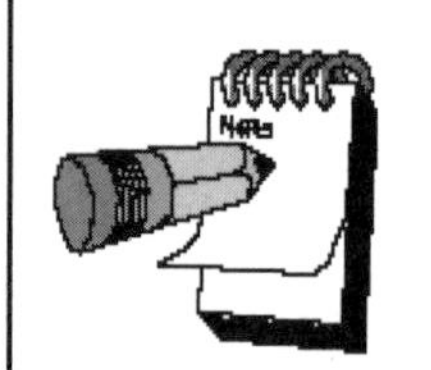

Note to Teacher

There is information about a few of the barriers to asset-building in the Talking Points on the next page. However, we recommend that you read *The Color of Wealth* (see Additional Resources on page 144) for background information on the items in the Barriers & Boosts Timeline (Chart 17d.

TALKING POINTS:

Government Barriers to Asset-Building

Slavery. Under slavery, people of African heritage did not even "own themselves" and were legally prohibited from owning property.

Discrimination in Land Grants. In the post-CivilWar South, Blacks were promised "40 acres and a mule" as restitution for slavery, but very few did obtain land and low interest loans to set up farms. Many remained in sharecropper arrangements that kept people in a permanent cycle of debt. At the same time, white households were benefiting from the "Homestead Act" which allocated land grants and provided low interest loans to farmers who were "opening the west." This often included taking land from indigenous Americans – and giving it to white settlers.

Laws Discouraging Asset-Building. Jim Crow laws included provisions sometimes called "Black Codes" that required that African-Americans have employers or be fined as vagrants. This discriminated against self-employed blacks and artisans.

Violence. Violence against African-American-owned businesses and Black people who seemed to be getting ahead economically served as major barriers to asset building. Race riots initiated by White people in the first half of the 20th century often resulted in the destruction of Black business districts and homes (e.g., in Rosewood, FL and Tulsa, OK, and many others are still being documented).

Black Farm Land Loss. In the years after the Civil War, some black households did acquire farms. But black farm ownership peaked in 1910 with 218,000 farms. Many whites also lost their farms in the years leading into the Depression, as there was tremendous consolidation of farmland and urban migration. Black farms were generally sold to white landowners, leading to a net increase in white ownership.

Urban Migration. Many Southern blacks left farms that were owned within their families to move to northern cities to work for wages. Between 1910 and 1970, 6.5 million blacks moved north, with 5 million of that 6.5 million occurring after 1940.

Social Security. Social Security, when it was established in the 1930s, exempted agricultural workers and domestic workers, excluding two occupations that were disproportionately done by people of color.

It is important to remember that despite these (and other) significant barriers placed before people of color, there was also struggle, resistance, and successful community and personal efforts to build economic independence.

Activity 17.3: Possible Solutions for Closing the Racial Wealth Gap

1. Divide students into small groups and hand each group the two-page handout, "Possible Solutions for Closing the Racial Wealth Gap."

2. Assign each group a different section of the handout. Group 1 reads "Affordable Housing and Home-ownership." Group 2 reads "Individual Development Accounts." Group 3 reads "KIDS Accounts." Group 4 reads "Income Assets."

3. Have students read their section and then work together brainstorming and answering the following questions: In terms of asset building for communities of color, what do you think of this program? What are the strengths and the drawbacks of the program? What would you add to the program? What other ways would you suggest to strengthen the program? How do these approaches deal with past barriers?

4. Ask a representative from each group to share an explanation of a "possible solution" that their group read about and then discuss the answers they prepared to the above questions.

Additional Resources

Dalton Conley, *Being Black, Living in the Red: Race, Wealth, and Social Policy in America.* Berkeley: University of California Press, 1999.

Howard Fast, *Freedom Road,* Armonk, NY: M.E.Sharpe, 1995. An engaging novel of the period of Reconstruction. To order: 800-541-6353.

Meizhu Lui, Bárbara Robles, Betsy Leondar-Wright, Rose Brewer, and Rebecca Adamson, *The Color of Wealth - The Story Beyond the Racial Wealth Divide.* New York: The New Press, 2006.

Thomas Shapiro, *The Hidden Cost of Being African American: How Wealth Perpetuates Inequality.* Oxford: Oxford University press, 2004.

Possible Solutions for Closing the Racial Wealth Gap

1. Affordable Housing and Homeownership

Owning a home is the primary asset for most Americans and has long been considered a stepping stone to building additional assets. Public policies that increase access to homeownership include: subsidized mortgages and mortgage insurance, down-payment assistance funds, second mortgage subsidy programs, and grants and low interest loans for home improvements. Stricter enforcement of fair housing and community reinvestment laws would remove barriers to homeownership and asset building for people of color.

According to a March 2006 study of housing trends over the last 25 years by the Center for Housing Policy, "low- to moderate-income working families with children are less likely to be homeowners now than they were in the late 1970s. The study also found that the gap between white families with children and families of color with children has worsened. "These comprehensive findings are particularly troubling," the study asserts, "because of the evidence that homeownership may play a positive role in helping children do better in school. Yet working families with children, and especially minority working families with children, are lagging far behind."* Given that housing was the principal asset-building program after World War II, it will likely remain an essential component of any major asset-building initiative, especially for younger households and people of color.

Homeownership is not the only tenure option that should be promoted, however, as it is not appropriate for all households at all stages of life. Nor should homeownership be considered the only "asset account" and "line of credit" for low- and moderate-income families, as it has many risks. A large and growing percentage of the population live in mobile homes or neighborhoods that do not have appreciating property values. Access to decent and affordable cooperative and rental housing would enable many people to save and meet other financial security goals. Public subsidies should be targeted to "third sector" housing ownership that includes community land trusts, housing cooperatives, mutual housing and other models that reduce housing costs and preserve long-term affordability.

Protecting residents who own homes against predatory lenders is another strategy to prevent "asset-raiding" and loss. Unscrupulous lenders are preying on lower income homeowners, peddling debt consolidation, refinancing and cash for second mortgages at high interest rates. Part of an asset-building campaign should be to publicize and protect existing low-income asset-owners from losing assets.

* Center for Housing Policy, *Locked Out: Keys to Homeownership Elude Many Working Families with Children*, March 2006 (www.nhc.org/index/chp-research-publications).

Possible Solutions for Closing the Racial Wealth Gap

2. Individual Development Accounts (IDAs)

Individual Development Accounts (IDAs) are matched savings accounts that enable low-income families in the United States to save, build assets, and enter the financial mainstream. IDAs reward the monthly savings of working-poor families who are building towards purchasing an asset — most commonly buying their first home, paying for post-secondary education, or starting a small business. IDAs make it possible for low-income families to build the financial assets they need to achieve the American Dream.

The match incentive — similar to an employer match for 401(k) contributions — is provided through a variety of government and private sector sources. Organizations that operate IDA programs often couple the match incentive with financial literacy education, training to purchase their asset, and case management.

The impact of these programs is being evaluated by the Corporation for Enterprise Development (CFED) and the Center for Social Development at Washington University. As of January 2003, over 500 IDA initiatives exist in communities across the country. Overall, at least 10,000 people are currently saving in IDAs. Thirty states included IDAs in their state Temporary Assistance for Needy Families (TANF) plans (as allowed by the 1996 welfare reform law) which excludes counting IDAs as assets for the purpose of qualifying for benefits. Thirty-four states, Washington, D.C., and Puerto Rico have passed some form of IDA legislation. Several national foundations have supported the American Dream Demonstration (ADD), a four-year, 14-site IDA policy demonstration.

IDAs are expected to reach an additional 30,000 to 40,000 working-poor people in the U.S. by the year 2003 through the federal Assets for Independence Act of 1998 (AFIA).

A large-scale publicly funded IDA program, with matching funds based on income, would provide significant opportunities for asset-poor households to build wealth. Participants could withdraw funds from IDAs in order to purchase a home, finance a small business or invest in education or job training. Even small amounts of money can make a substantial difference in whether or not individuals get on the asset-building train.

3. KIDS Accounts

In 2005, legislation was introduced in Congress called the America Saving for Personal Investment, Retirement, and Education Act (the ASPIRE Act of 2005). Modeled after a program known as "Baby Bonds" that was instituted in England in 2003, The ASPIRE Act would create a Kids Investment and Development Account ("KIDS" Account) for every child born in 2007 and beyond. Each child would receive a starter deposit of $500 from the government and children from households below the national median income would be eligible for a supplemental contribution up to an additional $500. Further contributions from any source could be deposited into the account and grow tax-free. Low- and moderate-income children would have their savings matched.

Once a child reaches 18, he/she would be able to use the account for a post-secondary education, a home, or save it until retirement. To ensure that families make good decisions regarding the account, financial education would be offered. Once an account holder reaches age 30, he/she must begin paying back the initial starter deposit from the government both to signal that the deposit was not something for nothing and to seed the next generation of KIDS Accounts.

Possible Solutions for Closing the Racial Wealth Gap

4. Income Assets

One of the main reasons that nonwhite people were shut out of asset building was because they were restricted to no-wage or low-wage jobs. From African slaves in the South to Latino day laborers on the street corners of Los Angeles, people of color have been denied fair compensation for their labor power. They have been limited to jobs that whites did not and do not want, were excluded from unions, paid taxes to work, and have always been the last hired and the first fired.

Jobs are needed that provide the cash income to cover the day-to-day needs with something left over to build savings, the basis for financial wealth. Today, income disparity lays the groundwork for future wealth disparities. Wealth disparity grows because of differences in income. Income includes not just wages and salaries based on working, but cash supports for those who are unemployed, retired, or parents of small children.

The present federal minimum wage of $5.15 an hour translates into an annual income of $10,712, not enough to keep a family out of poverty. Studies by the Economic Policy Institute reveal that an increase in the minimum wage would primarily benefit full- and part-time workers of low-income families, which are disproportionately headed by single women of color. It would require raising the minimum wage to $8.10 an hour (as of 2004 for a family of four) to move above the official poverty line. Around the country, people are organizing for more than the minimum wage; they are demanding a living wage. Since the cost of living varies across the country, communities are calculating costs particular to their cities. For example, in 2003, voters in San Francisco approved a city living wage of $8.50 an hour.

Unemployment Rates by Race, 2005

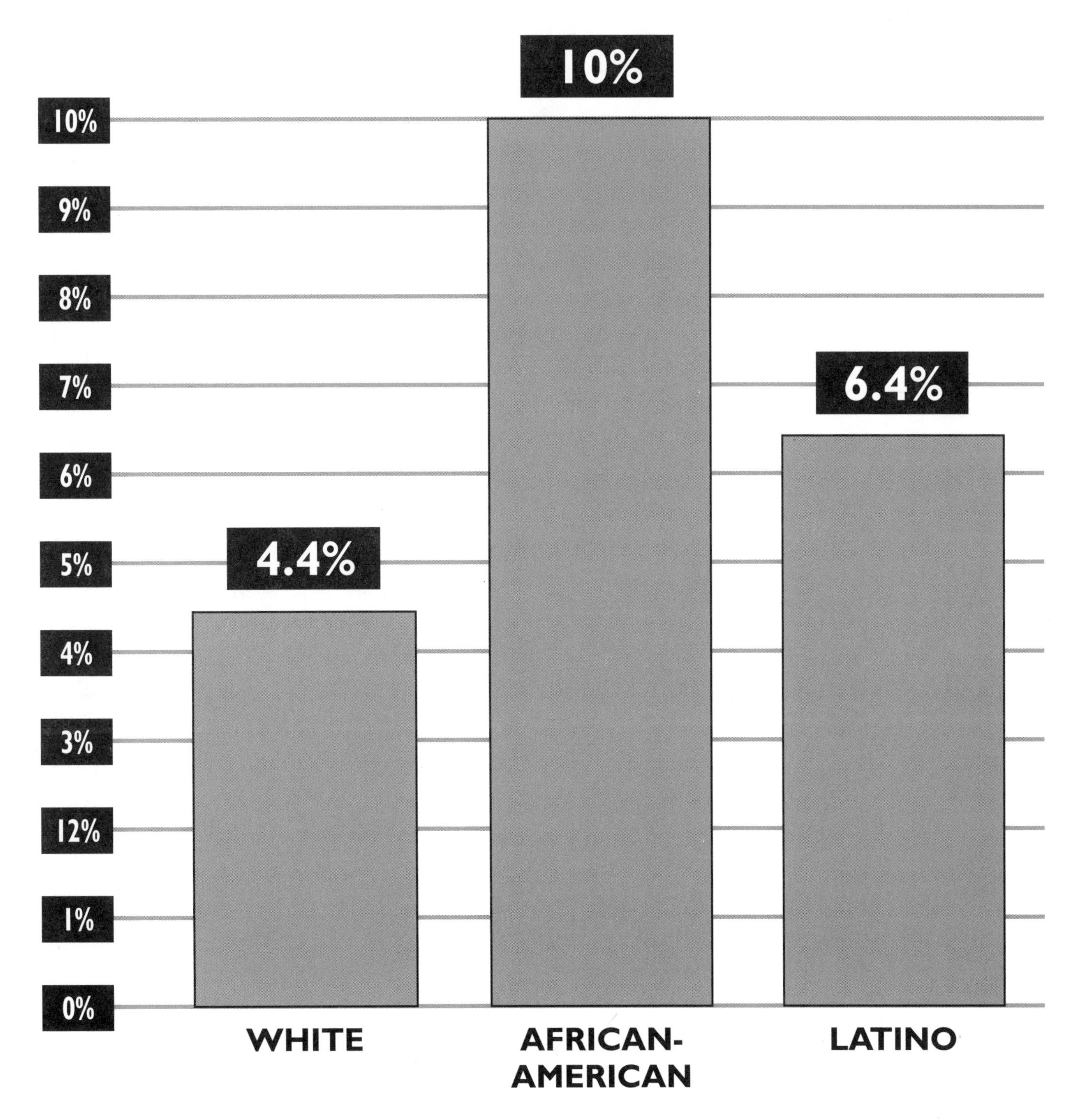

Source: **Economic Policy Institute,** authors' analysis from The State of Working America 2006-7, Table 4.2 and Figure 4G.

Chart 17a

Percentage of Families Whose Savings Would Run Out in 3 Months or Less

Many families are forced to live on the edge.

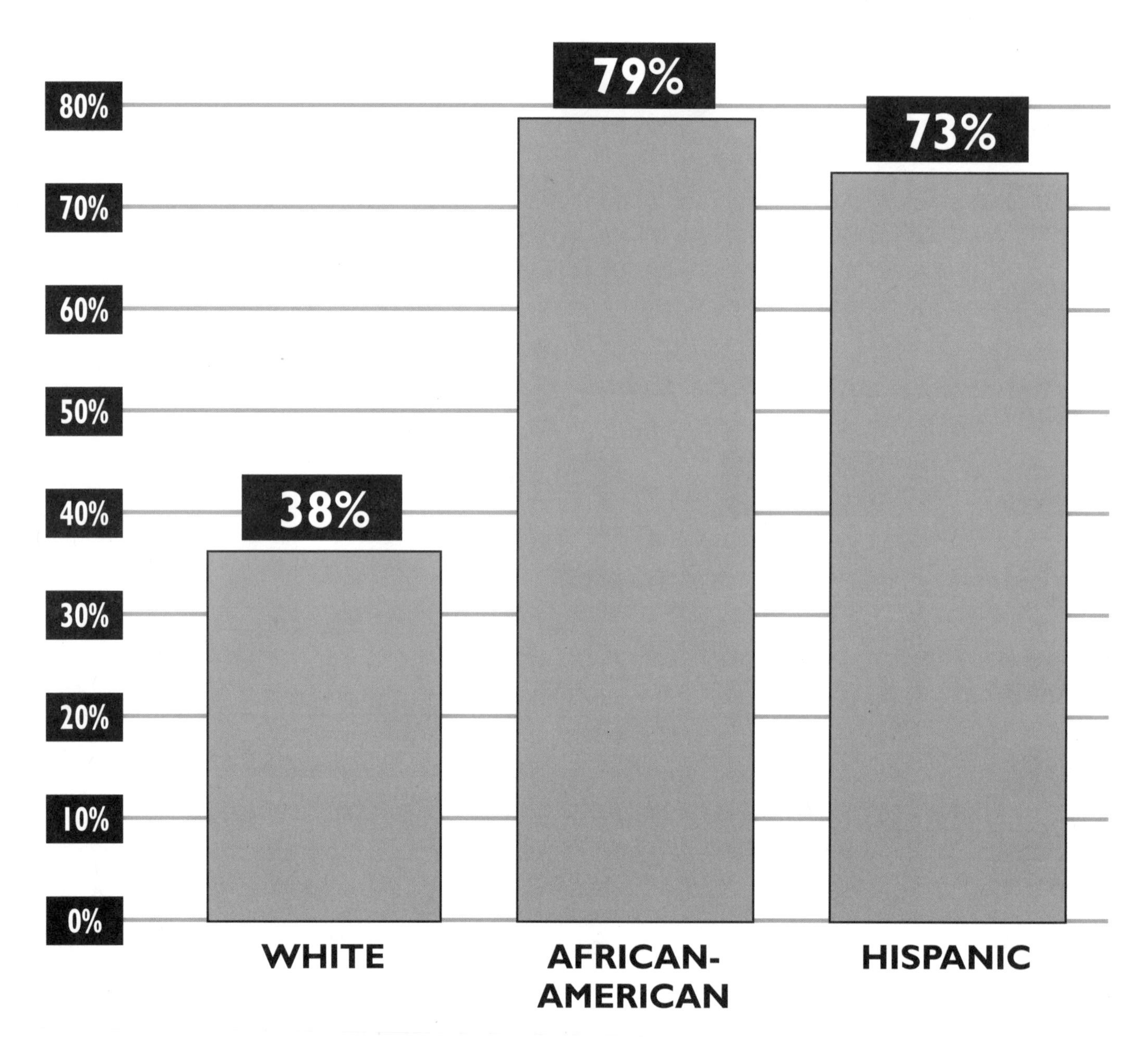

Source: Oliver, Melvin and Shapiro, Thomas M., *Black Wealth, White Wealth* (1995), p. 87.

Chart 17b

Median Net Worth of Households in 1998

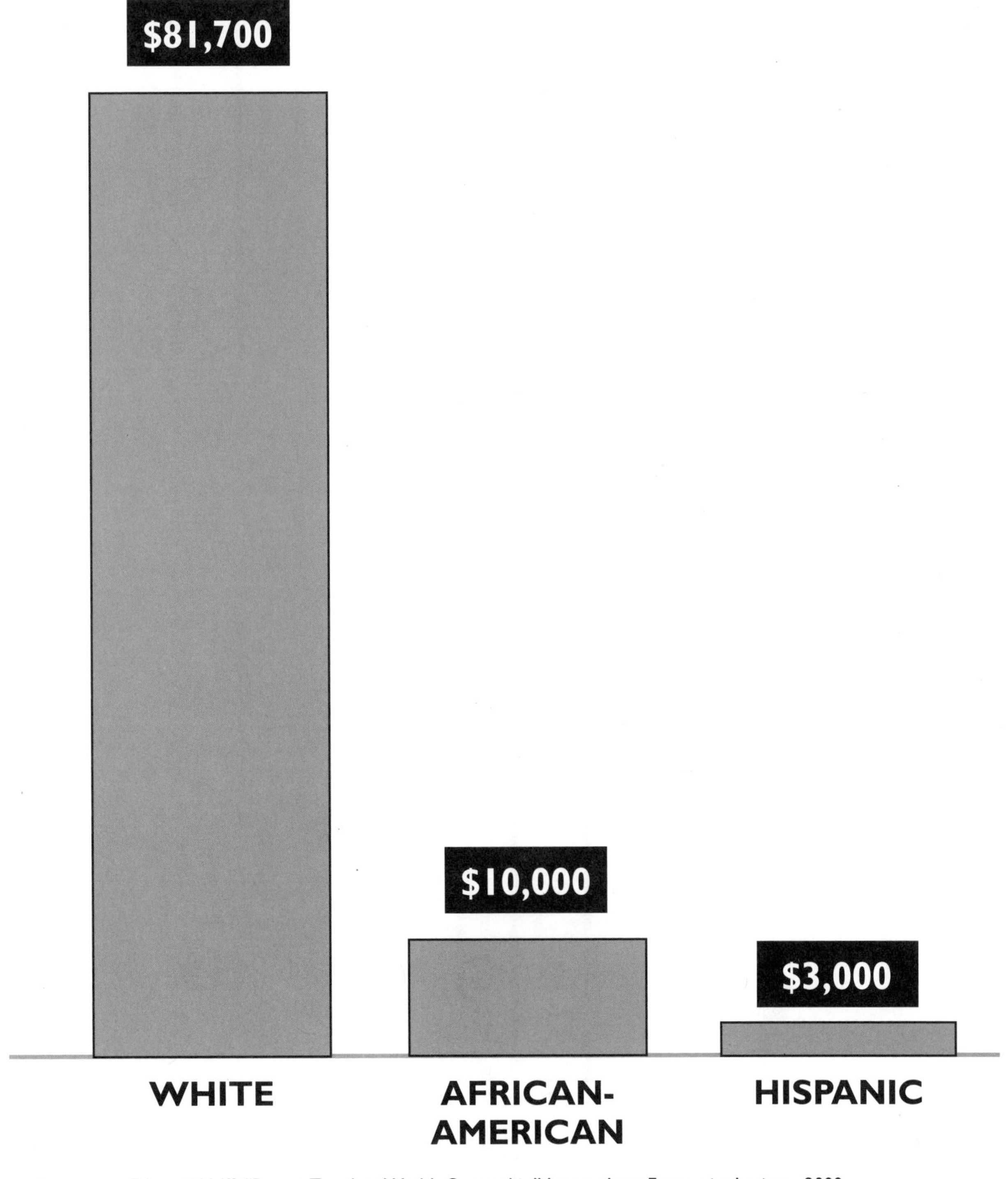

Source: Edward Wolff., "Recent Trends in Wealth Ownership," Jerome Levy Economics Institute, 2000.

Chart 17c

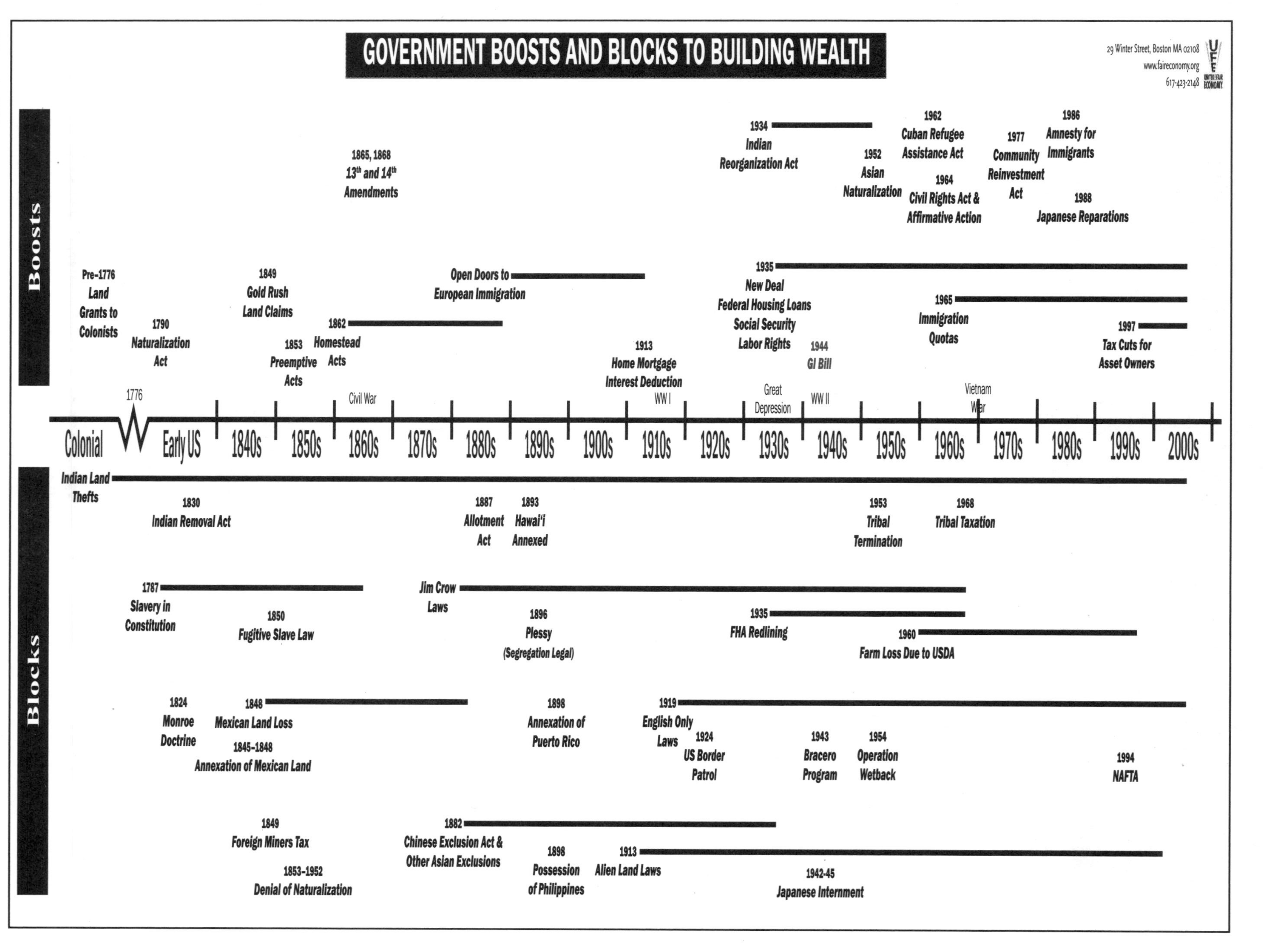

GOVERNMENT BOOSTS AND BLOCKS TO BUILDING WEALTH
29 Winter Street, Boston MA 02108
www.faireconomy.org
617-423-2148
UFE
UNITED FOR A FAIR ECONOMY
Boosts
Blocks
Colonial
1776
Early US
1840s
1850s
1860s
1870s
1880s
1890s
1900s
1910s
1920s
1930s
1940s
1950s
1960s
1970s
1980s
1990s
2000s
Civil War
WW I
Great Depression
WW II
Vietnam War
Pre-1776 Land Grants to Colonists
1790 Naturalization Act
1849 Gold Rush Land Claims
1853 Preemptive Acts
1862 Homestead Acts
1865, 1868 13th and 14th Amendments
Open Doors to European Immigration
1913 Home Mortgage Interest Deduction
1934 Indian Reorganization Act
1935 New Deal
Federal Housing Loans
Social Security
Labor Rights
1944 GI Bill
1952 Asian Naturalization
1962 Cuban Refugee Assistance Act
1964 Civil Rights Act & Affirmative Action
1965 Immigration Quotas
1977 Community Reinvestment Act
1986 Amnesty for Immigrants
1988 Japanese Reparations
1997 Tax Cuts for Asset Owners
Indian Land Thefts
1830 Indian Removal Act
1887 Allotment Act
1893 Hawai'i Annexed
1953 Tribal Termination
1968 Tribal Taxation
1787 Slavery in Constitution
1850 Fugitive Slave Law
Jim Crow Laws
1896 Plessy (Segregation Legal)
1935 FHA Redlining
1960 Farm Loss Due to USDA
1824 Monroe Doctrine
1848 Mexican Land Loss
1845-1848 Annexation of Mexican Land
1898 Annexation of Puerto Rico
1919 English Only Laws
1924 US Border Patrol
1943 Bracero Program
1954 Operation Wetback
1994 NAFTA
1849 Foreign Miners Tax
1853-1952 Denial of Naturalization
1882 Chinese Exclusion Act & Other Asian Exclusions
1898 Possession of Philippines
1913 Alien Land Laws
1942-45 Japanese Internment

Chart 17d

Objectives:

- *Analyze the role of political action committees in influencing public policy.*
- *Develop and make a presentation about the influence of big business and big money on public policy in the U.S.*

Concepts and Key Terms:

- *the price of influence*
- *Political Action Committees (PACs)*
- *interest groups*
- *lobbying, lobbyist*
- *public policy*

Instructional Time:

- *55 minutes*

Preparation:

For the Bellringer Activity 18.1:

- *Copies of each of the following handouts (one copy of each is included in this lesson): "Democracy for Sale," "Who's Paying For Our Democracy?".*
- *Three sets each of scissors, markers, tape, glue, different colored construction paper, and two pieces of poster board.*

Conducting the Lesson

Lesson 14 discussed the power shift and subsequent rule changes that have occurred since the 1970s. This lesson focuses on the impact of these rule changes on the political process. Teenagers are often wise (or cynical) enough to question the importance of any one person's vote in America's present day democracy. Many have a general sense that our democracy has become a game for the elite. However, when questioned further, many teens are unfamiliar with the inner workings of political action committees, corporate lobbyists and the like.

This lesson provides substance for the argument that our democracy is controlled by the people within it who have the most money. The purpose is not to leave students in despair, but to help them understand the influences of big money on public policy, in order to stop and/or prevent further undemocratic influences. After teaching this lesson, it is strongly recommended that you follow up with one of the following lessons suggesting ways we can stop such threats to our democracy.

Bellringer Activity 18.1: The Price of Influence

1. Break students into three small groups, providing each group with one copy of a particular handout for each member of the group. Each group should get scissors, markers, tape, glue, different colored construction paper, and two pieces of poster board.

2. Provide students with the following instructions:

    a. Read your handout silently. Highlight important parts of the handout or points that stand out to you.

    b. As a group, discuss the handout and decide how you can relay this information to your classmates.

    c. You will be given five minutes to present the information in your handout to your classmates.

d. You may use the materials provided to make your handout into a chart. You may use the board or the overhead. You can create a skit or a game. However, you must relay the important highlights of your article to your classmates. You must be able to answer questions about the material and all students in your group must participate in the designi and presentation of your material.

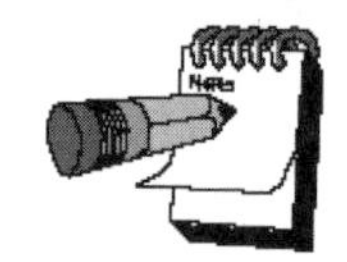

Note to Teacher

Read the three handouts and choose important points you want to make during students' presentations. In case they do not cover these points, you will have them handy and ready to discuss.

DEFINITIONS

Special interest groups try to influence public policy (often by passage or modification of legislation) in favor of their members and their shared viewpoints. Interest groups form for many reasons, however, most are founded on the basis of economic concerns, often on behalf of business, labor, agricultural, professional, and social interests.

A ***Political Action Committee (PAC)*** is the political arm of a special interest group. In 1974 there were approximately 600 PACs. Today, according to the Federal Election Commission with whom they are required to file, there are over 4,600 PACs that donate money to politicians and political causes.

Lobbying is the means used to bring pressure, usually on public officials, to influence public policy. Lobbyists are hired to speak with, write to, and otherwise convince officials to respond in the interest of their employers (special interest groups).

Democracy for Sale

Winning an election in the United States takes money. Lots of money! In 2004, winners in Senate races spent, on average, over $7.8 million. That's more than twice as much as the losers spent ($3.6 million).

In the House of Representatives, winners spent over $1,034,800 each, nearly four times as much as the losers did.

In most cases, spending more than the opponent is the way to victory. That means that candidates have to get the backing of interest groups who are able to give large contributions. Ultimately, this tilts policy-making in favor of those interest groups.

Incumbents — candidates who are already in office — have an easier time raising money, especially if they sit on powerful committees. This makes it difficult for challengers to raise enough money to mount credible campaigns and unseat incumbent candidates. In 2004, only one out of 26 incumbents running for reelection was defeated. In the House, only five out of 395 incumbents running for reelection were defeated.

Average Spending of Winners and Losers for Senate in 2004

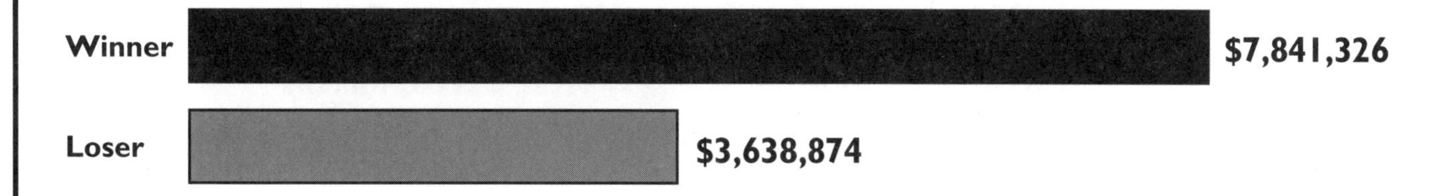

Average Spending of Winners and Losers for House of Representatives in 2004

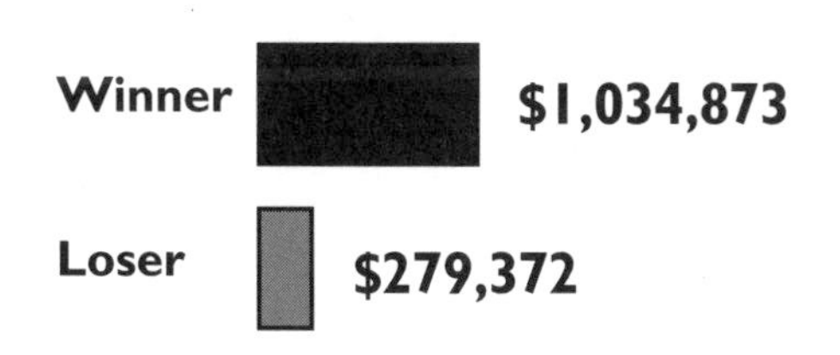

Source: Center for Responsive Politics (www.opensecrets.org)

Who's Paying For Our Democracy?

In 2004, businesses contributed nearly 25 times as much money to congressional campaigns as labor unions.

Total Contributions to Congressional Campaigns in 2004

Total Contributions to Congressional Campaigns in 2003-2004, by Sector

Finance, Insurance & Real Estate	$338.2 million
Lawyers & Lobbyists	$210.8 million
Miscellaneous Business	$208.6 million
Ideological/Single-Issues	$180.0 million
Health	$123.9 million
Communications/Electronics	$102.2 million
Construction	$71.9 million
Labor	$61.5 million
Agribusiness	$52.9 million
Energy & Natural Resources	$52.7 million
Transportation	$51.4 million
Defense	$16.1 million

Source: Center for Responsive Politics (www.opensecrets.org)

Lesson 19: The Consequences of Economic Inequality and What's Been Done about Them in the Past

Objectives:

- *Identify the consequences of economic inequality for our society, our democracy, our families, our civic life, our health and our environment.*
- *Review historical examples of responses to economic inequality and the gains of people's movements to address inequality.*

Concepts and Key Terms:

- *economic inequality, a historical perspective of movements addressing this subject*
- *consequences of economic inequality*
- *Populist movement*
- *Share Our Wealth movement*
- *labor movement*

Instructional Time:

- *55 minutes*

Preparation:

For the Bellringer Activity 19.1:

- *Ten magic markers*
- *Approximately ten (for a class of 30 students, fewer for a smaller class) large pieces of paper, taped to the walls, equal distance apart. Have the following words written on each poster: "The Consequences of Economic Inequality on: Our Society ... Our Democracy ... Our Civic Life ... Our Families ... Our Health ... Our Environment" Leave space after each subject area for students to write their answers.*

For Activity 19.2:

- *Chart 19a, What Have People Done in the Past?*

For Activity 19.3

- *Put the "Share Our Wealth" paragraphs on separate index cards.*

Conducting the Lesson

The previous lessons in this book have focused on the growth in economic inequality and the shift of power from the majority of the people in the US to a few extremely wealthy individuals and big corporations. In addition, the lessons focused on the impacts of this power shift on personal income and wealth. Lessons 19, 20 and 21 will build on knowledge gained in prior lessons. They are an integral part of motivating students towards action. We know that knowledge without action leads to despair and we do not want to leave our students feeling powerless. Therefore, this lesson will review what has been done in previous times to address similar problems. Lesson 18 challenges students to examine why they should care about the issue of economic inequality and Lesson 19 provides some avenues students can take to address this current growing economic inequality individually and collectively.

This lesson mentions the Abolitionist Movement of the 1850s, the Populist Movement of the 1880s, provides details of the 1930s Share Our Wealth Movement and reminds students of the Labor Movement and the role unions play in the balance of power between corporations and employees.

Bellringer Activity 19.1: The Consequences of Inequality

1. Working in small groups of approximately three or four, ask each group to gather around one of the posters taped to the wall. Provide each group with a marker and ask one student to act as scribe. Ask students to think carefully about the consequences of policy and rule changes and the resulting growth in economic inequality for each of the words written on the poster, and then record the group's answers.

2. When students have completed the task, ask each group to report its answers to the class. To keep students focused, have them move over and stand close to the group's poster being discussed.

3. When students are done, summarize the main themes into short phrases and compile one main list on the board. Ask what connections students see among the responses. Some possible responses:

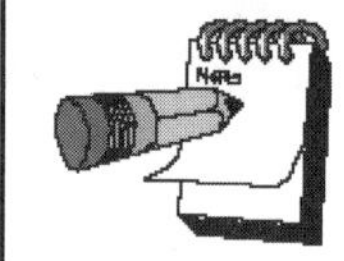

Note to Teacher

If your students have trouble brainstorming consequences of inequality, an option would be to put the possible responses on separate index cards (1. Our society, 2. Our democracy, etc.). Then break students up into six groups and give each group one of the cards. Have them read about the consequences and record specific scenarios expanding on their assigned consequence. Scenarios may be real-life stories or hypothetical situations.

The Consequences of Economic Inequality

Our Society
- Less-privileged people are scapegoated, resentment increases and society becomes divided.
- Due to extreme poverty and lack of hope, some people may turn to crime. As fear of crime escalates, people with more wealth isolate themselves in gated communities and society is further divided.
- The burden of paying for the national debt and for government services falls more heavily on lower and middle income people.
- Poverty and homelessness continue to increase.

Our Democracy
- Big money corrupts our democratic process.

Our Civic Life
- We are told that there is no money in the national budget for basic human services, yet we know corporate welfare is prolific. We lose faith in our government and don't fulfill our civic duties, leaving the government in the hands of the wealthy and their special interests.

Our Families
- Less time for family and community life.
- The real problems in our lives are not addressed.
- Parents try to buy happiness for their children. We become disillusioned with the drive for material possessions.

Our Health
- Our health suffers. (Read "Inequality is a Health Hazard" on page 159.)

Our Environment
- Our environment continues to be polluted and our natural resources destroyed for the sake of more profits for the wealthy.
- The wealthy protect their special interests, by lobbying against policies promoting long term sustainable management of our natural resources.

INEQUALITY IS A HEALTH HAZARD

Inequality, new data from the United Nations make clear, continues to be a matter of life and death. Japan, the nation with the world's most equal distribution of income and wealth, once again sports the world's longest life expectancy, at 82.2 years, according to the 2006 UN Human Development Report. The developed world's most unequal nation, the United States, now ranks 30th on the global life expectancy list, at 77.5 years, despite spending nearly as much on health care as the rest of the world combined! In 1970, a much more equal United States ranked 12th.

The United States also has the highest infant mortality rate, the highest teen pregnancy rate, and the highest child abuse rate of the top 25 industrialized nations.

Notes Dr. Stephen Bezruchka of the University of Washington School of Public Health: "Societies with a bigger gap between those on top and those on the bottom will be less healthy than societies where there is a smaller gap. Studies overwhelmingly show that for every health condition, for every disease, for every cause of death, those who have lower incomes have it much worse than those who have fat paychecks." Within the United States "greater inequality in the distribution of income was associated with not just higher rates of overall mortality, but also rates of premature death from heart attack, cancer, murder, and infant mortality." *

Poverty can affect health in a number of ways:

- income provides the prerequisites for health, such as shelter, food, warmth, and the ability to participate in society
- living in poverty can cause stress and anxiety which can damage people's health
- low income limits people's choices and works against desirable changes in behavior

* *The Health of Nations: Why Inequality is Harmful to Your Health* by Ichiro Kawachi and Bruce P. Kennedy (The New Press, 2002).

Activity 19.2: What Have People Done in the Past?

Provide this mini-lecture of examples of Americans' responses to social and economic injustice.

1. Write these words on the board and ask students what they have in common:
   - the weekend
   - the 8-hour work day
   - the 40-hour work week
   - the minimum wage
   - laws prohibiting child labor
   - laws extending the right to vote for women and minorities
   - Social Security
   - Medicare

   Answer: They are all the direct result of people organizing to establish rules and policies that address economic inequality and maintain fairness; and they are things we sometimes take for granted.

2. Ask students if they are familiar with the Populist Movement they may have learned about in history class. Show **Chart 19a, What's Have People Done in the Past?**

Explain that the Populists were unique in the ways in which they united rural farmers and urban workers. However, some Populists succumbed to racial and anti-Semitic views that contributed to their demise. But we do have a lot to learn about their commitment to creating real economic democracy.

3. In the wake of the Great Depression, The Share Our Wealth Movement gained momentum on the following platform:

   - Cap excessive wealth and income
   - A 30-hour work week
   - Universal Retirement Pension

What Have People Done in the Past?

The rules of our economy are often set up to benefit the wealthy. Repeatedly, popular movements have risen to challenge and change the rules so that the economy benefits everyone more equitably.

★ In the 1850s, before the Civil War, the **Abolitionist Movement** laid the groundwork to end legal slavery, if not the economic and social exploitation of former slaves.

★ In the 1880s, the **Populists** began a campaign for the first income taxes, which were to be directed at the wealthy. Thirty years later, the income tax was law, along with anti-trust and food safety regulations.

★ In the 1930s, **Labor Unions** organized millions of workers, improving wages and working conditions.

★ Also in the 1930s, the **Share Our Wealth Movement** campaigned for:
• a cap on excessive wealth & income
• a 30-hour work week
• a Universal Retirement Pension

. . . and helped the enactment of Franklin D. Roosevelt's New Deal legislation, which included Social Security, a highly-progressive income tax, the minimum wage, a 40-hour work week, the right to organize a labor union, and child labor laws.

Chart 19a

DEFINITION

A ***Pension*** is a stated amount of money paid regularly to a retired or disabled person. Pensions can be paid by the government or by private employers. The Share Our Wealth movement campaigned for a universal pension for all workers. This vision was incorporated into the Social Security program.

Activity 19.3: Share Our Wealth

1. To spend a few minutes discovering how the Share Our Wealth Movement functioned, have students conduct a read-around. Before doing the reading, use the talking points below to provide students with important background knowledge.

2. Ask for the number of volunteer readers needed.

3. Provide each volunteer reader with an index card containing one numbered paragraph of the words of Senator Long.

4. Ask the student with number one to begin reading. Keep track of what number was just read and call on number 2, 3, etc. until all paragraphs have been read. You may leave discussion until the end of the reading, or stop in between paragraphs as students desire.

5. When a volunteer reads the paragraph regarding taxing income over $8 million at 100%, remind them that $8 million in 1933 is equivalent to $109 million today.

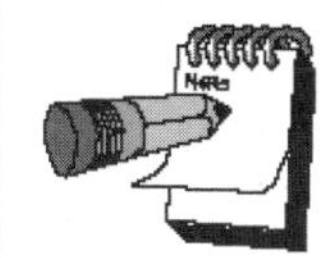

Note to Teacher

You may want to do some sort of disclaimer about Huey Long, who although an economic populist, was anti-Semitic and racist as well as corrupt. His economic ideas are, however, quite inspiring. The read-around was pulled together and excerpted from *Kingfish to America: Share Our Wealth. Selected Senatorial Papers of Huey P. Long,* edited by Henry M. Christman (New York: Schocken Books, 1985).

TALKING POINTS:

The last time wealth was as concentrated as it is today was in 1929 (the year of the great stock market crash). At that time, the wealthiest 1% had over 35% of the nation's private wealth. Compare this to today (2004), when the wealthiest 1% has over 33% of the nation's private wealth.

Some economists think this over-concentration of wealth in 1929 contributed to the stock market crash and, ultimately, to the Great Depression. Wealthy people had so much money that they were putting it into risky investments. Everyone else was losing ground, so they were defaulting (not paying) on their loans and had no money to spend to stimulate the economy.

During the era of the Great Depression, Huey Long, a larger-than-life politician who gained national attention as Louisiana's "Kingfish" — a nickname he gave himself — was a lively opponent of corporate wealth and privilege, targeting giants such as John D. Rockefeller's Standard Oil Company. From 1928 until 1932, Long served as Louisiana's governor — and in 1930 as senator as well — and launched an ambitious and successful program of public works. Long also ruled over a statewide political machine whose corrupt methods caused critics to regard him as a demagogue and political thug. Long was a radical populist with presidential ambitions who began a national campaign called "Share the Wealth," a campaign that included minimum salaries and caps on income and property. He railed against the influence of the wealthy few, organizing his own, alternative political organization, the Share-Our-Wealth Society, through which he advocated a populist program for redistributing wealth through sharply graduated income and inheritance taxes.

Excerpts from radio broadcasts and speeches of Huey Long

1. Total wealth in the United States...is about $400 billion or about $15,000 to a family. If there were fair distribution...our national wealth would be three or four times (greater) because a free, circulating wealth is worth many times more than wealth congested and frozen into a few hands as is America's wealth....

2. The fortunes of the multimillionaires and billionaires (should) be reduced so that no one person shall own more than a few million dollars....We should do this by a capital levy tax.... On the first million that a man (has) we would not impose any tax.

3. We would say, "All right for your first million dollars, but after you get that rich you will have to start helping the balance of us." ...On the second million a man owns we would tax that 1% so that every year the man owned the two million dollars he would be taxed $10,000. On the third million we would impose a tax of 2%. On the fourth million...4%. On the fifth million...8%. On the sixth million...16% On the seventh million... 32%. On the eighth million...64%. And on all over eight million we would impose a tax of 100%.

4. I am not asking any man in the United States Senate to do anything harmful to the rich people of this country. If you want to make the (lives of the rich) secure, provide a way to relieve the anxieties of 90 percent of the people in this country today who are in absolute fear of want and impoverishment.... If you love these rich people as much as I love them...provide a way to distribute (their wealth)....

5. We could distribute this surplus wealth, while leaving these rich people all the luxuries they can possibly use.... Leave them with every palace, with every convenience, with every comfort; but do not allow the concentration and stagnation of wealth to reach the point where it is a national calamity.

6. The Share Our Wealth Platform did not simply talk about redistributing wealth, but also about shortening the amount of toil in people's lives. The fourth part of the platform was: limit the hours of work to...prevent overproduction and to give the workers of America some share in the recreations, conveniences, and luxuries of life.

7. We must guarantee food and clothing and employment for everyone who should work by shortening the hours of labor to thirty hours per week, maybe less, and to eleven months per year, maybe less.... Let us all have work to do and have that much of heaven on earth.

Here are more excerpts of speeches by Huey Long where he talked specifically about the Share Our Wealth Societies:

8. Whenever a local society has been organized, please send me notice...so that I may send statistics and data which such local society can give out in their community, either through word of mouth in meetings, by circulars, or, when possible, in local newspapers....

9. Please understand that the Wall Street controlled public press will give you as little mention as possible and will condemn and ridicule your efforts....

10. Now be prepared for the slurs and snickers of some high-ups when you start your local Share our Wealth society. Also when you call your meeting be on your guard for some smart-aleck tool of the interests to come in and ask questions....

11. Enroll with us. We will send you a button if we have enough of them left. We have a little button that some of our friends designed with our message around the rim....

12. Many thousands of (societies) are meeting through the United States, and every day we are getting hundreds and hundreds of letters....

13. Where possible, I hope those who organize a society in one community will get in touch with their friends in other communities and get them to organize societies.... Anyone can have copies of this article reprinted in circular form to distribute....

14. By having their cooperation, on short notice we can all act as one person for the one object and purpose of providing that in the land of plenty there shall be comfort for all. The organized 600 families who control the wealth of America have been able to keep the 125 million people in bondage because (the people) have never once known how to effectually strike for their fair demands....

15. We can soon get about the work of perfecting a complete, unified organization that will not only hear promises but will compel the fulfillment of pledges made to the people.

TALKING POINTS:

People responded to the Share Our Wealth Movement. During the years 1934 and 1935, over seven and a half million people sent postcards and letters to the Share Our Wealth offices — significant at a time when the U.S. population was approximately 130 million and when the price of a stamp was a lot of money for many people.

Over 6 million people joined over 27,000 Share Our Wealth Clubs across the United States. This movement helped compel President Roosevelt to fulfill his campaign promises and become the champion of progressive taxation.

Biographer Henry Christman wrote of its impact: "The Share Our Wealth movement forced Roosevelt to the left [on the political spectrum], thereby expanding the scope of the New Deal and hastening its enactment."

Some final spoken words from Huey Long about the American people:

> *"They have the right to a living, with the conveniences and some of the luxuries of this life.... They have a right to raise their children in a healthy, wholesome atmosphere and to educate them, rather than to face the dread of their undernourishment and sadness by being denied a real life.... Share our wealth simply means that God's creatures on this lovely American continent have a right to share in the wealth they have created in this country."*

Activity 19.4: Teens Organize

1. Ask students to take out a sheet of paper and provide a written description of their idea of the average early 20th century labor organizer. You may need to give them hints of what was happening during the early 20th century, or what some of the more common jobs were.

2. Ask volunteers to read their descriptions. Do students suppose the organizers were: Males? Adults? White?

3. Explain that many children were involved in striking and protesting for the 8-hour work day and against child labor.

4. "But that was then and this is now," your teens respond. Share the following story:

> *In 1998, in Macedonia, Ohio, a 19-year-old employee of McDonald's walked out in protest when a manager mistreated another (middle-aged) worker. He organized all the other employees, mostly teenagers, to strike and picket the restaurant. He called the Teamsters Union, which helped the employees negotiate with management. They won a written contract that includes paid vacations, raises if the federal minimum wage goes up, classes in "people skills" for management, and a guarantee of respectful treatment.*

Students may know other examples of student organizing. Ask for volunteers to share some of these examples with the class.

5. Lesson 14 discussed the policies that were a factor in the decline of unions. The lesson focused on the role unions play in ensuring wage and salary fairness. Recall that unions provide for the balance of power between corporations and employees that results in:

- increased benefits
- safer working conditions
- fairness in wages and salary
- a stronger, more cohesive society

6. To wrap up, students can complete one of the following projects:

a. Provide students with history books and ask them to research the history of economic inequality in the US and movements that have risen to counter this economic inequality. Have students use their research to create a timeline of economic inequality. Alternative approaches include:

- Assign students specific time periods to research and then assemble one large timeline in class, on a long roll of paper, taped around the classroom. Group students together by time period and have them write stories on their section of the timeline describing specific events. (See the *Who Built America* video series under Additional Resources below, for ideas.) When students have completed the timeline, have them each explain their section to the class.
- Ask each student to develop their own timeline. Have them bring their timelines to class and ask each student to explain her/his work to the class.
- Ask students to work in pairs, and assign each pair a specific time period to research. Ask each pair to make a poster of their time period. In chronological order, have each pair present their poster to the class.

b. Have the class develop a set of questions they want to ask an older relative or neighbor about what it was like to live in a different time period. Focus the questions on the economic situation of the time period.

Note to Teacher

Some schools may have policies prohibiting students from taking home questionnaires or anything similar. Check with administrators before assigning the following homework.

Students often find it nice to have something to discuss with their elders. One student wrote years later to her teacher to express her new-found appreciation for the project in the event of her grandparent's death.

Ask a few teachers, guidance counselors, librarians or administrators to be available to discuss these issues with students who are unable to find an available or willing adult at home to discuss these matters. Make students aware of this option when explaining the assignment.

Sample questions:

- How does family life differ today than it did when you were growing up?
- What was your first job like?
- How have jobs and work in general changed from the time period you were growing up? (In pay, benefits, loyalty to the employer and in any other way?)
- How much did your first house cost?
- How does that compare to the prices of houses today, accounting for inflation? (In other words, what percentage of your income did it take to buy a house then compared to now?)
- What values do you recall when you were growing up that you see a change in today?
- What traditions did your family have that have changed from the time when you were growing up?

Type the questions and make copies for students to take with them. Ask them to interview a relative or a neighbor who has lived through several decades and experienced some of the economic policy changes focused on in the previous lessons. Add an assigned number of additional questions they must create on their own for use in the interview.

An alternative to written answers: Make this an oral history project. Ask students to use a videorecorder or a tape player to record the interview. This may take a bit of coordinating on the teacher's end. Check with your librarian to see if tape players are available for student loan. You may want to bring in a tape recorder of your own and some inexpensive blank tapes and have students sign up for an evening to borrow them.

Hold a discussion after the completion of the assignment and ask volunteers to share stories they learned during their interviews.

Additional Resources

Kawachi, Ichiro and Bruce P. Kennedy, *The Health of Nations: Why Inequality is Harmful to Your Health*, New York: The New Press, 2002.

Steinbeck, John, *The Grapes of Wrath*, Penguin Classic, 2006. A landmark of American literature, first published in 1939, that presents a portrait of the conflict between the powerful and the powerless, of one man's fierce reaction to injustice, and of one woman's stoical strength. The novel captures the horrors of the Great Depression and probes into the very nature of equality and justice and the hard realities of a nation divided into *haves* and *have-nots*.

Wilkinson, Richard, *The Impact of Inequality - How to Make Sick Societies Healthier*, New York: The New Press, 2005.

Who Built America, a 7-part video series on the history of America's working people using period graphics and reenactments of government testimony and readings from period magazines and newspapers. Includes, for example, the railroad strikes of 1877 and organization of the Grand Army of Starvation. Produced by The American Social History Project at the City University of New York. Phone: 212-966-4248, email: pbender@email.gc.cuny.edu.

Zinn, Howard, *A People's History of the United States*, New York: HarperCollins, revised and updated in 2003. This book is an attempt to balance the scales by writing about the parts of US history that aren't often covered in depth. It focuses particularly on the effects of government policy on the poor, women, and non-whites throughout US history, documents labor movements and equality movements in more depth than one normally sees, and points out the mixed and disappointing records of US cultural heroes.

"Well, they look pretty undocumented to me."

What Have People Done in the Past?

The rules of our economy are often set up to benefit the wealthy. Repeatedly, popular movements have risen to challenge and change the rules so that the economy benefits everyone more equitably.

★ In the 1850s, before the Civil War, the **Abolitionist Movement** laid the groundwork to end legal slavery, if not the economic and social exploitation of former slaves.

★ In the 1880s, the **Populists** began the first campaign for an income tax, directed at the wealthy. Thirty years later, an income tax became the law, along with anti-trust and food safety regulations.

★ In the 1930s, **Labor Unions** organized millions of workers, improving wages and working conditions.

★ Also in the 1930s, the **Share Our Wealth Movement** campaigned for:

- a cap on excessive wealth
- a 30-hour work week
- a Universal Retirement Pension

. . . and helped the enactment of Franklin D. Roosevelt's New Deal legislation, which included Social Security, a highly-progressive income tax, a minimum wage, a 40-hour work week, the right to organize a labor union, and child labor laws.

Chart 19a

Lesson 20: Economic Inequality, Why Should We Care? Because Knowledge Without Action Leads to Despair

Objectives:

- *Explore how students fit into the picture of an economy that is becoming increasingly unequal.*
- *Compare the difference between our political structure and our economic structure.*
- *Identify where the power lies in creating a more equal economy.*
- *Brainstorm economic policy remedies for closing the income and wealth gap.*

Concepts and Key Terms:

- *economic policy remedies*
- *political structure vs. economic structure*
- *increase in service sector jobs, decrease in manufacturing jobs*
- *the first generation to make less money than their parents*

Instructional Time:

- *55 minutes*

Preparation:

For Bellringer Activity 20.1:

- *thick pad of sticky notes, one per student*
- *markers, one per student*
- *Chart 20a, Entry Level Wages by Education Level, 2000-2005*

For Activity 20.2:

- *Chart 20b, Wheel of Shared Prosperity*
- *one large piece of paper, flip chart size, to compile a list of student ideas*
- *tape*

Conducting the Lesson

Bellringer Activity 20.1: Why Should You Care About Economic Inequality?

1. Start by asking students why should they care that wealth and power in the U.S. is concentrated in the hands of a few people and institutions. Pass around the pad of sticky notes and the markers and ask students to write an answer to this question: Why should I care about economic inequality in the U.S.?

2. When students are done, ask them to come up, one at a time, and explain their answer and then stick it on the board. Answers will vary within the class, often according to the socio-economic status of the group.

Some of the answers many students may have in common include:

- because we have to work one day and want to make a good living
- because we will have to pay taxes one day and we are not part of the 1% that owns more wealth than the bottom 90% combined and still receives huge tax breaks
- because we will have to pay taxes one day and we are not part of the 1% that owns 40% of the nation's wealth and receives huge tax breaks
- because we are consumers in this economy
- Because it is not healthy for the economy to have such a huge concentration of wealth and we don't want a recession similar to the 1929 depression to occur.

If students' answers do not come close to these, discuss their answers and then introduce the above suggestions. Use **Chart 20a, Entry Level Wages by Education Level, 1989-2005** and the following talking points to elaborate on the suggestions.

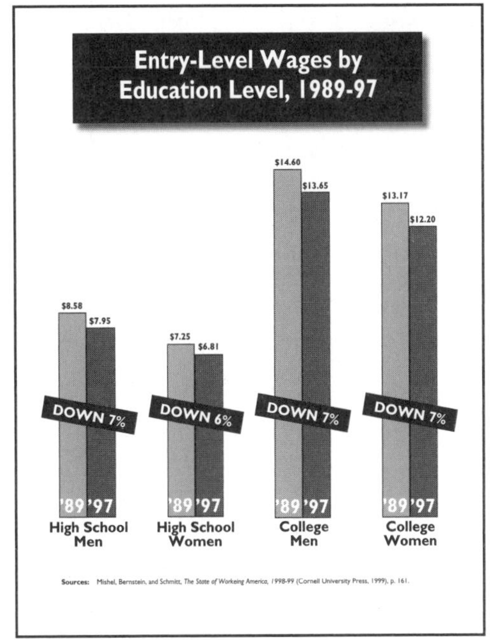

Chart 20a

TALKING POINTS:

We should care about economic inequality because we will have to work one day and we want to make a good living. The trend in the U.S. has been for each generation to do just as well or better financially than their parents. However this trend has come to an end with the current generation. This generation will start off with fewer opportunities than existed in the past. High school graduates finding a job for the first time in 2005 earned lower real hourly wages than they did in 2000. (Refer students to dollar figures on chart 20a.) More education doesn't solve the problem. Among first-time job seekers with a college education, average hourly wages also dropped. (Refer to the chart.)

We should care about economic inequality because we will have to pay taxes one day and we are not part of the 1% that owns more wealth than the bottom 90% combined and still receives huge tax breaks. As long as you are paying taxes, shouldn't you care how the money is spent, and how fair the tax process is? Why should you carry the burden of taxes while the extremely wealthy receive huge tax breaks. (Remind students of the budgeting activity in Lesson 16 or conduct that part of the lesson here).

We should care about economic inequality because we are consumers. Before students turn 18 and have the right to vote they can make a big difference just by how they shop. Students can make a difference by shopping responsibly.

3. Put the following quote on the board and ask students for comments, whether they agree or disagree.

"Knowledge without action leads to despair."

Activity #20.2: Economic Policy Remedies

1. This activity asks students to come up with economic policy remedies for closing the income and wealth gap. Before conducting the activity, make sure they have a clear understanding of our current political and economic structure, as well as the causes of economic inequality, using the following talking points.

TALKING POINTS:

Our political structure: The United States is a constitutional republic. Its government relies on representative democracy through a congressional system under a set of powers specified by its Constitution. However, majority rule is tempered by minority rights protected by law. There are three levels of government: federal, state, and local. Officials at all three levels are either elected by voters in a secret ballot or appointed by other elected officials. Executive and legislative offices are decided by a plurality vote of citizens in their respective districts, with judicial and cabinet-level offices nominated by the Executive branch and approved by the Legislature. The federal government is comprised of three branches – Legislative, Executive, and the Judiciary – which are designed to check and balance one another's powers.

Our economic structure: We have a capitalist economy. Capitalism generally refers to an economic system in which the means of production (capital, such as factories, farms, banks, etc.) are mostly privately or corporately owned and operated for profit, in which investment is determined by private decision, and in which distribution, production and pricing of goods and services are determined in a largely "free" market.

Our government currently regulates the free market. However, due to the power that the big owners of capital, including large corporations, have amassed, the rules imposed on the market tilt the economy to their benefit, raher than rewarding people strictly on the basis of their hard work. In the past, when wealth and power became highly concentrated in the hands of a few, people demanded that government place regulations and restrictions, such as taxes and anti-trust laws, to make the economy more equitable.

Recognizing the cause of inequality to be economic policies that favor the wealthy (the few) at the expense of everyone else (the many), we can now examine ways to change these economic policies.

2. Show students **Chart 20b, The Wheel of Shared Prosperity.** Ask THEM to brainstorm economic policy remedies for closing the income and wealth gap. You can conduct this activity in small groups or as a class. You may need to start the students out with one or two examples such as:

- raising the minimum wage
- expanding college loans and providing lower income families with more opportunities for higher education

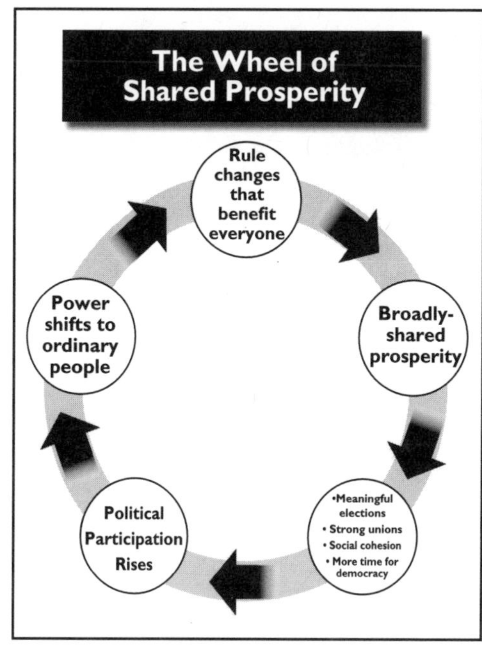

Chart 20b

3. Compile students' answers on a large piece of paper that you can tape up in the room and refer back to during this and the following lesson. One list of suggested policy remedies might include:

- passage of progressive taxation
- promoting unionization
- eliminating corporate tax loopholes
- raising the "no tax threshold"
- creating a "Wealth" tax
- increasing spending on education and health care
- expanding the earned income tax credit (EITC)
- creating a maximum wage, linking the top tax rate to a ratio of the minimum wage

Note to Teacher

The next lesson picks up here and provides in depth explanations of some of these policy remedies.

Suggested Homework:

Categorizing the Policies: Ask students to copy the compiled list to take home. Ask them to group each of the "policy remedies" under one of the following headings:

- policies that lift the floor (lift people out of poverty)
- policies that level the playing field
- policies that address the concentration of wealth and power

Entry-Level Wages by Education Level, 2000-2005

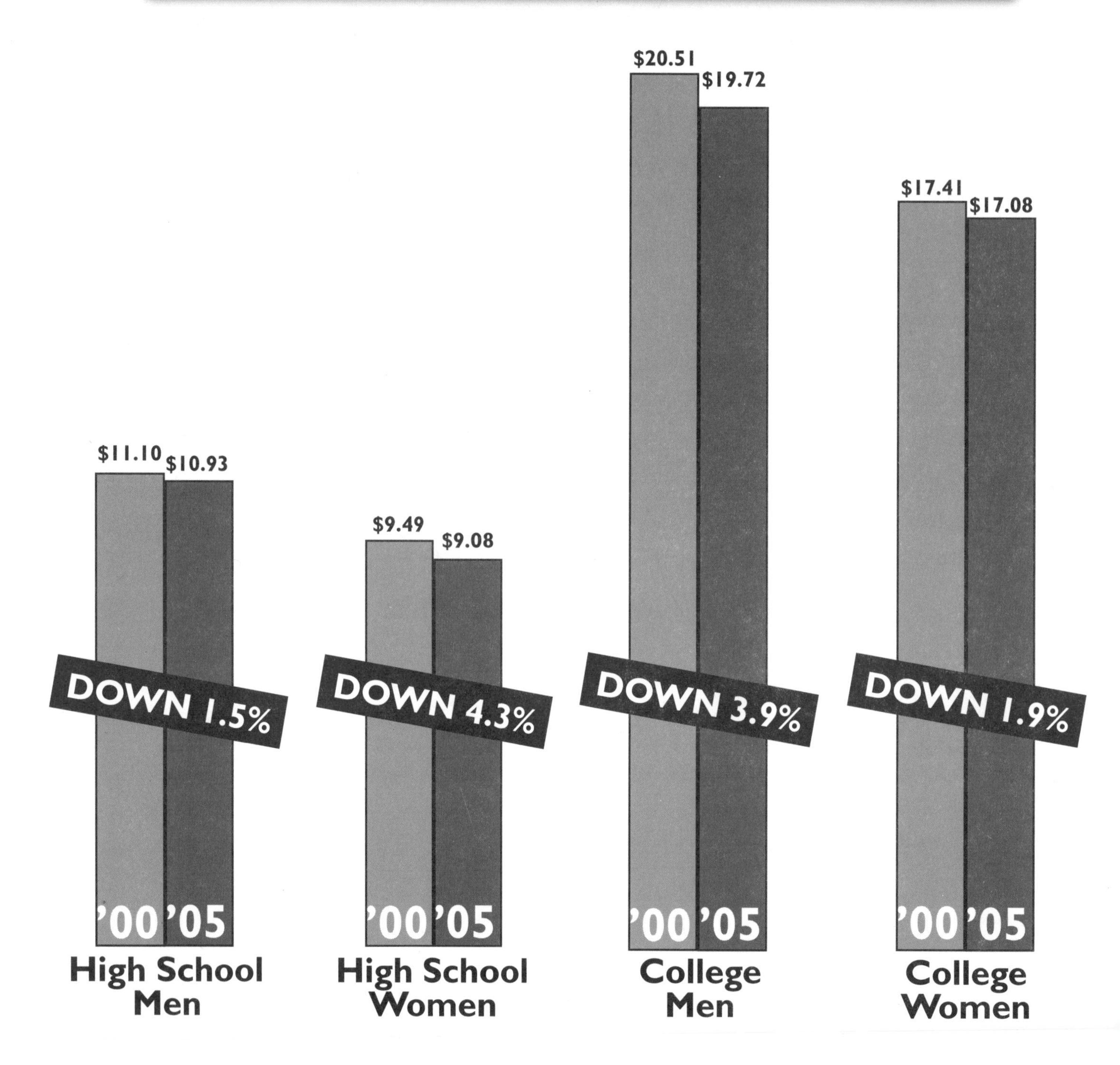

Note: Entry-level wage measured as wage of those from 19-25 years of age. In 2005 dollars.
Source: Mishel, Bernstein, and Allegretto, *The State of Working America, 2006/2007,* Table 3.2, page 153 (Cornell University Press, 2006).

Chart 20a

The Wheel of Shared Prosperity

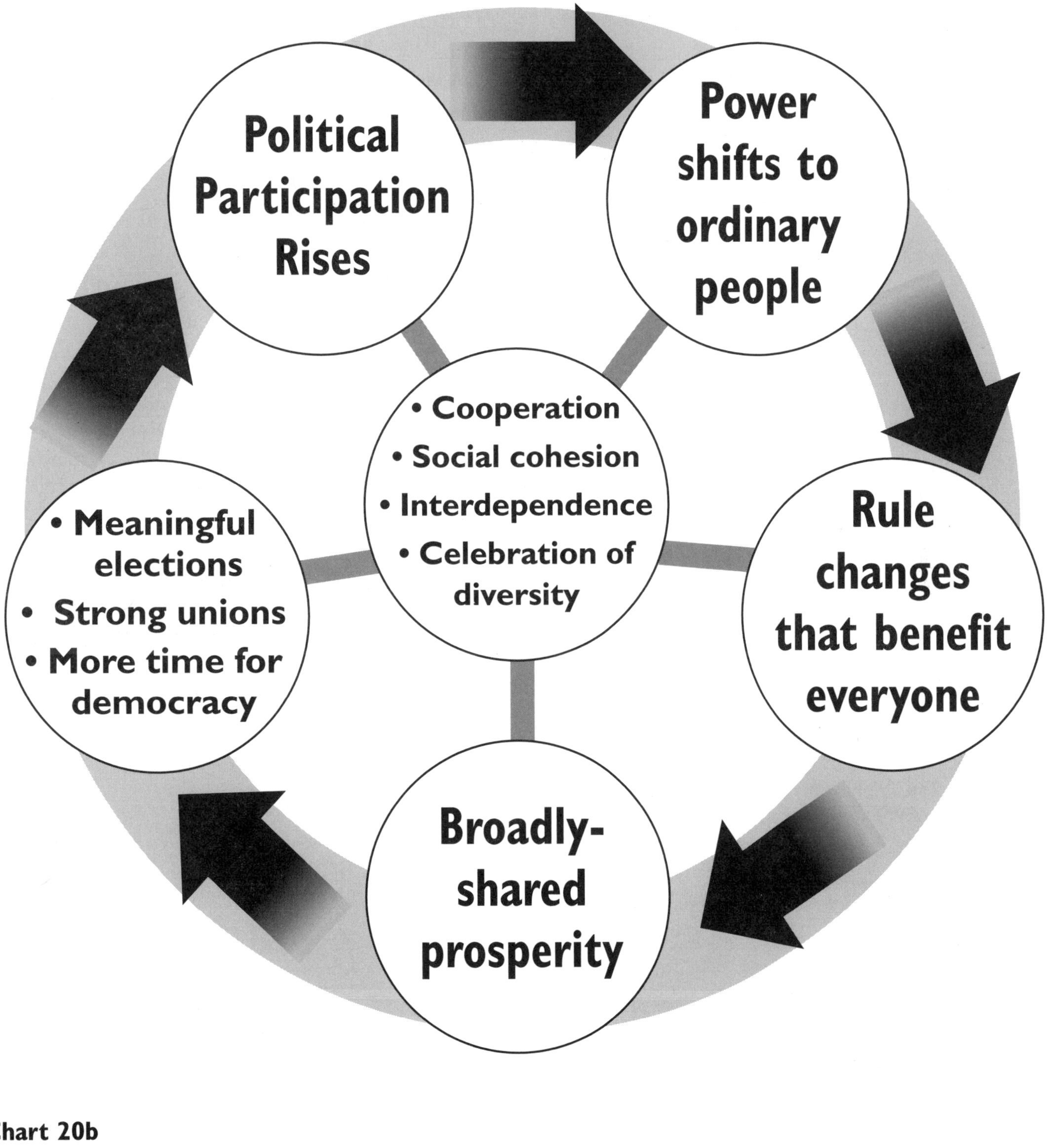

Political Participation Rises

Power shifts to ordinary people

Rule changes that benefit everyone

Broadly-shared prosperity

- Meaningful elections
- Strong unions
- More time for democracy

- Cooperation
- Social cohesion
- Interdependence
- Celebration of diversity

Chart 20b

Lesson 21: What Can You Do: Real Policies that Lift the Floor, Level the Playing Field, and Address the Concentration of Wealth and Power

Objectives:

- *Explore specific economic policies designed to lift the floor, level the playing field, and address the concentration of wealth.*
- *Review individual and collective actions that address the problem of economic inequality.*

Concepts and Key Terms:

- *economic policies addressing economic inequality*
- *lifting the floor*
- *leveling the playing field*
- *concentration of wealth, limiting it*
- *maximum wage campaigns*
- *local living wage campaigns*

Instructional Time:

- *55 minutes*

Preparation:

For Bellringer Activity 21.1:

- *Three large posters, with one of the following headings on each: "Policies that lift the floor," "Policies that level the playing field," "Policies that address the concentration of wealth and power"*
- *Tape*
- *Chart 21a, We Need New Rules to Reduce Wealth and Income Inequality*
- *The compiled list of suggested economic policy remedies from the previous lesson*

For Activity 21.2:

- *One index card per student*

Conducting the Lesson

Bellringer Activity 21.1: Categorizing Policies

1. If you did not assign the homework in the previous lesson, pick up here. Tape up the list of compiled economic policy remedies from the previous lesson and ask students to group their suggestions according to the following framework:
   - policies that lift the floor (lift people out of poverty)
   - policies that level the playing field
   - policies that address the concentration of wealth and power

If you assigned the homework in the previous lesson, ask students to take out their compiled lists and proceed from here.

2. Have the previous lesson taped to the board. Ask students to call out the policy remedies that should be placed under "Policies that lift the floor." Proceed to the next two categories.

3. When the list of policy remedies has been placed into the three categories above, conduct the following mini-lecture using these talking points and **Chart 21a, We Need New Rules to Reduce Wealth and Income Inequality** to explain the above categories.

We Need New Rules to Reduce Wealth and Income Inequality

Lift the Floor for Lower Income People
- ★ Higher minimum wage
- ★ Adequate incomes so families can save
- ★ Greater access to homeownership
- ★ Individual Development Accounts

Level the Playing Field for Everyone
- ★ Equal access to education and training
- ★ Publicly-funded asset accounts at birth
- ★ Fair trade policies that benefit wage-earners, consumers, communities, and the environment as well as investors
- ★ Fair taxes that treat income from investments and work the same
- ★ Expansion of business and corporate ownership

Address Concentration of Wealth and Power
- ★ Reduced subsidies for excessive pay and inequality
- ★ Progressive taxation of wealth and income
- ★ Campaign finance reform to get big money out of politics

Chart 21a

TALKING POINTS:

Lifting the floor. These are strategies that seek to bring people at the bottom up to at least a level where they have the ability to make use of their talents and pursue their dreams.

Higher minimum wage. The federal minimum wage has been stuck at $5.15 an hour since 1997. In 2005, Senator Edward Kennedy and Rep. George Miller proposed to raise the minimum wage to $7.25, which buys about 40 cents less today (December 2006) than it did in January 2005. That's why when Congress passes a raise to $7.25 it should continue to push for a minimum in the neighborhood of $8.00 by 2009 in order to preserve the purchasing power of that January 2005 target. Second, no matter what the amount of the next raise, inflation will start wearing it away, bit by bit, as soon as it is in place. Once the minimum has been raised to an appropriate and fair target wage, Congress needs to follow the lead of 10 states and add *indexing* to prevent the minimum wage from being eroded by inflation.

Adequate incomes so families can save. The modern living wage movement — the *living wage* is the level that would bring a family above the poverty line — was born in Baltimore in 1994, when the city passed an ordinance requiring firms working on city contracts to pay employees a rate above the minimum wage. Since then, over 120 communities, including New York, Chicago, L.A., Minneapolis-St.Paul, and Boston have followed suit, some setting wage floors more than twice the federal minimum wage, and some requiring various benefits. Many more local and statewide living wage campaigns are underway. The Living Wage addresses the problem of people working 40 hours a week and not being able to live above the poverty line. In addition, as in the past, the government should be doing more to help families purchase homes and build their savings, as was done with the Federal Home Mortgage Assistance Program following World War II.

Greater Access to Homeownership. Owning a home has long been considered a stepping stone to building assets. Public policies that increase access to homeownership include subsidized mortgages and mortgage insurance, down-payment assistance funds, second mortgage subsidy programs, and grants and low-interest loans for home improvements and weatherization. Stricter enforcement of fair housing and community reinvestment laws would remove barriers to asset-building for people of color.

Individual Development Accounts (IDAs). IDAs are like individual retirement accounts but are targeted to low- and moderate-income households to assist them in asset accumulation. Individuals who open an IDA receive matching funds, normally ranging from $1 to $3 for each dollar they deposit into their account. In addition, IDA programs normally include support services such as budget counseling and homeownership and entrepreneurial training to help participants achieve their goals.

Leveling the Playing Field for Everyone. Typically, most of the suggested strategies for addressing economic inequality are "lifting the floor strategies." However, opposition has focused on their cost. Strategies that level the playing field could fund lifting the floor strategies. It makes sense to tie these two types of strategies together. Some suggestions for leveling the playing field:

Publicly-funded asset accounts at birth. A program like this would, for example, guarantee every American child $1,000 at birth, plus $500 a year for the first five years, to be invested until retirement. Through compound returns over time, the account would grow substantially, provide a significant supplement to Social Security and other retirement funds, and enable many more people to leave inheritances to their children. This would strengthen opportunities for asset-building across generations. Such universal accounts could be funded by a modest wealth tax on assets in excess of $10 million, redistributing a small portion of the largess of the top half of one percent to address the generational inequalities of wealth.

TALKING POINTS, continued:

Fair trade policies. It is not anti-trade or anti-investment to oppose agreements such as NAFTA and CAFTA. Advocating speed limits does not mean that one is "anti-automobile." We can imagine what trade agreements that promoted the economic "high road" might look like: unrestricted trade between nations with high labor and environmental standards; social tariffs on products made in countries with gross human rights violations and low environmental standards.

Fair taxes. In a more equitable economy, income from going to work would not be taxed at a higher rate than income from stocks, bonds and investment real estate. This is currently the case with income taxes versus capital gains taxes. For most people, the capital gains tax rate (see definition below) is 15% and there have been repeated efforts to completely eliminate this tax. If a person works for a living, e.g., as a teacher, a factory worker, or a dentist, they will be taxed on their annual income at 25% if they make over $30,600, and 28% for income over $74,200. If a person is wealthy enough to make a living from buying and selling stocks, bonds and investment real estate, they will be taxed at only 15% on the hundreds of thousands or millions of dollars they make as an investor. How many people fall into this category? The few who are very wealthy. (See Lesson 11 for more on stock and bond ownership.)

Expansion of business and corporate ownership. There are a range of public policies that could promote broader ownership and reward companies that share the wealth with employees, consumers, and other stakeholders. These policies include encouraging employee ownership through government purchasing, licensing rights, public pension plan investments, loans and loan guarantee programs, and so on.

Addressing the over-concentration of wealth and power. These are strategies that seek to level the playing field by capping or restricting income and wealth from the top down. Some examples are:

Reduced subsidies for excessive pay and inequality. Corporations should not be allowed to take income tax deductions for executive compensation that exceeds 25 times their lowest paid workers' salaries.

Progressive taxation of wealth and income. The wealthiest one percent of the U.S. population now has more wealth than the bottom 90% combined. The current U.S. tax system leaves the vast differences in wealth and power largely untouched. A majority of advanced industrial countries — including those with high savings and growth and low levels of inequality such as Austria, Denmark, Finland, Germany, Luxembourg, the Netherlands, Norway, Spain, Sweden and Switzerland — provide for a direct annual tax on household wealth holdings, the United States does not.

Campaign finance reform. Those who have worked on the issue of big money in politics have identified several rule changes that would create a more equitable system of financing elections, including: Maximum contribution limits, campaign spending limits, a ban on contributions to political parties ("soft money"), and public financing of elections.

4. Share with students the following current proposals that further shift the tax burden off the wealthy few and onto the lower- and middle-income majority of taxpayers:

- implementing more "trickle-down" policies like cutting corporate taxes
- cutting capital gains taxes in half
- converting our progressive income tax to a flat tax
- abolishing the income tax and replacing it with a National Sales Tax

5. Ask students what types of policies do they think might give the top 5% a self-interest in seeing the living standards of other Americans rise? What actions do they suggest can be taken to increase equality that don't require using government intervention?

6. Elaborate on the subjects below. Most of the stories are directly or indirectly related to economic inequality, and all are examples of how people can organize to overcome obstacles and how there is strength and power in numbers.

- United Students Against Sweatshops (www.studentsagainstsweatshops.org) have 251 groups on college campuses that organize to stop schools from buying products made with sweatshop labor. As a result of their efforts, more than 160 colleges and universities have affiliated with the the Worker Rights Consortium (WRC), a non-profit organization created by students, labor rights experts, and workers from across the globe, with participation from college and university administrators. The WRC's purpose is to enforce manufacturing codes of conduct designed to ensure that factories producing clothing and other goods bearing school logos respect the basic rights of workers.

- Communities are addressing youth crime by keeping community centers open late for teens to have a place to congregate and play games.

- Women on college campuses across the country organize annually for "Take Back the Night" walks, holding rallies and speaking out on issues such as date rape and violence against women.

- Across the country, neighborhoods are organizing "Neighborhood Watch" groups. People are refusing to become part of gated communities and instead are taking power into their own hands for the safety of their neighborhood.

Activity #21.2 How Do We get There? Take a Longer View

1. Conduct a mini-lecture, using the talking points below, about actions that students can take that will have an impact on society and actions that they can take as individuals.

TALKING POINTS:

It has taken a long time for the owning class to get so much power — perhaps twenty to thirty years — and it will take time for us to organize to get it back. We need to think strategically about what efforts today will help us build a broader movement tomorrow; a strategy that will address the root causes of inequality. Remember, the Civil Rights Movement did not arise full-blown overnight.

As a Society:

- work to take money out of politics
- reframe current issues in terms of inequality
- expand the power of working people by aiding the creation of movement-building institutions, including unions and independent political parties

As an Individual:

- educate yourselves and others about this problem
- help raise awareness of economic inequality by monitoring the media and responding with letters to the editor
- inform our government that we want them to make things more fair; the government doesn't decide how much employers pay their employees but they can raise taxes on the wealthy, raise the minimum wage, pay government employees with fairer pay scales, and only do business with companies that pay living wages
- join campaigns for progressive rule changes (legislation) such as these:
    - income Equity Act - limits tax deductibility of CEO pay to 25 times the lowest paid workers' salary
    - minimum wage hike
    - local living wage campaigns
- engage in Direct Action, such as
    - poster and sticker campaigns
    - leafleting on Tax Day, Election Day, etc.
- build power
    - join or support a labor union
    - join an independent or third political party
    - work with religious congregations to educate and organize for a fair economy
    - join an interest group that promotes awareness of growing economic inequality, such as United for a Fair Economy

2. Ask students what they would tell an elected official to do if she/he were in the classroom right now. Ask them to think of at least two things and write them down on a piece of paper.

3. Explain to students that the class is going to write a letter to the President of the U.S. to tell him how you feel about economic inequality. The letter will be written one word at a time. Starting at one side of the room, the first person will say "Dear" the 2nd person "Mr. President" the 3rd person "We" etc., until everyone has added one word. You may go around a second time if the class desires.

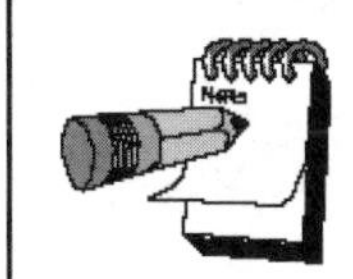

Note to Teacher

This activity can be serious and fun. If the letter turns out to be a good letter you can type it up, correct grammar if necessary, give copies back to the students to read, approve and sign, then actually mail the letter to the President.

Remind students to pay attention so they will know what has been said before it is their turn. Record the letter as it is being made (on the board or on a flip chart easel). If the words are not visible, stop at some point and read what has been written up to that point. Ask students to try to incorporate the ideas they wrote in response to the question above.

4. Two alternatives: Write a letter to a corporate CEO of the students' choice. Or, have a form letter pre-addressed to the Governor, the President, or our Representative in Congress and give students the form to complete on their own time. Pass around sample letters to give students ideas of what to write.

Optional Activity:

This activity is optional based on students' level of interest and the academic setting in which the materials are being presented.

1. Hand each student an index card. Ask them to write down three ACTION STEPS they will take personally to address the problem of economic inequality.

2. Ask them to write TARGET DATES next to each ACTION. Instruct students to stand as they finish writing and find a partner who is standing.

3. In pairs, students explain their action steps and solicit feedback. The pair may serve as reminder buddies for each other. Each buddy will check to see that the action steps have been taken by the target date.

Additional Resources:

Jared Bernstein, *All Together Now - Common Sense for a Fair Economy*, Berrett-Kohler Publishers, 2006.

Robert Polin and Stephanie Luce, *The Living Wage: Building a Fair Economy*, The New Press, 1999.

Institute for Policy Studies (IPS) - For more than four decades, IPS has transformed ideas into action for peace, justice, and the environment. The Institute has strengthened and linked social movements through articulation of root principles and fundamental rights, research and analysis on current events and issues, and connections to policymakers, academics, and activists at all levels. As a multi-issue think tank that has worked with the movements that shaped the late 20th Century, from Civil Rights onwards, IPS offers a cross-cutting analysis with a historical perspective.

We Need New Rules to Reduce Wealth and Income Inequality

Lift the Floor for Lower Income People

- ★ Higher minimum wage
- ★ Adequate incomes so families can save
- ★ Greater access to homeownership
- ★ Expansion of Earned Income Tax Credits

Level the Playing Field for Everyone

- ★ Equal access to education and training
- ★ Publicly-funded asset accounts at birth
- ★ Fair trade policies that benefit wage-earners, consumers, communities, and the environment as well as investors
- ★ Fair taxes that treat income from investments and work the same
- ★ Expansion of business and corporate ownership

Address Concentration of Wealth and Power

- ★ Reduced subsidies for excessive CEO pay
- ★ Progressive taxation of wealth and income
- ★ Campaign finance reform to get big money out of politics
- ★ Accountability for corporations receiving public subsidies

Chart 21a

Resources for Teachers

Additional copies of *Teaching Economics as if People Mattered* are available for $20 plus shipping and handling from United for a Fair Economy. Call 617-423-2148 x110 or email sschnapp@faireconomy.org.

Overhead transparencies of the charts in TEAIPM and full-size flip charts may also be purchased from United for a Fair Economy.

- A set of 8.5" x 11" transparencies are $15 plus shipping and handling.
- A set of 24" x 36" flip charts are $125 plus shipping and handling.

Responsible Wealth (www.responsiblewealth.org), a project of United for a Fair Economy, is a network of businesspeople, investors and affluent individuals in the top 5 percent of income and assets who are concerned about growing economic inequality and are taking action to promote a fair economy. Contact Mike Lapham at 617-423-2148 x112 or email: mlapjam@responsiblewealth.org.

Rethinking Schools (www.rethinkingschools.org), 1001 E. Keefe Ave., Milwaulkee, WI 53212. Phone: 800-669-4192. Fax: 414-964-7220. *Rethinking Schools* is an online and print resource that is committed to equity and to the vision that public education is central to the creation of a humane, caring, multiracial democracy. While writing for a broad audience, *Rethinking Schools* emphasizes problems facing urban schools, particularly issues of race. Throughout its history, *Rethinking Schools* has tried to balance classroom practice and educational theory. It is an activist publication, with articles written by and for teachers, parents, and students. Yet it also addresses key policy issues, such as vouchers and marketplace-oriented reforms, funding equity, and school-to-work.

Teaching for Change (www.teachingforchange.org), NECA, PO Box 73038, Washington, D.C. 20056. Phone: 800-763-9131. Fax: 202-238-0109. Established in 1989, Teaching for Change operates from the belief that schools can provide students the skills, knowledge and inspiration to be citizens and architects of a better world — or they can fortify the status quo. By drawing direct connections to 'real world' issues, Teaching for Change encourages teachers and students to question and re-think the world inside and outside their classrooms, build a more equitable, multicultural society, and become active global citizens. Teaching for Change's professional development workshops, publications, parent-empowerment program, and catalog of innovative K-12 resources serve as a lifeline for teachers, other school staff and parents.

About the Author

Tamara Sober Giecek is currently Assistant Director of Government Relations for the Virginia Education Association. Formerly a public high school social studies teacher at James River High School (JRHS) in Chesterfield, Virginia teaching United States and Virginia Government and Economics, and World History. Tamara was nominated "JRHS Teacher of the Year" by her peers during her 2nd year of teaching. She holds a Masters of Art in Social Science Education and a Bachelor of Science in Political Science, both from Florida State University. Tamara has written government and economic curriculua for Chesterfield County Public Schools.

Notes